13.50
7P

From Dr. Mather
to Dr. Seuss

Mary Lystad

From Dr. Mather
to Dr. Seuss
200 Years of American
Books for Children

Schenkman Publishing Co.   Cambridge, Massachusetts

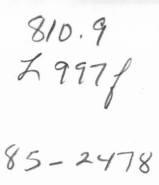

Pages 263-264 contain permissions and acknowledgments and constitute an extension of this page.

Library of Congress Cataloging in Publication Data

Lystad, Mary H
  From Dr. Mather to Dr. Seuss.

    1. Children's literature, American—History and criticism. 2. Literature and society—United States.
3. Social values in literature. I. Title.
PN1009.Z6L9   810'.9'9282   79-16949
ISBN 0-8161-9007-0 cloth
ISBN 0-87073-210-2 paper

This publication is printed on permanent/durable acid-free paper
MANUFACTURED IN THE UNITED STATES OF AMERICA

To Bob

Contents

Illustrations

Foreword

Social historians who seek to interpret a country's past are looking more closely at its books for children. For children's books reflect the attitudes and values of a people, as older generations socialize their young and declare their values and aspirations for both themselves and the future of their society.

Changes in book content over the decades of our country's history reflect changes in people's feelings about what is significant in their world and what is to be prized in human relationships and human achievement. Children's books, first published in New England in 1646, were often written by proper English men and women. Those written in this country emulated the instructive nature of their British counterparts and consisted largely of catechisms, primers, spellers, Latin grammars, geographies, and other school books. Much intellectual activity in the New England colonies was directed by the Puritan clergy, forceful men such as Cotton Mather, and the books had fervent religious overtones. After the American Revolution, the emergent spirit of patriotism was reflected in children's books, and biographies of George Washington and Benjamin Franklin became popular. English books reprinted in America were altered to include American place names and American heroes.

By 1850 the style and character of literature for children in America was beginning to change. Soul-saving didacticism gave way to an increasing interest in the family. The Victorian family, as eloquently portrayed by Louisa May Alcott, became the center of social life. It was there that children learned social roles (preferably those of the middle class) and learned some academic skills. The family was often the unit of economic activity and of recreation, which took the form of reading aloud.

As 1920 approached, a strong interest in children as children began to appear in literature for the young. There was a humanistic concern for the child's own dignity, needs, and desires. A real effort was made to satisfy them and to liberate the content of books from the do's and don'ts of the more rigid middle-class-oriented society. The first sustained criticism of children's books was also initiated in this period by Anne Carroll Moore in *The Bookman* (1918). The following year the Macmillan Company became the first publishing house to establish a children's book department. In the 1920's, due in part to significant technological advances in printing, the children's picture book came of age. The modern picture book, as examplified by Dr. Seuss's exuberant productions, serves both to entertain and to afford practice in reading. By the 1950's other technological advances allowed television to rival the book as a communications medium, and debates continue about their relative merits.

This volume examines in detail changes in book content over the past two hundred and more years of the United States growth and development. It is concerned with changes in beliefs about the nature of children and the nature of society, of perceptions of proper ways of socializing children, and of definitions of social values. The methodology adopted is that of content analysis of a random sample of books in the collection of the Rare Books Division of the Library of Congress. One thousand books were rated on a set of fifty social-psychological variables. The books were also examined for the quality of images and ideals they mirrored.

The oldest book examined was published in 1698: *A New Primer or Methodical Directions to Attain the True Spelling, Reading and Writing of English (Whereunto are Added, Some Things Necessary and Useful Both for the Youth of this Province, and Likewise for those, who from Foreign Countries and Nations Come to Settle Amongst us)*, was written by Francis Daniel Pastorius (1651–1719), printed by William Bradford in New York, and sold by the author in Pennsylvania. The latest books examined were written in 1977.

The first chapter of this book presents the overall conceptual framework of the study and the procedures used to implement it. Six subsequent chapters provide detailed analysis of attitudes, values, and social behaviors during varying periods of America's history—from the period which emphasized Adam's fall to that which emphasized fun that is funny. Following are two chapters with longitudinal analyses of changing social values and changing views of childhood. The final chapter discusses the beginning of our third century and raises questions about what lies ahead.

The immediacy of the present often obscures the relevance of the past and beclouds visions of the future. This book, dealing with a range of American values and institutions, is designed to set forth questions, considerations, and ideas that have not previously been in sharp focus. It provides information on differences in orientations over decades and over centuries. Some of these differences are significant, involving the very fabric of social order and social conscience; others are merely humerous or nostalgic, involving fad and fashion. The book also reveals similarities over time—in particular, a continuing deep concern for children and for their future. It is such concern which has prompted this work.

MARY LYSTAD
January, 1979

Chapter 1

American Books for Children: A Framework for Study

This study of American books for children focuses on the social values they express and the social behavior they proscribe. Some general questions are addressed. The first question concerns the value of egalitarianism. Have the social backgrounds of characters in books become more culturally diverse and their social conditions more equal in accordance with the spirit of the new country over the years? The second question concerns the value of self-expression. Have the needs of characters changed over the years, becoming less concerned with survival and more with self-fulfillment as the country grew and prospered? The third question concerns the value of freedom of choice around the way needs were satisfied. Are there more social institutions available to individuals through which to satisfy needs, and are these social institutions viewed as more adaptable over time? A final question concerns satisfaction of needs. Are needs met more often by characters in books in later years, accompanied by greater feelings of self-worth and control over the environment?

Each of these questions is looked at historically. Did such values, important as a *reason* for forming a new country, become expressed more clearly and more strongly in books for children as the country grew? Did the country, as it progressed, hold up to its children other ideas and hopes for the future?

There have been some value analyses of recent children's books within the sociological context of race, class, and sex differences; the findings show considerable role stereotyping (Lystad [7],* Weitzman [9], and Zimet [10]). There has also been an historical study of socialization patterns emerging from books for and about children in the colonial periods (Kiefer [2]). But a look at social values and social behavior preferred in children's books over a long time span has not heretofore been undertaken.

The framework used for analyzing stories for children within contexts of values and behavior focuses on the social orientation and generalizability of the value as well as on the relationship of values to the psychological needs of the individual. It also includes analysis of behavior, looking at patterns of social

*Numbers in brackets refer to the list of references at the end of each chapter.

relationships as seen in the social institutions involved and social outcomes experienced (for other studies using this framework, see Lystad [4, 5, 6, 7]). In this study stories were looked at in terms of five different areas: orientation of the book, social characteristics of the actors in the book, needs of these actors, social relationships employed to satisfy needs, and finally, the resulting social satisfaction.

The major categories of analyses, by area, for each of the books studied are as follows:

Orientation of the Book

1. Purpose (instruction in morals and religion; instruction in social behavior; elementary instruction: primers, spellers, ABC's; advanced instruction: scientific information, arts and humanities; amusement; understanding)
2. Author (sex; religious background)
3. Publisher (place; religious affiliation)
4. Style (fiction, nonfiction; prose, poetry)
5. Type of Orientation (reality, fantasy)
6. Treatment of Subject (matter-of-fact, humorous)
7. Characteristics of Locale (urban, suburban, rural, out of this world)
8. Locale in Relation to Main Character (home, school or work, community, away from community, out of this world)

Social Characteristics of the Actors

1. Type of Actor (human, animal, supernatural)
2. Type of Social Involvement (family, other primary group members, secondary group members, supernatural)
3. Racial and Ethnic Characteristics (white, black, Spanish-speaking Americans, American Indians, Asian-Americans)
4. Sex Characteristics (male, female)
5. Age Characteristics (children, adolescents, adults)
6. Social Class (upper, middle, lower)
7. Type of Animal Actors (animals as people in fur, animals as animals but talking, animals as animals)
8. Supernatural Actors (God; good guys: Santa Claus, elves, fairies; bad guys: witches, ghosts, vampires)
9. Main Character (child, adolescent, adult)
10. Affect Shown (positive, negative)
11. Complexity of Figures (acts as a whole, shows interaction of intellectual and emotional processes)

Needs of Human Actors

1. Basic Human Needs (eternal salvation, physiological, safety, love, play and adventure, self-esteem as shown by a desire for strength and achievement and by desire for reputation and prestige, self-actualization*)
2. Problems in Solving Need (physical threats, psychological threats, incompetency of the actor)
3. Human Needs in Relation to Self (concern with self alone, with other humans, with God)
4. Human Needs in Relation to Time (past, present, future on earth, future after life)

How Needs are Satisfied

1. Social Institutions (political, economic, leisure, family, religious, education)
2. Family Institution (who is in the home, who makes family decisions, who takes care of the child, who disciplines the child, amount and kind of adult interaction with child)
3. Social Responsibility of Actors (to oneself, to the family, to other persons, to God)
4. Use of Stimulants (drugs, alcohol)
5. Cognitive Relationship between Human Actors (rational, irrational)**
6. Affective Relationship between Human Actors (intimate, apart)**
7. Goal Orientation of Human Actors (individual, group, God)**
8. Social Stratification between Human Actors (hierarchical, nonhierarchial)**
9. Manner in which Needs are met (self-direction, conformity to adult or to supernatural norms)

**These basic aspects of social relationships are adapted from Levy's scheme for the analysis of any social relationships [3]. Two other basic aspects of social relationships mentioned by Levy but not used here are the membership criteria aspect and the substance definition aspect; they are omitted because the data provided in the stories are insufficient to differentiate the subcategories.

*This list of needs was adapted from Maslow's list of human needs [8]. A category of "eternal salvation" was added because of its primacy as an area of concern in the early periods studied, and a category of "play and adventure" was added since these activities do indeed represent an important need of childhood.

10. Needs and Social Change (orientation toward change, orientation to status quo)

Satisfaction of Needs

1. Satisfactions (success due to actor alone, to family, to persons outside of family, to God or magic; lack of success due to actor's inadequacies, inadequacies of others, or God's indifference)
2. Main Actors view of self (good, bad)
3. Main Actors view of People (people control their own lives, people control their own lives but need help of others, people do not control their own lives)
4. View of World in General (friendly, uncertain, hostile)
5. Spectre of Death (present, absent)

The contents of one thousand books were analyzed using this framework. Quantitative ratings were made on each variable, and a reliability check over time produced 91 percent agreement. From the universe of the Rare Book Collection of the Library of Congress a random sampling of books was made, five for each of our country's first two hundred years. In the early years, before 1796, the sample was sometimes less than five books per year, but, to provide adequate sampling for the Revolutionary period, it also included a number of books published before 1776. Books printed in England (and there are some great treasures from the eighteenth and nineteenth centuries) were omitted from the sample, since concern was with American publishing. Also omitted were the few American publications in foreign languages, which included a number of North European editions of the Bible and of folk tales.

The Rare Book Collection

This study of children's books in the Rare Book Division of the Library of Congress, was greatly facilitated by the 1975 publication of a two-volume work containing the complete card catalogue, by date and by author, of the Rare Book Collection [11]. The Rare Book Division, through gifts, purchase, and deposit, contains 17,000 old and rare juveniles, most of which were published in America in the English language (Haviland [1]).*

The children's book collection was begun in 1934 by V. Valta Parma, the Library's first curator of Rare Books, who searched the Library's general

*The Library of Congress itself holds the largest collection of children's books in the country, comprising an estimated 100,000 books in the general library. These include, in addition to American and British publications, many shelves of foreign-language books acquired either through exchange or through purchase.

collection for suitable candidates for Rare Book custody. Though this collection is lacking in some important eighteenth- and nineteenth-century books, it is strong in later years. It is particularly good in works of fiction, especially the works of Jacob Abbott, Louisa May Alcott, Samuel Griswold Goodrich ("Peter Parley"), William Taylor Adams ("Oliver Optic"), Horatio Alger, Jr., Mrs. C. R. Alden ("Pansy"), Charles A. Fosdick (Harry Castlemon), Rebecca Sophia Clarke (Sophie May), Harriet Mulford Stone Lothrop (Margaret Sidney), and Susan Warner.

Especially notable are three hornbooks, dated 1729, c.1750, c.1760. The book published c.1750 is a small jewel. Made of ivory, it has the ABC's in small letters, followed by a flower, incised on one side, the ABC's in capital letters, followed by a similar flower, incised on the other side. There are numerous New England Primers, six of them published before 1800. There are two copies of *Cock Robin's Death and Funeral,* printed in Boston in the late seventeen hundreds. And there is one of the three known copies of Goodrich's *The Tales of Peter Parley About America* (Boston, 1827), perhaps the first popular American book aimed at entertaining as well as instructing the child. There are a number of beautifully illustrated copies of *The Butterfly's Ball.*

Included in the collection are small paperbound books from the earliest years of the nineteenth century, among them toy books with multicolored covers, which offered entertainment in the stories of Blue Beard, Dick Whittington, and other chapbook heroes. Also included are examples of the prolific publishing by the American Sunday School Union in Philadelphia and by other denominational publishing houses. These church-related presses provided a large pool of sober and didactic matter designed to protect the young from his or her natural instincts. A large, homogeneous group of Americana in the collection is the McGuffey series with almost all first editions of the books that sold 122,000,000 copies and had a profound influence on American education. And, of course, all the major twentieth-century authors and illustrators are included. Finally, early American magazines for children in the Rare Book Collection include *Our Young Folks, Parley's Magazine, Peter Parley's Annual, Riverside Magazine for Young People,* and *The Chatterbox.*

The Rare Book Division does not have the most extensive collection of early-American children's books in this country; the American Antiquarian Society's Collection in Worcester, Massachusetts, is larger for those books published before 1821. The Rosenbach Collection (housed at the Free Library of Philadelphia) and the Connecticut Historical Society Collection in Hartford are also extensive in the early years. The Rare Book Collection, though, continues to grow. Each year a small group of first issues of books significant for authorship, content, or illustrations and format is selected for inclusion. Such inclusion will be continued so that the Rare Book Collection remains an important repository of Americana.

Why Were the Books Written

The first question posed about these children's books dealt with the purpose for which they were written. In early years, instruction in morals and religion is an objective very clearly stated on the title pages, lest anyone have his doubts.

The Heidelberg Catechism, or Method of Instruction in the Christian Religion as the Same is Taught in the Reformed Churches and Schools, in Holland. To which is Added, A Compendium of the Christian Religion for those who Intend to Approach the Holy Supper of the Lord. Translated for the use of the Reformed Protestant churches in America. 5th ed. Albany. Printed by Charles R. & George Webster, No. 37 (on the North Side) of State-Street, near the English church, 1789.

Select Songs for Children, in Three Parts. I. Divine Songs, Attempted in Easy Language. II. Moral Songs, in the Most Familiar Manner. III. Psalms in Verse, Spiritual Hymns, and Serious Little Poems. By I. Watts . . . New York: Printed by J. Harrison, Yorick's Head No. 3, Peck-slip, 1794.

Principles of Politeness, and of Knowing the World; by the Late Lord Chesterfield. Methodised and Digested under Distinct Heads, with Additions, by the Rev. Dr. John Trusler; Containing Every Instruction Necessary to Complete the Gentleman and Man of Fashion, to Teach him a Knowledge of Life, and Make him Well Received in all Companies. For the Improvement of Youth: yet not Beneath the Attention of any. Philadelphia: Printed and sold by R. Aitken, at Pope's Head, three doors above the Coffee house, Market street, 1781.

A Little Pretty Pocket-Book, Intended for the Instruction and Amusement of Little Master Tommy, and Pretty Miss Polly. With two Letters from Jack the Giant-Killer; as also a Ball and Pincushion; the use of which will Infallibly make Tommy a Good Boy, and Polly a Good Girl. To which is Added, a Little Song-Book, Being a New Attempt to Teach Children the Use of the English Alphabet, by Way of Diversion. The 1st Worcester ed. Printed at Worcester, Massachusetts. By Isaiah Thomas, and sold, wholesale and retail, at his bookstore, 1787.

The Youth's Instructor in the English Tongue; or The Art of Spelling Improved. Being a More Plain, Easy and Regular Method of Teaching Young Children, with a Greater Variety of Very Useful Collections than any Other Book of this Kind and Bigness Extant. In Three Parts. The First, Containing Monosyllables, Expressing the

Most Natural and Easy Things to the Apprehension of Children; with Common Words, and Scripture Names. The Second, Being an Introduction More Particularly for Children of a Higher Class. The Third, Rules in Arithmatick, With Forms of Bills, Bonds, Releases, &c. very Useful for All Persons. The Whole Being Intermix'd with Variety of Exercises, in Prose and Verse, Adapted to the Capacities of Children. For the use of schools. Collected from Dixon, Bailey, Owen, Strong and Watts. Boston: Printed and sold by Kneeland and Adams, in Milkstreet, 1767.

Geography Made Easy: Being an Abridgment of the American Geography. Containing Astronomical Geography; Discovery and General Description of America; General View of the United States; Particular Accounts of the Thirteen United States of America . . . To which is Added, a Geographical Account of the European Settlements in America; and of Europe, Asia and Africa. Illustrated with eight neat maps and cuts, newly engraved . . . By Jedidiah Morse . . . 3d ed., cor . . . Boston: Printed by Samuel Hall, No. 53, Cornhill, 1791.

Introduction to the History of America . . . Designed to Instruct American Youth in the Elements of the History of Their Own Country. With a correct map of the United States of America. Philadelphia: Printed and sold by Young and M'Culloch, at the Corner of Second and Chestnut-Streets, 1787.

Table 1.1 gives a categorization of book purpose by publication date. The earlier years saw instructional orientation of several types, dealing with proper behavior to ensure a good life on earth and a good life in the hereafter. The later years had fewer instructional orientations and more books designed to provide understanding and amusement. Most of the intellectual activity of pre-Revolutionary America was in the hands of Puritan clergy, men of the force of Cotton Mather, and the books had a strong religious perspective. The spectre of death was ever present—children were born not to live but to die, and these stories taught them how to die in a befitting manner. One of the most popular of the early spiritual guides was "A Token for Children, being An Exact Account of the Conversion, Holy and Exemplary Lives and Joyful Deaths of several Young Children," written by the celebrated English nonconformist divine, James Janeway, in 1671–1672, and first published in Boston in 1700. To this book Cotton Mather added "A Token for the Children of New-England, or, Some Examples of Children, in whom the Fear of God was remarkably Budding before they died; in several parts of New-England. Preserved and Published for the Encouragement of Piety in other Children." This book went through many editions and was widely read both prior to and after the Revolu-

*Table 1.1. Purpose of Books by Publication Date (percent)**

	INSTRUCTION				UNDER-STANDING	AMUSE-MENT	N
Publication Date	Religious Behavior	Social Behavior	Primers/ Spellers/ ABC'S	Scientific Information			
1721–1795	58	30	20	34	0	4	100
1796–1815	55	50	17	28	0	9	100
1816–1835	64	31	7	17	0	7	100
1836–1855	77	49	4	20	0	3	100
1856–1875	68	56	2	11	0	17	100
1876–1895	41	37	2	10	1	33	100
1896–1915	17	37	5	14	4	42	100
1916–1935	2	11	3	8	9	71	100
1936–1955	1	6	2	12	22	58	100
1956–1975	2	3	3	9	27	56	100

N.B. The percentages per time period add up to more than 100% because a number of books, especially in the early years, contained more than one discernible purpose.

*p<.001

tion. The main character of such books is the child himself, weak in nature. Parents and teachers appear in the stories to help him overcome his obvious faults in the face of a fearsome and vengeful God.

The religious overtones occur in fiction as well as nonfiction, in poetry and in prose. Even the alphabet lesson was often religiously inclined. *The History of the Holy Jesus,* sixth edition (Boston: Printed by J. Bushell and J. Green, 1749) includes the following familiar alphabet:

In Adam's Fall
We sinned all.

Thy Life to mend,
This Book attend.

The Cat doth play,
And after slay.

A Dog will bite
A Thief at Night.

An Eagle's Flight
Is out of Sight.

The idle Fool
Is Whipt at School.

As runs the Glass,
Man's life doth pass.

My Book and Heart
Shall never part.

Job feels the Rod,
Yet blesses God.

Our King the good
No Man of Blood.

The Lion Bold
The Lamb doth hold.

The Moon gives light
In Time of Night.

Nightingales sing
In Time of Spring.

The Royal Oak
It was the Tree
That sav'd his
Royal Majesty.

Peter denies
His Lord and cries.

Queen Esther comes
In Royal State,
To save the Jews
From dismal Fate.

Rachel doth mourn
For her First born.

Samuel annoints
Whom God appoints.

Time cuts down all,
Both great and small.

Uriah's beautious Wife,
Made David seek his Life.

Whales in the Sea,
God's Voice Obey.

Xerxes did die
And so must I.

Youth forward slips,
Death soonest nips.

Zaccheus he
Did climb the Tree,
His Lord to see.

Throughout the nineteenth century the religious message continues strong. The writers for various church presses carry the message of God and righteousness, as, for example, Daniel Wise in *Willow-grove Cottage; or, The Orphan's Victory* (Philadelphia: American Sunday School Union, c.1849):

> Go then, to Christ, and repent of your former sins. Confess them to Almighty God, with deep and unfeigned sorrow. Believe in the Lord Jesus Christ, and then live in the service of your saviour, and you shall be happy in this world, and in the world to come you shall have everlasting life. (p. 69)

The Victorian novelists also carry the religious message. Martha Finley in *Elsie on the Hudson and Elsewhere* (New York: Dodd, Mead and Co., 1898) writes:

> "I wish I knew how to turn many to righteousness. What's the way to do it?"
> "To tell them the sweet story of Jesus and his love," she answered in low, moved tones. "Tell them how he suffered and died that we might live. But first you must give your own self to him." (p. 37)

Another important purpose for writing books directed at the young in the eighteenth and nineteenth centuries was instruction in social behavior. During the early days of our country's history and throughout the growth of industrialization, life was hard and tenuous for most people. Children assumed social responsibility early. They worked in the home, in the fields, and later in the factories. They shared—beds and books and the few homemade toys. They were urged to contribute to their social world. In *Mama's Lessons for Her Little Boys and Girls* (Providence: Geo. P. Daniels, 1834) children are told:

> Take pains; and while you have work, or a task to do, think of it.
> Then you can soon do it; and when it is done you will be glad; and
> can go out and play, or swing, as happy and as long as you please.
> But *learn* first. (p. 18)

They were urged to care especially for family members, as shown in the Rev. Theron Brown's *Stories for Sunday* (New York: American Tract Society, c.1880):

> "My little boy must try to be a comfort to me, and grow fast and
> strong and good, so that when he is a man he can take all the care of
> me that his father would have done." (p. 90)

Instructional materials in the form of primers, spellers, and ABC's are represented in the collection more frequently in the earlier years because of their rarity. Proportionately they are just as much a part of the later publishing scene, as the growth of the American educational system encouraged the publishing of curriculum materials. But these later school-related books are found only in the Library's General Collection, not being deemed of sufficient literary merit to be included in the Rare Book Collection.

Although the most frequent ABC of the early years began with

> In Adams fall,
> We sinned all,

there were even in the eighteenth century some amusing rather than admonishing alphabets, such as *Tom Thumb's Play Book* (Boston: A. Barclay, c.1760):

A was an Archer,
and shot at a Frog.

B was a Butcher,
and had a great Dog.

C was a Captain,
all cover'd with Lace.

D was a Drunkard,
and had a red Face.

E was an Esquire,
with Pride on his Brow.

N was a Nobleman,
gallant and bold.

O was an Oysterwench,
and a sad Scold.

P was a Parson,
and wore a black Gown.

Q was a Queen,
and wore a fine Crown.

R was a Robber,
and wanted a Whip.

F was a Farmer,
and follow'd the Plow.

S was a Sailor,
and liv'd in a ship.

G was a Gamester,
and he had ill Luck.

T was a Tinker,
and mended a Pot.

H was a Hunter,
and hunted a Buck.

V was a Vinter,
a very great Scot.

I was a Joiner,
and built up a House.

W was Watchman,
and guarded the Door.

K was a King,
and he govern'd a Mouse.

X was expensive,
and so became poor.

L was a Lady,
and had a white Hand.

Y was a Youth,
did not love School.

M was a Merchant,
to a foreign Land.

Z was Zany,
and look't like a Fool.

Often the ABC's combined gentleness with wisdom. *My Little Darlings Pictorial ABC* (New York: McLoughlin Bros., c.1883) states:

A,B,C, and D,
Pray playmates agree,
E,F, and G,
Well so it shall be.
J,K, and L,
In peace we will dwell.
M,N, and O,
To play let us go,
P,Q,R, and S,
Love may we possess.
W,X, and Y,
Will not quarrel or die,
Z, and &
go to school on command.

From the earliest time in this country there was concern with providing arts and science information to the young, particularly science. Geographies and histories were very popular in the early years; they described both America and other countries of the world. Biographies of American statesmen, especially of George Washington and Benjamin Franklin, were also popular. Perhaps the most famous of the earlier science writers was Samuel Griswold Goodrich. His *Tales of Peter Parley about America* (1827) and *Tales of Peter Parley about Europe* (1828) were followed by a long succession of books in this genre. He wrote numerous books of geography, history, and travel and many biographies of famous men and women, all packed with detailed information and moral values. In 1833 he published and edited *Parley's Magazine,* a substantial children's periodical which ran until 1844. Over a period of thirty years (1827–1857), no less than seven million copies were sold of about 120 different Goodrich titles.

Goodrich titles in the Rare Book Collection include:

The Child's Book of American Geography: Designed as an Easy and Entertaining Work for the Use of Beginners. With sixty engravings and eighteen maps. Boston, Waitt & Dow (etc.) 1831.

The First Book of History. For children and youth. By the author of Peter Parley's tales. . .Cincinnati, C. D. Bradford and Co., New York, Collins and Hannay, 1831.

A Book of Mythology for Youth, Containing Descriptions of the Deities, Temples, Sacrifices and Superstitions of the Ancient Greeks and Romans. Adapted to the use of schools. Boston, Richardson, Lord and Holbrook, 1832.

A Book of Quadrupeds, for Youth, Embracing Descriptions of the most Interesting and Remarkable Quadrupeds in all Countries, with Particular Notices of those of America. . . New York, P. Hill, 1832.

The First Reader for Schools. By S. G. Goodrich. Boston, Otis, Broaders and Co., 1839.

Famous Men of Ancient Times. By the author of Peter Parley's tales. Boston, Bradbury, Soden & Co., 1843.

A Glance at the Physical Sciences; or, The Wonders of Nature, in Earth, Air, and Sky. By the author of Peter Parley's tales. Boston, Bradbury, Soden & Co., 1844.

Enterprise, Industry, and Art of Man, as Displayed in Fishing, Hunting, Commerce, Navigation, Mining, Agriculture, and Manufacture. By the author of Peter Parley's tales. . . Boston, Bradbury, Soden & Co., 1845.

A Glance at Philosophy, Mental, Moral, and Social. By the author of Peter Parley's tales. Boston, Bradbury, Soden & Co., 1845.

History of the Indians, of North and South America. By the author of Peter Parley's tales. Boston, C. H. Peirce and G. C. Rand, 1848.

A Comprehensive Geography and History, Ancient and Modern. By S. G. Goodrich. New York, Huntington and Savage (etc.), c. 1850.

A History of Africa. By S. G. Goodrich. Louisville, KY., Morton and Griswold, 1850.

The Balloon Travels of Robert Merry and his Young Friends over Various Countries in Europe. Ed. by Peter Parley (pseud.). New York, J. C. Derby and Co.; Boston, Phillips, Sampson and Co.; etc., etc., 1855.

A Gem Book of British Poetry: With Biographical Sketches. By Samuel G. Goodrich. Elegantly illustrated. Philadelphia, published by E. H. Butler and Co., 1855.

There have, of course, been many arts and science books published in the twentieth century as our social interest in these matters increased and as scholarly work on them grew. Again, most of these books would be found in the General Collection of the Library rather than in the Rare Book Collection, which selects out for these later years books of special literary excellence.

Toward the end of the 1800's books were written not only to instruct the little reader as to how he should behave, or to provide him with academic skills, but to give him understanding of individual human values and social needs. A number of authors have paid special attention to the inner person and his personal feelings—feelings of love and friendship, of anger and fear. By the middle of the twentieth century authors were also openly discussing social problems. Problems of divorce, death, mental retardation, mental illness, senility, race, poverty, crime, drug addiction, and alcoholism became the subjects of novels for young people and, to a small extent, of picture books for children. The need for love and understanding in human and animal societies is eloquently expressed in E. B. White's *Charlotte's Web* (1952). This need is shown in the book on several levels. Charlotte is a spider whose love of a fellow creature in the barn, a pig, motivates her to save his life in a wise and witty manner. Love and respect between animals in the barnyard are echoed in love and respect among humans, adults, and children around the barnyard. In this story a range of human emotions—joy, sorrow, anger, concern—is actually present; love comes through as a unifying force in the actions of living creatures.

More recently, the essential dignity and humanity of one who is both black and old is dealt with poignantly in Sharon Mathis' *The Hundred Penny Box* (1975). The young hero accepts his great-great aunt's needs and values as they are. He begins to understand what it's like to be a nonrunner in a fast-paced, achievement-oriented society.

Amusement as a legitimate purpose of books became important in the latter part of the nineteenth century. Clement Moore's *A Visit From St. Nicholas* has been tantalizing children for many generations. Written in 1822 for Moore's own children, the book went into many editions in the late 1800's and the early 1900's, and several well-known illustrators (F.O.C. Darley, Thomas Nast,

Aldren Watson, Roger Duvoisin) helped interpret the lively and engaging plot.

In 1900 came the fantasy which America has taken to heart, Frank Baum's *The Wizard of Oz*. Baum said that the book was written "solely to please children of today. It aspires to being a modernized fairy tale, in which the wonderment and joy are retained and the heartaches and nightmares are left out." Baum wrote thirty-nine *Oz* books filled with rare and absurd creatures still enormously popular today. The movie version of *The Wizard* is a much anticipated annual TV special.

Also in the amusement category are books by Walt Disney. Disney's major medium was film; he brought old stories to life and created new ones, which then often appeared in book as well as film versions. Disney's books in the Rare Book Collection appear as early as 1933 *(Mickey Mouse in King Arthur's Court)* and as late as 1956 *(The Walt Disney Story of our Friend the Atom)*.

Finally, Dr. Seuss (Theodor Seuss Geisel) has provided children with forty odd books of amusement. One of the most important picturebook author-artists of modern times, he has produced books that have delighted and instructed literally millions of children. His opening success, *And to Think that I Saw it on Mulberry Street* (1937), is as full of joy and imagination as those that appeared four decades later. Children know him best, though, for *The Cat in the Hat* (1957), a creature who roams in and out of homes promoting "Lots of good fun that is funny!" Dr. Seuss pioneered in the publishing of beginner readers—short books with large type and small vocabularies that a child could start and finish himself with a minimum of reading skills. These beginner readers are used extensively in schools, sometimes in place of textbooks.

Authors, Publishers, Artists

In the late eighteenth and early nineteenth centuries the authors of books for children were for the most part learned males, sometimes doctors of divinity, sometimes self-taught scholars. It was these men of Protestant faith who spoke the gospel of the Lord and promoted specific social behavior for children. They wrote the early prayer books and primers and histories and geographies to orient children to an afterlife as well as to a life on earth. There were Cotton Mather in the early eighteenth century, and in the nineteenth, Samuel Goodrich and also Jacob Abbott, author of histories, pious tracts, and adventure stories, as well as Noah Webster, whose spellers and readers were standard fare in many a one-room wooden school.

In the second half of the nineteenth century female authors were slightly more frequent than male authors, and their family-centered Victorian novels were very popular. Louisa May Alcott gave us the March family, Martha Farquharson (Martha Finley) gave us Elsie Dinsmore, Sophia May (Rebecca Clarke) gave us Little Prudy, and Margaret Sidney (Harriet Mulford Lothrop)

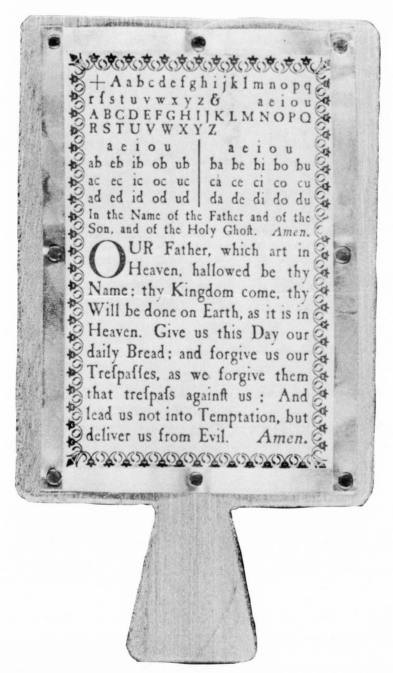

Ill. 1: Hornbook. c.1760. Paper on wood. [3″ x 5¼″]

Ill. 2: Samuel Griswold Goodrich. *The Life of Benjamin Franklin.*
Philadelphia: Thomas, Cowperthwait and Company, 1848. [1½'' x 1½'']

gave us the Five Little Peppers. Boys were not forsaken during this period;
Mark Twain (Samuel Clemens), Oliver Optic (William P. Adams), Horatio
Alger, Jr., and William Sylvester Ellis provided them with adventure and
assertiveness training. Both female and male authors, well schooled in the
Protestant ethic, confirm the value of hard work, close family ties, and
religious fervor.

In the 1900's male authors are found somewhat more frequently than female
authors, but there is no significant difference between the kinds of books
written by authors of one sex or the other. Religious affiliation of authors is less
important than humanistic concerns for social and economic rights of all
persons, individual self-expression, and individual acts of morality. Esther
Forbes, Scott O'Dell, E. B. White, and Laura Ingalls Wilder all show
humanistic concerns for a child's needs and wants. Furthermore, a number of
talented writers of minority-group backgrounds—such as Lucille Clifton,
Nikki Giovanni, Virginia Hamilton, and John Steptoe—are adding insights
and vitality derived from different cultural values and lifestyles.

The publishers of children's books, like the publishing field itself, have
remained largely in the northeastern area of the country. Table 1.2 gives the
geographic distribution of publishing houses in the sample by publication date.
Boston and Philadelphia were the early leaders of the publishing field. One gets

34

There was an old woman, she liv'd in a shoe,
She had so many children she didn't know what to do,
She gave them some broth without any bread,
She whipt them all soundly and put them to bed.

Ill. 3: *Mother Goose's Melodies*. Boston: Munro and Francis, 1833
[3½'' x 4½'']

the flavor of their humble operations from the addresses noted on their books:

Chesterfield, Philip Dormer Stanhope, Earl of. *Principles of
Politeness, and of Knowing the World.* Philadelphia: Printed and
sold by R. Aitken, at Pope's Head, three doors above the Coffee
house. Market-street, 1781.

Dodsley, Robert. *Select Fables of Esop and Other Fabulists.*
Philadelphia: Printed and sold by Joseph Crukshank, in
Market-street, between Second and Third-streets, 1786.

Webster, Noah. *An American Selection of Lessons in Reading and
Speaking.* Printed at Boston, by Isaiah Thomas and Ebenezer T.
Andrews. At Faust's statue, no. 45, Newbury street. Sold,
wholesale and retail, at their bookstore; by said Thomas at his
bookstore in Worcester, and by the booksellers in town and country,
1790.

The History of the Seven Wise Masters of Rome. Boston: Printed
and sold by J. White, near Charlestown-Bridge, 1794.

*Table 1.2. Geographic Location of Publishing Houses by Publication Date
(percent)*

Publication Date	Boston	Philadelphia	New York City	Other North East	North Central	South	West	N
1721–1795	34	26	7	33	0	0	0	100
1796–1815	23	26	7	34	0	10	0	100
1816–1835	24	17	18	38	0	3	0	100
1836–1855	24	26	31	15	2	2	0	100
1856–1875	31	28	32	3	1	4	1	100
1876–1895	46	12	38	1	3	0	0	100
1896–1915	28	12	34	0	23	2	1	100
1916–1935	7	11	63	6	9	0	4	100
1936–1955	3	1	84	5	7	0	0	100
1956–1975	9	2	78	5	3	0	3	100

It was not until the twentieth century that New York City became the main focal point of publishing in this country.

The North Central region in the United States has accounted for some activity, mostly in the city of Chicago. There has also been publication in the South, particularly in the border States of Delaware and Maryland. Some activity has occurred over the years in the West, and San Francisco has shown considerably more activity in the 1970's.

Most publishers in our country have been profit-making commercial presses. In the 1800's church-related presses came to the fore, comprising, from 1836 to 1855, 29 percent of the total sample and, from 1856 to 1875, 28 percent of the total sample. The church presses were, by and large, related to Protestant denominations; very few were outlets for Jewish or Catholic groups.

The American Sunday School Union was the most prolific of the church-related publishers. It was formed in 1824 through a merger of the resources of various denominations, and it provided for a confederated system of religious instruction. To execute the program of religious education nationwide, auxiliary branches of the Union sprang into existence in almost every state and territory. In 1830 the Union resolved to establish a Sunday school in every neighborhood in the western states that was without one, and in 1833 it adopted a similar resolution with respect to southern states. For such purpose it employed about 350 missionaries to travel the country and revitalize decaying schools or establish new ones.

The object of the Union was twofold: to provide children with oral instruction and to furnish suitable reading material for both the school and the home. The union published hundreds of volumes for its libraries as well as an infinite variety of educational works, magazines, and journals. Accounts of conversions, directions for the observance of Sunday, temperance works, stories concerning charity to the poor and kindness to animals, and warnings against idleness and frivolous play were the most commonly treated subjects.

Going back to the earlier history of books in America, one finds that the first important publisher of American children's literature was the famous Englishman, John Newbery, for it was his children's books which were widely imitated in this country and which provided the impetus for books specifically for the young. His books were all small and bound in Dutch flowered boards, the format often copied here. The major American publisher to be linked with John Newbery was Isaiah Thomas, one of America's first great printers and the founder of the American Antiquarian Society of Worcester. Thomas set out to imitate the Lilliputian library of Newbery. He copied the binding and illustration as well as the texts of the books. Newbery's methods of self-advertisement in the text of his books were copies by Thomas, such methods being adopted by printers and publishers for many years to come.

The growth of several large firms is rooted in the early nineteenth century—Harper and Brothers, for example, began publishing in New York in 1827. G. P. Putnam, Charles Scribner's Sons, and Dodd, Mead followed in New York. E. P. Dutton and Lothrop, Lee & Shepard first located in Boston and later moved to New York. In Boston two famous juvenile houses, through mergers, gained association with distinguished forebears—Little, Brown acquired Roberts Brothers, and Houghton Mifflin absorbed Ticknor and Fields. In the nineteenth century, Philadelphia was the home of numerous small commercial presses as well as the American Sunday School Union and other Sunday School presses.

Some mention should be made of illustrators who, though less well known and influential than authors and publishers, have nonetheless contributed substantially to American books for children. With Isaiah Thomas' editions of the John Newbery publications, the art of woodcutting in this country received a real impetus, for these books introduced the delightful cuts of Thomas and John Bewick and their pupils and followers. These illustrations inspired Alexander Anderson, the father of woodcutting in the United States, to forsake copperplate engraving and to devote himself to the art of woodcutting. Anderson made the woodcut illustrations for many of the children's books published throughout the East in the early nineteenth century. He illustrated for William Durell and Samuel Wood of New York, for Sidney Babcock of New Haven, for Munroe and Francis of Boston, and for other prominent printers and publishers. He was followed by Nathaniel Dearborn, Abel Bowen, Gilbert, and many other noted craftsmen, who made cuts for toy books as a means of practicing their art.

F.O.C. Darley was perhaps the best known of early American book illustrators. He employed his talents in a great variety of materials, from the playful *A Visit from St. Nicholas* to many historical tomes on America's founding.

Ill. 4: *Yankee Doodle*, illustrated by F.O.C. Darley. New York: Trent, Filmer and Co., 1865. [8¼'' x 10¾'']

Ill. 5: Maurice Sendak. *Higglety Piggelty Pop!* New York: Harper and Row, 1967. [4⅜'' x 4⅝'']

Howard Pyle was a prolific writer and illustrator of the late nineteenth and early twentieth century. His first published book, the incomparable *Merry Adventures of Robin Hood,* which he both wrote and illustrated, appeared in 1883. He also produced four volumes retelling the Arthurian cycle. Later he illustrated many books written by other authors and concerned mainly with American history and heritage.

Some artists became as much identified with books as their authors. W.W. Denslow's illustrations for Baum's *The Wizard of Oz* series and Garth Williams illustrations for White's *Charlotte's Web* and *Stuart Little* have become as closely linked with the characters as verbal descriptions. These illustrators also produced books on their own, but generally with less success than accompanied the books they had illustrated for others.

The twentieth century saw tremendous technical advances in color reproduction, developments which produced true color at affordable cost. In the

1920's the child's picture book came of age, and a number of talented illustrators, who often wrote books as well, used picture books as a serious medium. Among these distinguished modern illustrators are Marcia Brown, Wanda Gág, Robert McCloskey, Nonny Hogrogian, and Leo and Diane Dillon. Perhaps the most outstanding illustrator of the later time is Maurice Sendak. Equally at ease in black-and-white and blazing color, Sendak continues to explore, experiment, enlarge his horizons.

The ensuing chapters provide a closer look at American children's books throughout the country's history from before the Revolution to America's bicentennial year. Explored in detail for successive time periods are the kinds of books published, the characters found within their pages, expressions of needs of these characters, ways in which needs are satisfied, and actual satisfactions shown. Both quantitative analysis of the thirty-eight selected variables discussed earlier and qualitative analysis of further contextual materials are provided.

References

1. Haviland, Virginia. "Serving Those Who Serve Children." *The Quarterly Journal of the Library of Congress* (October 1965).
2. Kiefer, Monica. *American Children through their Books: 1700-1835.* Philadelphia: University of Pennsylvania Press, 1948.
3. Levy, Marion J. *The Structure of Society.* Princeton: Princeton University Press, 1952.
4. Lystad, Mary. "Traditional Values of Ghanaian Children." *American Anthropologist* 62 (1960): 454–464.
5. Lystad, Mary. "Paintings of Ghanaian Children." Africa 30 (1960) 30: 238–242.
6. Lystad, Mary. "Adolescent Social Attitudes in South Africa and Swaziland." *American Anthropologist* 72 (1970): 1389–1397.
7. Lystad, Mary. *A Child's World As Seen in his Stories and Drawings.* Washington, D.C.: National Institute of Mental Health, 1974.
8. Maslow, A. H. *Motivation and Personality.* New York: Harper, 1954.
9. Weitzman, Lenore; Effler, Deborah; Hokada, Elizabeth; and Ross, Catherine. "Sex-role Socialization in Picture Books for Preschool Children." *American Journal of Sociology* 77 (1972): 1125–1150.
10. Zimet, Sara, ed. *What Children Read in School: Critical Analysis of Primary Reading Textbooks.* New York: Grune and Stratton, 1971.
11. *Children's Books in the Rare Book Division of the Library of Congress.* Totowa, New Jersey: Rowan and Littlefield, 1975.

Chapter 2

1721-1795: "In Adam's fall,/ We sinned all."

In the earliest years of our country's development children's books were written to instruct—to teach primarily about proper religious behavior, but also to teach about other desired social behaviors and about academic subjects. Only a very small proportion of these books were written to amuse the child.* The religious behavior required included piety, obedience, humility, good works, prudence, hard work, deference. Such requirements were necessary because sooner or later the child would die, and he had to be prepared to die with a pure heart so as to avoid hell and damnation. Many of the early religious books were written by Englishmen and published in America without changes in the texts. Some of the books contained supplements by American authors; Cotton Mather's addition to James Janeway's *A Token For Children* being among the more famous.

Instructions in social behavior were also imported from England. The definitions of proper conduct mirrored the concerns of the British upper classes. Eight editions of Philip Dormer Stanhope, Earl of Chesterfield's *Principles of Politeness, and of Knowing the World* are in the Rare Book Collection, beginning with that of 1781. Among the subjects discussed are modesty, lying, cleanliness of person, dress, elegance of expression, address, phraseology, and small talk. The purpose of the instruction is "to complete the gentleman and man of fashion, to give him knowledge of life and to make him well received in all companies." The book focuses on the instruction of young men but points out that it is "yet not beneath the attention of any." Later versions did include instruction for young women. Another popular book of social and academic instruction is John Hamilton Moore's *The Young Gentleman and Lady's Monitor and English Teacher's Assistant*. There are seven editions in the Rare Book Collection, beginning with one dated 1790.

Primers were plentiful in this early period; containing religious and social instruction as well as ABC's and spelling words, they were used in the home and in the school. *The New England Primer* was the most widespread book of

---

*For further descriptions of eighteenth century American children's books see Earle [3], Halsey [6], Keifer [8], Shipton [11], and the *New England Magazine* [13].

A TOKEN

FOR

CHILDREN.

THE FIRST PART

◄◄◄◄◄◊►►►►

EXAMPLE. I.

Of one eminently converted, between eight and nine years old, with an account of her life and death.

MRS. SARAH HOWLEY, when she was between eight and nine years old, was carried by her friends to hear a sermon, where the minister preached upon *Mat.* xi. 13. *My yoke is easy, and my burden is light;* in the applying of which scripture, the child was mightily awakened, and made deeply sensible of the condition of her soul, and her need of Christ: She wept bitterly to think what a case she was in; and went home and got by herself into a chamber, and upon her knees she wept and cried to the Lord as well as she could, which might easily be perceived by her eyes and countenance.

B

Ill. 6: James Janeway. *A Token for Children . . . to Which is Added a Token for the Children of New England. . . .* Eighteenth century. [3″ x 5½″]

easy lessons; there are ninety-six in the Rare Book Collection. But there were other primers:

> Fox, George. *Instructions for Right-Spelling, and Plain Directions for Reading and Writing True English.* With several delightful things, very useful and necessary, both for young and old, to read and learn. Boston, Printed by Roger & Fowle, 1743.

> *The Child's New Play-Thing:* being a spelling-book, intended to make the learning to read, a diversion instead of a task. Consisting of a new-invented alphabet for children. A variety of lessons in spelling, of one, two, three, four, five, six, and seven syllables, with Scripture-histories, fables, stories, moral and religious precepts, riddles, &c. With entertaining pictures to each story and fable, The whole adapted to the capacities of children, and designed for the use of schools, or for children before they go to school; to which is added,—Three dialogues, shewing First, How a little boy shall make every body love him. Second, How he shall grow wiser than the rest of his school-follows. And third, How he shall become a great man. Philadelphia: Printed by W. Dunlap, 1763.

> Benezet, Anthony. *The Pennsylvania Spelling-Book,* or Youth's friendly instructor and monitor . . . Second edition, improved and enlarged. Philadelphia, Printed by Joseph Crukshank, 1779.

As regards instruction in science and the arts, American writers were prolific very early in our country's history. Jedidiah Morse and Noah Webster were among the more influential of the textbook writers. There are eleven editions of Morse's American geography.

> *Geography Made Easy:* being an abridgment of the American geography, containing astronomical geography, discovery and general description of America, general view of the United States; particular accounts of the thirteen United States of America . . . To which is added, a geographical account of the European settlements in America; and of Europe, Asia and Africa. Boston, Printed by Samuel Hall, 1791.

There are seventy editions of various Webster books in the Rare Book Collection. Some of the Webster titles included are:

> *An American Selection of Lessons in Reading and Speaking.* Calculated to improve the minds and refine the taste of youth. And also to instruct them in the geography, history, and politics of the United States. Being third part of a Grammatical institute of the English language. 3d. ed . . . enl. Philadelphia, Young and M'Cullock, 1787.

The American Spelling Book: containing an easy standard of pronounciation. Being the first part of a Grammatical institute of the English language. Thomas and Andrew's 2d ed. With additional lessons, corrected by the author. Boston, Printed by Isaiah Thomas and Ebenezer T. Andrews, 1790.

A Dictionary of the English Language: abridged from the American dictionary. For the use of primary schools and the counting house. New York, White, Gallaher, & White, 1830.

The Elementary Primer, or First lessons for children: being an introduction to the Elementary spelling book. New York, M'elrath and Bangs, 1831.

A Grammatical Institute of the English Language: comprising an easy, concise and systematic method of education. Designed for the use of English schools in America. In three parts. Part second containing a plain and comprehensive grammar, grounded on the true principles and idioms of the language. Thomas and Andrew's 1st ed. With many corrections and improvements by the author. Boston, Printed by I. Thomas and E. T. Andrews, 1790.

History of the United States, to which is prefixed a brief historical account of our English ancestors, from the dispersion of Babel, to their migration to America, and of the conquest of South America, by the Spaniards. New Haven, Durrie and Peck; Louisville, Kentucky, Wilcox, Dickerman, and Co., 1832.

Instructive and Entertaining Lessons for Youth; with rules for reading with propriety, illustrated by examples; designed for use in schools and families. New-Haven, S. Babcock and Durrie and Peck, 1835.

The Little Reader's Assistant; containing: I. A number of stories, mostly taken from the history of America, and adorned with cuts. II. Rudiments of English grammar. III. A federal catechism being a short and easy explanation of the Constitution of the United States. IV. General principles of government and commerce. V. The farmer's catechism, containing plain rules of husbandry. All adapted to the capacities of children. 2d. edition. Hartford, Printed by Elisha Babcock, 1791.

A Philosophical and Practical Grammar of the English Language. New-Haven, Printed by O. Steele and co., for Brisban and Brannan, New York, 1807.

The Pictorial Elementary Spelling Book; being an improvement on

the American spelling book. With about one hundred and sixty original illustrations. New York, G.F. Cooledge and brother, 1844.

In the early years there were precious few books on amusements, but the
sample does include two Tom Thumb "play books" and a Cock Robin. These
books had dual purposes, to instruct as well as to amuse, the major focus being
on humor and play. *Cock Robin's Death and Funeral* (Boston: Sold at the Bil-e
& Heart in Cornhill, 1780) offers the following ABC:

A was an artful Body
B a beauty was,
C a comely wench but coy,
D a dainty Lass.
E lov'd Eggs
F was fair and fat.
G had Grace and Wit at Will,
H wore a gold-lac'd Hat.
J was little Jackey's Name.
K was Kitty fair,
L lov'd Learning and got fame,
M was Mammy's Dear.
N was Naughty oft a-crying,
O was an only Child
P was pretty Peggy fighting,
Q was a Quaker mild.
R was rude and in Disgrace,
S stands for Shammy still,
T takes Vow of his Place,
W was Wanton Will.
X exceeding well done,
Y was young and tall,
Z and so you have them all.

In 37 percent of these books the author is unknown. In 58 percent of the
books the author was male, in 3 percent female, and in 2 percent of undeter-
mined sex. The anonymity of authors is related to the purpose of these books,
which were oriented to the honor and glory of God rather than the honor and
glory of the authors. The religious background of the authors was overwhelmingly Puritan. No dissident religious views were expressed.

All of the books were published in New England. Boston, leading the list of
cities, published 34 percent of the books. Philadelphia had 26 percent of the
publishing houses and New York 7 percent. There were other smaller cities
with thriving houses during the period: Hartford, New Haven, New London,
and Norwich in Connecticut; Salem and Worcester in Massachusetts;

Portsmouth in New Hampshire; and Providence in Rhode Island. During this time period only 2 percent of the publishing houses were affiliated with religious organizations.

The style of writing varied. Of the books in the sample, 47 percent employed prose only, 8 percent employed poetry only, and 45 percent employed a combination of prose and poetry. The prose was not necessarily difficult to read but was almost always repetitious and tedious. The combination of prose and poetry was livelier; poetry was usually rhymed.

Of the books, 24 percent could be classified as fiction, 53 percent as nonfiction, and 23 percent as both. Works of fiction included a large number of moral tales which exhorted persons to follow the straight and narrow and often reminded them through painful accounts of death and dying that we are not long on this earth. One of the most popular of the moral tales was the *History of Little Goody Twoshoes,* about a poor little orphan girl who, through piety and good works, enriches the lives of the unfortunate in her community and herself progresses from rags to riches. The original story is often attributed to the famous English writer, Oliver Goldsmith (see American Antiquarian Society [14] for a more detailed history of this book). There are fifteen copies in the library's collection.

Works of nonfiction include the religious books, books on social behavior,

Ill. 7: *The History of little Goody Twoshoes.* c.1795. [2½" x 2¼"]

and school books. Most of these volumes do include short fictional passages, as well as nonfiction treatises, to make the material more palatable. *The New England Primer* and Noah Webster's many academic endeavors are prime examples of the genre, but there are a number of prolific imitators.

The settings were primarily reality-oriented (80 percent). Very little fantasy was allowed because fantasy did not serve the sombre instructional purposes of most books and, it was felt, only encouraged playfulness in the child. For the same reasons, almost all of the books were matter-of-fact rather than humorous.

Settings were generally on this earth but often included more than just this country. Settings in England and the European continent were frequent. In 28 percent of the books, however, the locale shifted back and forth from this earth to otherworldly places. In a large proportion of the books individuals, even young individuals, died and went to heaven or hell, and these settings were sometimes vividly described. Heaven was certainly the preferred landing place.

When one views the setting in relation to the main character, the home and neighborhood appear as the locale in 53 percent of the books. The church, the school, and the family were the most important social groups, and the individual stayed largely within these contexts. Other contexts included places outside of the community or town (24 percent) or out of this world (23 percent).

The vast majority of books reviewed during this period (89 percent) were concerned with human actors. In some cases (38 percent) human actors interacted only with each other. In more cases (42 percent) they interacted significantly with God as well. Many of the books focused on the relationship of God and man — the need for the individual to note well and to follow God's proscriptions. A number of books recounted the lives of holy people who died early and, presumably, went straight to heaven. The actors, it might be added, were in general not persons of wealth. On the contrary, money and riches were looked on with considerable suspicion. Ahimaaz Harker, in *A Companion for the Young People of North America.* (New York: Printed by J. Holt at the Exchange, 1767) writes:

> The rich are exposed to innumerable Dangers, Simple nature in its contracted sphere, loves indulgence; how much more then will its career be accelerated, when flattering Riches, so sweet to our taste, gives greater Latitude to our Desires. (p. 281)

In general, individuals in these books interacted within a family or other primary group settings such as neighborhood, classroom, or church. There was little interaction in large secondary groups. Life revolved principally about parent and child, and the roles between them were often discussed. Noah Webster, in *A grammatical Institute of the English Language* (Hartford: Printed by Hudson and Goodwin, 1785), explains:

Perhaps there is no situation in life in which it is so difficult to behave with propriety as in the contest between parental authority and parental love. This is undoubtedly why we see so few happy families. Few parents are both loved and respected because most of them are either the dupes or the tyrants of their children. (p. 80)

The History of Master Jackey and Miss Harriot, the first Worcester edition (Worcester, Mass.: Printed by Isaiah Thomas, 1787) states:

The grand Design in the nurture of Children is to make Them Strong, Hardy, Healthy, Virtuous, Wise, and Happy; and these good Purposes are not to be obtained without some Care and Management in their Infancy.

A Present to Children (Norwich: Printed by Thomas Hubbard, 1794) admonishes:

A Wise Son makes a glad Father, but a foolish Son is the heaviness of his Mother. . . .

In the books of this sample the actors all seemed to be white Protestant, and undoubtedly the targeted reader was white Protestant as well. There were no minority actors identifiable either through the stories or through the illustrations. More books were written solely about boys than solely about girls, and the importance of boys is also shown where both sexes are present. In well over half the instances, boys are characterized as being more active and more productive than are girls. They think of more things to do, and they set about doing them.

Close to half the books focused on adult characters alone. Children existed only to learn roles of adulthood, and what better way to learn than to read in detail about how adults think and feel and behave. Only a small number of this sample (5 percent) focused upon the child alone; 1 percent focused on the adolescent alone. Little import was attached to economic class differentials. When such differentials were described, the poor were being assisted by the rich. The destitute widow, and there were many in the books, was discovered by a wealthy person of good and generous nature. Usually, she was stumbled upon in the woods in front of her small home. Sometimes food and clothing were provided; sometimes the widow and child were brought into the benefactor's commodious home to be fully cared for with respect and love.

Animals occur infrequently in major roles in the stories; when they appear they do so as animals rather than as people in fur or as talking beings. They are usually domesticated and helpful in the agrarian setting. Rarely do fairies and like supernatural beings appear. In over half the stories God appears, a stern and just and good and unbending leader. Isaac Watts in *The First Set of Catechism and Prayers . . .* 12th ed. (Boston: Printed and sold by S. Kneeland, 1762) writes:

Can you tell me Child,
   Who made you?
The great God who made
   Heaven and Earth.

What does God do for you?
He keeps me from Harm
by Night and by Day,
and is always doing me Good.

And what must you do for this
great God who is so good to you?
I must learn to know him first, and then
I must do everything to please him. (p. 5)

The major characters in the stories, those whose needs and activities are described in some detail, are, in two cases out of three, adults, in the one case children. Adults, warts and all, are described in some detail. Negative as well as positive emotion is displayed. Complex feelings and complex decisions based on feelings are shown. Proscriptions of behavior sometimes vary for adult men and women. In most cases the behavior is linked to the Lord's will, as in Lord Chesterfield's *Principles of Politeness and of Knowing the World* (Norwich, Connecticut: Printed and sold by John Trumbull, 1785):

   The Woman is loved, that hath a fair face; the Man is blessed who
   fears the Lord: Rewards are laid up for him who keeps God's Commandments. (p. 5)

And given man's lowly nature, unquestioned acceptance of the burdens of this world was required. *The Poor Orphans Legacy* (Philadelphia: Printed by B. Franklin, 1734) states:

   Be cheerfully content with your Lot in the World; bring your
   Mind to your Condition, and never grudge that you cannot bring
   your Condition to your Mind: Consider for your Help, that whatever
   afflicting Circumstances be in your Condition, you deserve
   infinitely worse for your sins. (p. 30)

Usually several needs were expressed by the major actors. The needs varied from, on the one hand, salvation in the next world to, on the other hand, self-actualization and fulfillment in this world.

Over half of the books (58 percent) emphasized salvation. Care was to be taken of one's actions in this world, an imperfect environment at best, to prepare for a perfect eternity. In his introduction to *A Token for Children* (Boston: Printed and sold by Z. Fowle, 1771), James Janeway writes:

   To all Parents, School-Masters and School-Mistresses, or any who
   have any Hand in the Education of Children

Dear Friends,

I have often thought that Christ speaks to you, as Pharoah's Daughter did to Moses's Mother, Take this Child and Nurse it for me. O
Sirs, Consider, what a precious Jewel is committed to your Charge,
what an Advantage you have to shew your Love to Christ, to stock
the next Generation with noble Plants, and what a joyful Account
you may make if you be faithful: Remember Souls, Christ and Grace
cannot be overvalued. I confess you have some Disadvantages, but
let that only excite your Diligence; the Salvation of Souls, the Com-
mendation of your Master, the Greatness of your Reward and everlasting Glory will pay for all. Remember the Devil is at work hard,
wicked Ones are industrious, and corrupt Nature is a rugged knotty
Piece to hew. But be not discouraged, I am almost as much afraid of
your Laziness and Unfaithfulness as any thing. Do but fail to work
lustily, and who knows but that rough stone may prove a Pillar in the
Temple of God? In the Name of the living GOD, as you will answer
it shortly at his Bar, I command you to be faithful in Instructing and
Catechising your young Ones. If you think I am too peremptory, I
pray read the Command from my Master himself, Deut. 6, 7. Is not
the Duty clear? and dare you neglect so direct a Command? Are the
Souls of your Children of no Value? Are you willing that they
should be Brands of Hell? Are you indifferent whether they be
damned or saved? Shall the Devil run away with them without Con-
troul? Will not you use your utmost Endeavour to deliver them from
the Wrath to come? You see that they are not Subjects uncapable of
the Grace of God. Whatever you think of them, Christ does not
slight them: they are not too Little to die; they are not too Little to go
to Hell; they are not too Little to serve their great Master; too Little
to go to Heaven; for of such is the Kingdom of God: And will not a
Possibility of their Conversion and Salvation put you upon the
greatest Diligence to teach them? Or are Christ and Heaven, and
Salvation, small Things with you? If they be, then lay about with all
your Might: The Devil knows your Time is going apace, it will
shortly be too late. O Therefore what you do, do quickly, and do it, I
say with all your Might: O pray, pray, pray, and live holily before
them, and take some Time daily to speak a little to your Children one
by one, about their miserable Condition by Nature. I knew a Child
that was converted by this Sentence from a godly School-Mistress in
the Country, Every Mother's Child of you are by Nature Children of
Wrath. Put your Children upon learning their Catechism, and the
Scriptures, and etting to pray and weep by themselves after Christ.
Take heed of their Company, take heed of pardoning a Lie; Take
heed of letting them mispend the Sabbath. Put them to beseech you,

upon imitating these sweet Children; let them read this Book over an hundred Times, and observe how they are affected, and ask them what they think of those Children; and whether they would not be such? And follow what you do with earnest Cries to God, and be in Travail to see Christ formed in their Souls. I have prayed for you, I have oft prayed for your Children, and I love them dearly, and I have prayed over those Papers; that God would strike in with them, and make them effectual to the Good of their Souls. Encourage your Children to read this Book, and lead them to improve it. What is presented, is faithfully taken from experienced solid Christians, some of them no way related to the Children, who themselves were Eye and Ear Witnesses of God's Works of Wonder, or from my own Knowledge, or from Reverend godly Ministers, and from Persons that are of unspotted Reputations for Holiness, Integrity, and Wisdom; and several Passages are taken verbatim in Writing from their dying Lips. I may add many other excellent Examples, if I have encouragement in this Piece. That the young Generation may be far more excellent than this, is the Prayer of One that dearly loves little Children.

James Janeway (p. 3–5)

In his introduction to the addendum to this volume, *A Token For the Children of New-England,* Cotton Mather explains:

A TOKEN FOR THE CHILDREN OF NEW-ENGLAND

If the Children of New-England should not with an Early Piety, set themselves to know and Serve the Lord JESUS CHRIST, the GOD of their Fathers, they will be condemned, not only by the Example of pious Children in other Parts of the World, the publish'd and printed Accounts whereof have been brought over hither; but there have been Exemplary Children in the Midst of New-England itself, that will rise up against them for their Condemnation. It would be a very profitable Thing to our Children, and highly acceptable to all the godly Parents of the Children, if, in Imitation of the excellent Janeway's Token for Children, there were made a true Collection of notable Things, exemplified in the Lives and Deaths of many among us, whose Childhood hath been signalized for what is virtuous and laudable.

In the Church-History of New-England is to be found the Lives of many eminent Persons, among whose Eminencies, not the last was, Their fearing of the Lord from their Youth and Their being loved by the Lord when they were children.

> But among the many other Instances, of a Childhood and Youth delivered from Vanity by serious Religion, which New-England has afforded, these few have particularly been preserved. (p. 107–108)

Very few of the books focused on physiological needs (2 percent) or safety needs (7 percent) of individuals, though there were a few cases of children lost in the woods without sustenance and without protection from either the elements or wild animals. There was, however, significant mention (15 percent) of the need for love and affection, primarily between parent and child. Children were to love and respect their parents, and parents were to love and direct their children. Harsh punishment was rarely mentioned, though there was one case of child abuse where a father tied the arms and legs of his son with a piece of string in order to force him, for disciplinary reasons, to sit still all day in *The Good Child's Delight or the Road to Knowledge* [Philadelphia: Printed by W. Young, 1795]).

In addition to the more basic needs for physical and psychological survival in this world, as well as security with God in the next, there was concern for expressive needs—for play, strength and achievement, reputation, and self-actualization, needs which refer to quality of life rather than to mere "getting along." Real need for play, as compared to the occasional diversionary activity, occurred in only a few cases (4 percent). Play was not thought of as essential to children; rather, it was thought of as time-wasting and thus somewhat sinful.

Strength and achievement, on the other hand, together constituted a need expressed in 69 percent of the books. It was found in religious as well as school books, fiction as well as well as nonfiction, poetry as well as prose. There were many multipurpose books for the young designed to impart knowledge in a number of related areas:

> *The Youth's Instructor in the English Tongue: or, The Art of Spelling Improved.* Being a more plain, easy and regular method of teaching young children, with a greater variety of very useful collections than any other book of this kind and bigness extant. In three parts. The first, containing monosyllables, expressing the most natural and easy things to the apprehensions of children, with common words, and Scripture names. The second, being an introduction more particularly for children of a higher class. The third, rules in arithmatick, with forms of bills, bonds, releases, &c. very useful for all persons. The whole being intermix'd with variety of exercises, in prose and verse, adapted to the capacities of children. For the use of schools. Collected from Dixon, Bailey, Owen, Strong and Watts. Boston: Printed and sold by Kneeland and Adams, 1767.

> Wood, John. *Mentor or The American Teacher's Assistant,* being a selection of essays, instructive and entertaining, from the most im-

proved authors in the English language. Intended to diffuse a true taste for elegance in style and sentiment, by exhibiting to the youth of our schools, just models of composition; and with a view to the improvement and amusement of young persons at classical and other schools, and to facilitate the invaluable arts of reading and writing. New York: Printed by John Buel, 1795.

The need for reputation and prestige is evident in 14 percent of the books. It is manifested in discourses on proper social behavior. There are scores of books on manners — explaining how to dress, speak, walk, particularly for boys. The major writers were two British gentlemen, Lord Chesterfield and John Hamilton Moore. Their works were reprinted in America and widely distributed to ensure good breeding in the New World.

In only a few books (5 percent) was there mention of the need for self-actualization, for pursuit of one's own set of ideologies and values. Even so, it was mentioned largely in relation to stories of our country's founders who, by virtue of their own strong commitment to freedom, justice, and opportunity, overcame many obstacles to create a new country.

In two-thirds of the books problems were expressed in meeting needs, because of the general ability of the individual to achieve a goal by himself. He needed the help of God or other humans. Sometimes there were specific threats to achievement of his ends — psychological threats of complete rejection by others or physiological threats of hunger or cold. But primarily it was man's weak and imperfect nature that was the basic cause of his difficulties. Children were thus encouraged to fear the Lord and listen carefully to their elders, for success was attainable only through their help. In *Virtue and Vice: or, The History of Charles Careful and Harry Heedless* (Boston: Printed and sold by Samuel Hall, 1795), the child is told:

> From this little history, we hope our young readers Will see the necessity of being good, obeying Their parents and friends, Minding Their learning, being cautious in Their actions and never apt to do things of Their own heads, when They have the opportunity of consulting Their elders. (p. 61)

Human needs were expressed more in terms of needs of the group than in terms of needs of the individual. The need for food and shelter was a community concern, and those more fortunate were supposed to assist those less fortunate. Love, of course, involves intense group interrelationships. And strength and achievement, while encouraged, was encouraged for the purpose of the group good. The idea of achieving just for one's own honor and glory was not apparent. Certainly there was no idea of doing one's own thing for the fun of it.

The orientation to needs and goals was primarily a future orientation. The future on earth and the future after earth were important. Delayed gratification in the present, to achieve satisfaction at a later time period, was expected. The child was not encouraged to be a child. He was, in effect, asked to wait for adulthood and even for death to achieve real happiness.

Religious institutions were the most frequently used social organizations for achieving goals; they were evidenced in 57 percent of the books. The church was seen as an important link between the individual and his needs, but there were other important links—family and school—as seen in these songs of Isaac Watts, *Select Songs for Children, in Three Parts . . .* I. Divine songs; II. Moral songs; III Psalms in verse (New York: Printed by J. Harrison, 1794):

DIVINE SONGS
Song 6
Lord, I ascribe it to thy grace,
And not to chance, as others do,
That I was born of Christian race,
And not a heathen or a Jew. (p. 7)

Song 23
Let Children that would fear the Lord,
Hear what their teachers say;
With rev'rence meet their parent's word,
And with delight obey. (p. 20)

Educational institutions were discussed in 43 percent of the books. Educational and religious institutions were, of course, certainly interrelated. In order to read the Bible one first had to learn to read. And academic learning not only brought piety; it also kept the young child busy and out of mischief.

The family as an institution was focused upon in 32 percent of the books. The family was looked upon primarily as carrying out the mission of the church through its teaching of dogma and through holy example. In all but two books the family household described was a nuclear family — mother, father, children. In one case the household included guardian and child; in still another case it included the child living with other relatives. In no case did the household take in the extended family of parents, children, grandparents, and other relatives, all living together.

Who made family decisions in the books? In 84 percent of the sample the father and mother did it jointly. This was true whether or not the decision was about family finances or childrearing. In 13 percent of the cases the father alone made the decision, in 3 percent the mother alone made the decision.

Both parents generally cared for the child, but in those cases where only one parent took charge it was more likely to be the father. This finding is related to the fact that books were more oriented to boy children than to girl children. And boys often spent time with their fathers in an apprenticeship situation — boys hunted with their fathers, discussed politics and economic affairs with their fathers, sometimes helped in the family business, certainly helped on the family farm.

Care of the child was considered important, requiring organization and hard work on the part of parents. The amount of parent-child interaction was substantial. Children rarely appeared alone in the stories. They most often appeared with adults, and the adults were shown taking time with them, primarily to teach them morals and manners. In 84 percent of the cases both parents disciplined the child; in 13 percent it was the father, and in 3 percent it was the mother. The discipline was rarely physical, such as spankings, putting in the corner, and the like. It was most often psychological, involving threats of God's wrath and social ostracism, as in these lines from *The Children's Bible: or, An History of the Holy Scriptures* (London: Printed, and Philadelphia: Reprinted and sold by Andrew Steuart, 1763):

> But setting aside God's displeasure; pray, what will you get by
> acting contrary to these commandments? will it gain you fine cloaths
> or money? or will people carress you or love you better for it? by no
> means, but, on the contrary, your father and mother will not care for
> you; your masters will correct, or leave you to your own naughty
> dispositions, which will be worse; and everyone will avoid and hate
> you. (p. vii)

The social responsibility of the individual in the institution was primarily to others—to God, to family, and occasionally to other persons (72 percent of the cases). Sometimes the responsibility was to God alone (26 percent of the cases). George Fox, in *Instructions for Right Spelling, and Plain Directions for Reading and Writing True English* (Boston: Printed by Roger and Fowle, 1743), declares:

> Christ is the Light. Christ is my Way. Christ is my Life. Christ is
> my Savior. Christ is my hope of Glory.

And in a few cases responsibility was to self alone (2 percent) — to study hard in order to better one's position in life. High on the list of social responsibilities was abstinence, primarily from alcohol, but also from mind-altering drugs.

The cognitive relationship between persons was, in more than half the books, based on rational and humanistic concerns for individuals and for society. Children were encouraged to be diligent and obedient and prudent so as to turn into responsible adults. In almost half the cases, however, the relationship was based on supernatural concerns. Satisfying God was the major goal because the individual was on this earth for only a short period; existence after this earth was what mattered.

Individuals tended to have intimate (25 percent of the cases) or both intimate and apart relationships with one another (75 percent of the cases). In a society in which people lived in small communities, everyone knew everyone else. There might be status differences (especially between adult and child), but the relationships remained intimate. Both adult and child were very much involved in each other's worlds and knew what was expected in terms of social behavior. Not surprisingly, in books where family institutions were present, there tended to be more intimate-only behavior. Although sternness and discipline were stated modes of relationship, warmth and love were there as well.

In the majority of the books, the primary goal orientation of individuals was to satisfy the needs of the group rather than the needs of the individual. In a fourth of the cases it was to satisfy the needs or prerogatives of God alone. This goal orientation remained true whether the main character was adult or child. The group itself was nonstratified in 67 percent of the cases, stratified but with social mobility in 23 percent of the cases, and stratified with no apparent mobility in 10 percent of the cases. In this new land across the ocean from England there was little patience for kings and queens, lords and ladies, dukes and duchesses.

The ways in which needs were met, not surprisingly, involved conformity to established group norms—either adult natural norms or supernatural norms. Social change was encouraged in only 5 percent of the cases. *The Good Child's Delight or the Road to Knowledge* (Philadelphia: Printed by W. Young, the corner of Chestnut and Second Streets, 1795) admonishes:

> Caution is to be observed in all our actions, but more so in any
> new attempt; and those who will not look before they leap, must
> expect often to fall short of the end proposed. (p. 64)

And *A Present to Children* (Norwich: Printed by Thomas Hubbard, 1794) states:

> Better is a little, with the fear of the Lord, than great treasure and
> trouble therewith.
>
> Come unto Christ all ye who labour and are heavy laden, and he
> will give you rest.

In most cases (96 percent) needs were indeed satisfied. They were satisfied by the individual actor alone in 10 percent of the cases, by his family in 5 percent of the cases, by his God in 29 percent of the cases, and by a combination of natural and supernatural beings in the remaining cases. Little could be done without following God's commandments and without accepting God's grace and mercies. In four books needs were not satisfied; in two instances God's displeasure was the reason, and in two instances the individual's own inadequacies constituted the reason.

The individual, for the most part, was possessed of an insecure self-image; he could succeed only with a lot of assistance—from family, from the supernatural. His view of humans, in general, was less than positive; they, too, were seen as capable of accomplishing their goals primarily through help from others. The view of the world was of a fairly hostile place, with death just around the corner. It was essentially through the critical help of God and his fellow man that the individual could hope to survive.

In addition to this overview of a random sample of one hundred books for the period 1721–1795, detailed analysis will be made of two books, both of which are representative of the subject matter and the presentation of the period, and both of which were enormously popular: *The New England Primer* and Noah Webster's *An American Selection of Lessons in Reading and Speaking*. These books employed fiction as well as nonfiction styles; they were concerned with spiritual, social, and academic needs of the child; and they pointed the way to satisfaction of these needs through traditional institutions of church, family, school.

The New England Primer

In the Rare Book Room of the Library of Congress are ninety-six copies of the *New England Primer*, a book that has been called the most important volume in the eighteenth-century nursery (Rosenbach [10]). Its authorship has been ascribed to Benjamin Harris, a London bookseller and printer, who suffered the pillory in 1681 for printing *A Protestant Petition* and who came to Boston in 1686. The earliest extant issue of the book is that printed by S. Kneeland and T. Green in Boston, 1727, though many earlier editions have apparently simply disappeared. The earliest Rare Book edition is 1773. Estimates suggest that well over six million were printed between the years 1680 and 1830, and, in any case, the book went through important editions for 150 years. (See historical studies by Eames [2], Ford [4], Heartman [7], Livermore [9], and Winship [12]).

The *Primer* is small enough to fit in a child's pocket; it was that volume to which the child turned after his hornbook, and it was the first to provide children with religious education in a form which the child could assimilate. The basic part of its teaching was *The Shorter Catechism of the Assembly of Divines at Westminster*, which children were supposed to learn by heart. The *Primer* made a bold attempt to hold the attention of children by the introduction of pictures. The alphabet couplets placed near the beginning of every edition were always accompanied by illustrations.

Over the centuries of its intense use, the alphabet changed somewhat in content, and the different alphabets used reflect the change in tone and content. The 1749 edition contained an "Alphabet of Lessons for Youth" which stated:

> F Foolishness is bound up in the Heart of a Child,
>   but the Rod of Correction shall drive it from him.

> G Grieve not the Holy Spirit.

while by 1800 the growth of secular subjects allowed this alphabet to appear (published in Hartford, 1800):

> A was an Angler, and fished with a hook.
> B was a Blockhead, and ne'er learn'd his book.
> C The Cat doth play and after slay. (p. 5)

The opening lesson included the alphabet, followed by lists of words of two, three, four, and five syllables. The words chosen for inclusion were not usually names of familiar objects; rather, they were abstractions relating to religious or social behavior.

Following the alphabet of lessons came The Lord's Prayer and the Ten Commandments (they did not change over the editions). Then appeared the account of the martyrdom of the Reverend John Rogers, with a picture of Rogers being burned at the stake, under the watchful eyes of his wife and nine children. The inclusion of Rogers' martyrdom was to keep alive the memory in the new land of those persecutions which came with the development of protestanism in England. Rogers was the first of the ministers executed in Queen Mary's reign.

The *Primer* also contained Dr. Watts's beautiful cradle hymn, with its loving and reassuring lines (1773 edition):

> Hush, my dear, lie still and slumber,
>   Holy angels guard thy bed;
> Heavenly blessings, without number,
>   Gently falling on thy head.
> Sleep, my babe, thy food and raiment,
>   House and home, thy friends provide;
> And without thy care or payment,
>   All thy wants are well supply'd.

The major portion of the rest of the *Primer* was filled by the Westminster Shorter Catechism. It included the Dialogue between Christ, Youth, and the Devil, in which Youth succumbs to the Devil, repents at the sight of death, but is too late to save his own life or to enjoy an afterlife with God.

The individual actors in the *Primer* include both humans and supernatural beings, who sometimes interact with each other in dialogue. Human interaction with other humans involves principally family members. The humans depicted are white Protestants. Males and females appear without any status differentials indicated between them, and indeed social-class differentials are also absent. Both God and the devil appear, and the human is shown as a complex intellectual being with negative as well as positive feelings toward these supernatural beings.

The most important human need depicted is the need for eternal

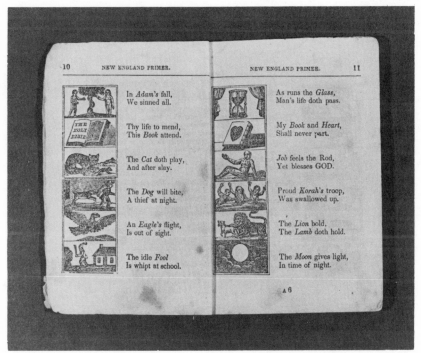

Ill. 8: The New England Primer. Eighteenth Century. [3″ x 4½″]

salvation—we are born not to live, but to die, and we must learn how to die suitably. Why? Because it is the afterlife that really counts (as seen in a 1773 edition):

Q1 What is the chief End of Man?

A. A Man's chief End is to glorify God and enjoy him for ever.

Q2 What Rule hath God given to direct us how we may glorify and enjoy him?

A. The Word of God which is contained in the Scriptures of the Old and New Testament, is the only Rule to direct us how we may glorify and enjoy him.

Q3 What do the Scriptures principally teach?

A. The Scriptures principally teach what Man is to believe concerning God and what Duty God requireth of Man.

Q4 What is God?

A. God is a Spirit, infinite, eternally unchangeable, in his Being, Wisdom, Holiness, Justice, Goodness and Truth.

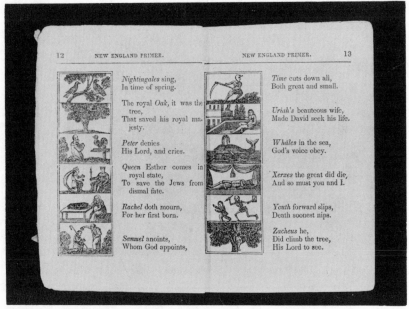

Ill. 9: The New England Primer. Eighteenth Century. [3″ x 4½″]

Another need certainly in evidence is the need for strength and achievement on this earth, and the vocabulary drills address that point. They must have seemed endless to the child (1773 edition):

Words of Two Syllables
Ab sent
Ba bel
Ca pon
Dai ly
Ea gle
Fa ther

Words of Three Syllables
A bu sing
Bar ba rous
Cal cu late
Dam ni fy
Ea ger ly
Fa cul ty

Words of Four Syllables
A bi li ty

Ill. 10: The New England Primer. Eighteenth Century. [2″ x 1⅞″]

Be ne fit ed
Ca la mi ty
De li ca cy
E dy fy ing
Fe bru a ry

Words of Five Syllables
A bo mi na ble
Be ne dic ti on
Ce le bra ti on
De cla ra ti on
E du ca ti on
For ni ca ti on

Concern is primarily with God, but responsibilities to other persons are to be considered in one's actions. Needs relate to the future—in this life and in the next.

The family, the church, and the school are all institutions which carry out God's work and prepare the child for adult roles and for eternal salvation. Social responsibility is mainly to God, and the religious belief system is all pervasive. Needs are met by conformity to supernatural norms, not by self-direction or innovation. There is no orientation to social change.

Needs of the individual are indeed to be satisfied if the individual obeys the word of God. But success is due largely to God's benevolence, because the individual himself is indeed weak. He can do nothing without help. The world is shown as a somewhat hostile place, with death always nearby. But hope of eternal life with God, without trials and tribulations, remains to the end.

The New England Primer was probably the first American children's book to be widely read abroad. Puritan children in England and Scotland read it, and its power and influence lasted for well over a hundred years and through hundreds of editions. While original sin and human frailities were discussed at length, not too much effort was made to be specific on a subject which would be hard for young minds to understand. However, the idea of early death and the need to prepare for it was a theme constantly mentioned and spelled out in great detail. Infant and child mortality was, of course, comparatively high at that time, and medical services were far less advanced and far less available. Parents thus felt the need to teach their children early to be ready for death.

There is a whole group of similar writings about the need to prepare for death and avoid eternal damnation. Cotton Mather, in *The Family Well-Ordered* (1699), published a sermon addressed directly to children in which he portrayed hell as a place of complete darkness, warning children not to "make light of their parents" if they wished eternal "light." Mather also added "A Token for the children of New England, or, Some Examples of Children in whom the Fear of God was remarkably budding before they died; in several parts of New England," to Janeway's *A Token for Children*. This former work describes, among others, the lives of John Clap, who died at the age of thirteen, Priscilla Thornton, who left this world having first given demonstrations of an exemplary piety, and Daniel Williams, whose dying speeches have been conscientiously collected.

An American Selection of Lessons in Reading and Speaking

Noah Webster (1758–1843), the lexicographer whose name became a virtual synonym for the word *dictionary*, was teacher, journalist, essayist, lecturer, and patriot. He was born at West Hartford, Connecticut. He entered Yale College in 1774, interrupted his studies to serve briefly in the Revolutionary War, and graduated in 1778. He taught school, clerked, and studied law, being admitted to the bar in 1781.

While teaching in Goshen, New York, in 1782, Webster became dissatisfied with texts for children that ignored American culture, and he began his lifelong efforts to promote a distinctively American education. His first step was *A Grammatical Institute of the English Language*, the first part being *The American Spelling Book* (1783), the famed "Blue Backed Speller," which has never been out of print. It provided much of Webster's income for the rest of his life, and its total sales have been estimated to be as high as 100,000,000 copies. *A Grammatical Institute of the English Language* (1784) and *An American Selection of Lessons in Reading and Speaking* (1785) completed the Institute. The grammar was based on Webster's principle, enunciated later in his dictionary, that "grammar is formed on language, and not language on grammar." Although he did not always follow this principle, and often relied on analogy, reason, and true or fanciful etymology, his inconsistencies were no greater than those of his English contemporaries. He spoke of American English as "Federal English," always contrasting the superior usage of the yeoman of America with the affectations of London. The *Reader* consisted mainly of American selections chosen to promote democratic ideals and responsible moral and political conduct.

Webster wrote on many subjects—politics, economics, medicine, and physical science—in addition to language. He noted the living language as he traveled, but with varying degrees of approbation according to the fit between what he heard and what he himself used. His early enthusiasm for spelling reform abated in his later works, but he is largely responsible for the differences that exist today between British and United States spelling.

In 1806 Webster published his *Compendious Dictionary of the English Language*. Though it was no more than a preparation for his later dictionary, it contained about 5,000 more words than Samuel Johnson's dictionary (1755) and a number of innovations, including perhaps the first separation of *i* and *j*, of *u* and *v*, as alphabetical entities. He started work on *The American Dictionary* in 1807, acquiring at least a passing acquaintance with about twenty languages and traveling in France and England in 1824–25 in search of materials unavailable to him in the United States. The first edition of *The American Dictionary of the English Language* was published in two volumes in 1828, when Webster was seventy years old. It numbered 2,500 copies in the United States and 3,000 in England, and it sold out in little more than a year, in spite of harsh attacks on its "Americanisms," its unconventional preferences in spelling, its tendency to favor American rather than British usage and spelling, and its inclusion of nonliterary words, particularly technical terms from the arts and sciences. It contained about 70,000 entries and between 30,000 and 40,000 definitions that had not appeared in any earlier dictionary. Despite his frequent disparagement of Johnson, his indebtedness where the literary vocabulary is concerned is apparent in both definitions and citations. *The American Dictionary* was relatively unprofitable and the 1841 revision was generally unsuccessful. The rights were purchased from Webster's estate by George and Charles Merriam. (For historical analyses of Webster's and other early-American schoolbooks see Carpenter [1] and Freeman [5].)

Webster's spelling book, geographies, and histories were intended to do more than just impart academic skills. They advocated precepts to encourage social conduct befitting God-fearing proper young gentlemen and women. In *An American Selection of Lessons in Reading and Speaking* (Printed at Boston by Isaiah Thomas And Ebenezer T. Andrews, 1790) a lot was offered—geography, history, and politics; rules of elocution; rules of social behavior; observations on family life.

In Chapter One of *An American Selection* Webster gives specific advice on how to conduct social relationships. The emphasis on group needs rather than individual desires is paramount:

> To be very active in laudable pursuits, is the distinguishing characteristic of a man of merit.
>
> There is an heroic innocence, as well as an heroic courage.
>
> There is a mean in all things. Even virtue itself has its stated limits, which not being strictly observed, it ceasest to be virtue.
>
> It is wiser to *prevent* a quarrel beforehand, than to *revenge* it afterwards.
>
> It is much better to reprove, than to be angry secretly.
>
> No revenge is more heroic, than that which torments envy, by doing good.
>
> The discretion of a man deferreth his anger, and it is his glory to pass over a transgression.
>
> Money, like manure, does no good till it is spread. There is no real use of riches, except in the distribution; the rest is all conceit.
>
> A wise man will desire no more than what he may get justly, use soberly, distribute cheerfully, and live upon contentedly.
>
> A contented mind, and a good conscience, will make a man happy in all conditions. He knows not how to *fear*, who *dares to die*.
>
> There is but one way of fortifying the soul against all gloomy passages and terrors of the mind; and that is, by securing to themselves the friendship and protection of that Being who disposes of events, and governs futurity.
>
> Philosophy is then only valuable, when it serves for the law of life, and not for the ostentation of science. (p. 18)

In Chapter Nineteen of *An American Selection* Webster discusses "Family Disagreements the frequent cause of Immoral Conduct." In doing so he gives a glimpse of ideal home life of the period and some problems in achieving same, problems which have probably not changed substantially over the years:

After all our complaints of the uncertainty of human affairs, it is undoubtedly true, that more misery is produced among us by the irregularities of our tempers, than by real misfortune.

And it is a circumstance particularly unhappy, that these irregularities of the temper are most apt to display themselves at our firesides, where everything ought to be tranquil and serene. But the truth is, we are awed by the presence of strangers and are afraid of appearing weak and ill-natured, when we act in the fight of the world; and so, very heroically, reserve all our ill-humor for our wives, children and servants. We are meek, where we might meet with opposition; but feel ourselves undauntedly bold where we are sure of no effectual resistance.

The perversion of the *best* things converts them to the *worst*. Home is certainly well adapted to repose and solid enjoyment. Among parents and brothers, and all the tender charities of private life, the gentler affections, which are always attended with feelings purely and permanently pleasurable, find an ample scope for proper exertion. The experienced have often declared, after wearing themselves in pursuing phantoms, that they have found a substantial happiness in the domestic circle. Hither they have returned from their wild excursions in the regions of dissipation, as the bird, after fluttering in the air, descends into her nest, to partake and to increase its general warmth with her young cries. (pp. 72-73)

Individual actors in *An American Selection of Lessons in Reading and Spelling* are, for the most part, adult humans. God's name is used with reverence and respect. And animals are depicted primarily in a natural rural habitat. Individuals are shown usually at home or at work. Interpersonal relationships are stressed, and the importance of justice and respect and humility to others is emphasized. Social involvement is with both primary and secondary groups. The individuals are whites, male and female. They show both positive and negative affect and complex intellectual behavior.

The human needs focused upon were need for eternal salvation, for love in the family setting, for strength and achievement. There was no problem anticipated in achieving needs, if only the person worked at it. Human needs did not relate to the individual alone but to the welfare of the group and to God's will. Needs were oriented to the future on this earth, when the child would take on adult responsibilities, and to the life hereafter where he would meet his Maker.

Several social institutions came into play in satisfying needs. The history and geogaphy portions of the book concerned political and economic groupings. Family activity was discussed directly, and religion remained an underlying factor in all of social behavior. Education as an institution was the focus of the lessons provided; the book was aimed at the American one-room and larger schools.

In human interaction, social responsibility was to one's family and to one's God. Use of stimulants was abhored. Actors behaved rationally and were in close contact with one another. Conformity to both adult and supernatural demands was expected and, concomitantly, social change was not encouraged.

Satisfaction of needs came about through the help of others and the help of God; an individual was not able to achieve on his own. The view of the world in general was of an uncertain place—with the individual in need of a lot of support and the spectre of death at hand.

An American Selection like *The New England Primer*, is sober and task-oriented. Both books are aimed at providing the child with skills needed to participate meaningfully in the society and moral reasons for such participation. Those editions that have come down to us are generally ragged and torn, showing the effects of hard use. Books were not plentiful. They could not be bought in the local grocery but were reserved for booksellers. They were bought by parents to help them produce proper children, by reminding the child that

> In Adam's Fall
> We sinned all.

and that only through considerable personal effort was there hope for eternal salvation.

References

1. Carpenter, Charles. *History of American School-Books*. Philadelphia: The University of Pennsylvania Press, 1963.
2. Eames, Wilberforce. *Early New England Catechisms*. Worcester, Massachusetts: C. Hamilton, 1898.
3. Earles, Alice. *Child Life in Colonial Days*. New York: Macmillan, 1899.
4. Ford, Paul L. *The New-England Primer: A History of Its Origin and Development*. New York: Dodd, Mead, 1897.
5. Freeman, Ruth S. *Yesterday's School Books*. Watkins Glen, New York: Century House, 1960.
6. Halsey, Rosalie V. *Forgotten Books of the American Nursery*. Boston: Charles E. Goodspeed, 1911.
7. Heartman, Charles F. *The New-England Primer Issued Prior to 1830*. New York: R.R. Bowker, 1934.
8. Kiefer, Monica. *American Children Through Their Books: 1700–1835*. Philadelphia: University of Pennsylvania Press, 1948.
9. Livermore, George. *The Origin, History and Character of the New England Primer*. New York: C.F. Heartman, 1915.

10. Rosenbach, Abraham, S.W. *Early American Children's Books*. Portland, Maine: The Southworth Press, 1933.

11. Shipton, Clifford K. *Isaiah Thomas, Printer, Patriot and Philanthropist, 1749-1831*. Rochester, New York: Printing House of Leo Hart, 1948.

12. Winship, George P. *Notes on a Reprint of the New-England Primer Improved, for the Year 1777 for the More Easy Attaining the Truth*. Cambridge: Printed by C.P., 1922.

13. "The Early History of Children's Books in New England." *New England Magazine*, 26 (1899):147–160.

14. *The History of Little Goody Two-Shoes, an essay, and a list of editions*. Worcester, Massachusetts: American Antiquarian Society, 1940.

Chapter 3

1796-1835: "Let the poor witling argue all he can,/It is Religion still that makes the man."

The majority of books in this period, as in the previous, focused on moral instruction (60 percent). Many editions of *The New England Primer* and of the Bible were published, as well as numerous other religious texts. Several British women writers, typifying the hell-and-damnation school of strict Puritanism, were reprinted in America, among them Anna Barbauld, Hannah More, Elizabeth Turner, Maria Edgeworth, and Jane and Ann Taylor. These writers were influential in the development of the church press in America—such as that of the American Sunday School Union and American Tract Society —which became increasingly important transmitters of moral standards until the turn of the twentieth century.* The books were clear about where one's duty lay. In *The Child's First Book; Being an Easy Introduction to Spelling and Reading* (Boston: Printed for W. P. and L. Blake, 1802) the reader is admonished:

> Be a good child
> Love and fear God
> Do not lie nor swear
> Play not with bad boys. (p. 46)

Ann Taylor Gilbert in *Hymns for infant minds* (Boston: S. T. Armstrong, 1810) writes:

> Thank the goodness and the grace
> Which on my birth have smiled,
> And made me in these latter days,
> A happy Christian child. (p. 11)

Along with instruction in religious behavior came instruction in social behavior, found in 38 percent of the books. The Sunday school presses were particularly active in telling people how to conduct their daily lives with gravity and moderation. Their special concern was temperance, and the following grim

*For additional readings on books of this period, see Halsey[3], Kiefer[5], Meigs[6], Rosenbach[9], and the *New York Public Library*[11].

scene from *The Reformed Family* (Philadelphia: American Sunday School Union, c.1835) is typical:

> A few years before, John had been unfortunate in business. Then the first drop of spirits was brought into the house, and his happy little home was turned into an abode of misery and vice. Had his wife been a Christian woman; had she then affectionately, but firmly, remonstrated against it, the evil might have been prevented; but she said nothing, and as one after another of her usual comforts was abridged, she would take, with him, "a little spirit" to console her for the want of them, or rather to make her forget she had ever possessed them. (pp. 11-12)

Exemplary behavior is described in the following passage from *I am Afraid There is a God!*, 6th ed. (Boston: Published by Ford and Damrell. Temperance Press, 1834):

> My father was a respectable mechanic in the town of ——————. On the subject of religion, there existed the most perfect unanimity between my father and my mother; and their whole lives were ample illustrations of their confidence in the promises of God and of their firm and sustaining belief in the precepts and doctrines of Christianity. My parents were both members of the Temperance Society, and earnest promoters of the cause, to the extent of their limited influence and ability. (p. 7)

Instructional books—primers, spellers, histories, and geographies—were also important during this time, 34 percent of the books falling into this category. Very important were histories and geographies about America and biographies of American heroes (see Johnson [4] and Nietz [7] for information on texts of the period). Two important writers of this genre were Samuel Griswold Goodrich (pseudonym, Peter Parley) and Mason Locke Weems.

Goodrich was horrified as a child by fairy tales such as *Little Red Riding Hood* and *Jack The Giant Killer;* he thought such tales were too frightening and fanciful, and he resolved at an early age to try to give children true stories to read. The first of his many famous Peter Parley books was *Tales of Peter Parley about America,* written in 1827, and a long succession of books about geography, history, science, travel, and biography followed—all packed with information and moral values. Goodrich has been described as one of the first of America's didactic writers for children; there are 239 editions of his works in the Rare Book Collection of the Library of Congress.

Parson Weems's claim to fame rests on one book: *The Life of George Washington.* This biography of Washington by the one-time Rector of Mount Vernon Parish stressed love of God and of country, hard work, and other clear and simple virtues. Weems's purpose was both moral teaching and historical information; but the history was secondary, a means of getting across basic precepts in an interesting manner. There are twenty-one editions of this book in the Rare Book Collection, including several foreign-language translations.

Also in this period were books strictly for entertainment (8 percent of the cases). Found were *Cock Robin's Courtship and Marriage*, *The History of Tom Thumb*, and several editions of *Cinderella*, one of which, *Cinderella, or, The Little Glass Slipper* (Cooperstown, New York: H. and E. Phinney, 1828), explains:

> The story of Cinderella, or the Little Glass Slipper, is one of these wonderful Tales of Fairies, which, although entirely divested of truth, contains so many curious incidents, both instructive and entertaining, that it forms a pleasing fund of amusement to youthful readers. (p. 5)

With regard to the authors, there were three times as many male as female writers during this period. Males in general had more education and were more prominent in the educational field. Six percent of the writers were ministers. More publishing houses were located in Boston (24 percent) and Philadelphia (22 percent) than in any other Eastern city. Seven percent of the publishing houses were church sponsored, and the proportion grew during the period.

There was a much greater use of fictional writing at this point. Edification of little minds was still the primary goal, but it was felt that story material would liven things up—35 percent of the books were fiction, 43 percent were nonfiction, and 22 percent were both fictional and nonfictional. There was more prose than poetry in the time period, with fewer religious songs or rhymed monologues; 64 percent of the books included prose only, 9 percent poetry or song only, and 27 percent both.

The settings were almost always reality-oriented (83 percent), human beings interacting in familiar human, often humdrum, situations. A mixture of fantasy and reality occurred in 11 percent of the cases, and in 6 percent of the cases fantasy won out—in the form of absurd animal stories or classic fairy tales.

By far the majority of these books (96 percent) were matter-of-fact rather than humorous. Children were looked upon as little adults who were to pay attention to their work rather than just play. They were also suspected of flightiness and distractability—humor would only divert them more. The thought of play and laughter as important parts of children's developmental needs rarely occurred to the authors of these books and was rarely addressed.

The location for the majority of books was rural or semiurban America, which was where both the writers and the readers resided. But in 25 percent of the cases other countries were depicted. Authors such as Samuel Griswold Goodrich, Jedidiah Morse, and Noah Webster tried to make other peoples and their customs and ideals come alive to the American child in geographies and histories. The breadth of such offerings can be seen in this partial listing of the works by Goodrich:

The Tales of Peter Parley about Europe. Boston, 1828.

Peter Parley's Tales about Asia. With a map and numerous engravings. Boston: Gray and Bowen and Carter and Hendee, c.1830.

The Tales of Peter Parley about Africa. With engravings. Boston: Gray and Bowen, 1830.

Peter Parley's Tales about the Islands in the Pacific Ocean. Boston: Gray and Bowen, 1831.

Peter Parley's Tales about Ancient and Modern Greece. New York: Collins and Hannay; Boston: Richardson, Lora, and Holbrook, etc., 1832.

Peter Parley's Tales about South America. Baltimore: J. Jewett, 1832.

Peter Parley's Tales about Ancient Rome, with Some Account of Modern Italy. Boston: Carter, Hendee and Company, 1833.

Peter Parley's Rambles in England, Wales, Scotland, and Ireland. New York: Samuel Coleman, 1839.

A Pictoral History of France. For the use of schools. Revised and improved edition, brought down to the present time. Philadelphia: E. H. Butler and Company, 1855.

Locale of the book, as related to the main character, is found in two-thirds of the cases to be the community in which he carries on his day-to-day activities. Described are his home, school, work, or church encounters. Not infrequently described are situations in which the individual assists those in the community who need his help, be that person a close relative or a stranger. Usually, it is the family to whom one comes for help, as in *The Snow Drop:* by a lady (Salem: Whipple and Lawrence, 1824):

> However, as was her usual practice when in trouble, she went to her mamma. It was natural; to whom else could she go? What earthly friend so sympathizing and so kind? Much as you love your mother, my dear little reader, your love for her does not amount to the love she feels for you. You do not think how many hours fatigue she has felt on your account. When you were a tender babe, how has she watched your features, and, perhaps, in her over anxiety, has sometimes fancied you were ill when in reality you were not. (p. 11)

But other people are to be cared for besides family members, as shown by

Elizabeth Turner in *The Daisy; or, Cautionary Stories in Verse* . . . (Philadelphia: Published by Jacob Johnson, no. 147 Market-street, 1808):

> Do you see the old beggar who stands at the door?
> Do not send him away—we must pity the poor;
> Oh! see how he shivers!—he's hungry and cold!
> For people can't work when they grow very old.
> Go, set near the fire a table and seat;
> And Betty shall bring him some bread and some meat,
> I hope my dear children will always be kind
> When ever they meet with the aged or blind. (p. 164)

In the majority of the books of the period humans appear as the only actors. A fourth of the books showed supernatural beings interacting with humans, and a few showed animal actors with humans. Human actors interacted principally with primary group members—with families, friends, teachers.

The family was the most visible group in the books, with parent and child coming together for many simple day-to-day tasks of housekeeping and working, as well as complex day-to-day tasks of teaching and learning. In these books children's nurses and servants were sometimes present, but they did not take the role of parents. Rather, they were there only to carry out the instructions of parents. And the caution was often given children that they should not abuse nurses or servants or treat them with disrespect. George Chipman writes in *The American Moralist* (Wrentham, Mass: Printed by Nathaniel Heaton, jun., for the author, 1801) of the child's duty with regard to family: "The first thing I recommend is obedience to parents." And *The Child's First Book* (Boston: Printed for W. P. & L. Blake, at the Boston book-store, 1802) states:

> Be grateful to thy Father,
>   for he gave thee life,
> and to thy Mother, for she
>   sustained thee.

George Alfred reminds the reader in *The American Universal Spelling; Containing a New and Complete System of Orthography* . . . (Staunton, Va.: Printed by Isaac Collett, at the office of the Republican farmer, 1811):

> If you have sisters or brothers, it is your duty to love them; they
> will love you for it, and it will be pleasing to your parents and
> pleasure to yourselves. (p. 157)

Mentor, or Dialogues, Between a Parent and Children (Lexington, Ky.: Printed by T. Smith, 1828) discusses the relationship between parents and children in this manner:

> Child: What is the reason parents are so anxious about their children?

Parent: God has made parents fond of their children, and children
fond of parents, for very good purposes. Children are helpless and
require someone to take care of them; they need food, clothing and
education, which necessarily require much expertise and trouble.
Then if God had not caused parents to love their children, dis-
posed their hearts to do all this for the helpless little ones, what
would become of them?

Human actors in the books also interacted substantially with peers and with
neighbors, showing love and concern for their fellow man. Eleanor Fenn in
Fables in Monosyllables (by Mrs. Teachwell, pseud.) (Philadelphia: Printed for
Thomas Dobson, at the Stone house no. 41, South Second Street, 1798) writes:

This was wrote to teach you to be good
If you be good your friends will love you
If you be good, God will bless you.

And Samuel Willard in *Franklin Primer: Containing a New and Useful
Selection of Moral Lessons*, 4th ed. (Boston: Printed by J. M. Dunham, 1803)
admonishes children:

Love to learn your book
Be kind to all your mates.
A good boy will be a good man.
Love good boys, and play with none that
swear, or lie, or cheat, or do ill things,
or call bad names, for fear you will learn
their ways, and be as bad as they. (p. 17)

George Alfred in *The American Universal Spelling Book; Containing a New
and Complete System of Orthography* (Staunton, Virginia: Printed by Isaac
Collett, 1811) cautions children:

If you would be happy you must be good. A good man has a
tender concern for his neighbor. We were not made for ourselves
only. Vice soon or late brings on pain and woe. A modest person is
loved by all wise men. (p. 55)

In addition to parents interacting with children, teachers interacted with
students, directing and encouraging them in good conduct as well as academic
affairs. Mrs. Taylor in *Familiar Letters Between a Mother and her Daughter
at School* (Boston: James Loring, 1827) writes:

She (teacher) takes great pains to check in us a spirit of competition and rivalry; while she endeavours to inspire us with the genuine
love of knowledge, and with a true taste for our acquirements; urging
us to be more ambitious to excell *ourselves,* than to excell each
other. (pp. 13-14)

Consideration of and kindness to others is a recurring value expressed in all of the different types of human interaction shown. Such behavior is usually linked to God's will, and while God is not often an active participant in human social relationships, he is nearly always in evidence as the guiding force behind them. Abner Kneeland writes in *The American Definition Spelling Book,* 1st edition . . . (Keene, New Hampshire: Printed by John Prentiss, for the author, 1802):

> Religion is that sense of God on the soul, and our obligation to, and dependence on him, as to make it our principle study to do that which we think will be well pleasing in his sight, and to avoid everything we think will offend him. As he is the fountain of goodness and justice; of course, religion must be the foundation of all Christian and moral virtue to do good to all; and to avoid giving offence to, or injuring willingly, even those who are enemies and persecutors. (p. 179)

In most of the books of this period the persons described in the text or portrayed in the illustrations were white Anglo-Saxon Protestants. But there was a beginning awareness of minority racial figures, blacks and American Indians appearing in 7 percent of the books. Considerable stereotyping and disparagement of minority people was shown throughout the period. In *Mentor, or Dialogues, Between a Parent and Children* black slaves are pictured in this manner:

> Child: If there were no slaves in the country, how should we get the work done?
>
> Father: It would be done by the free people.
>
> Child: Would it not cost more?
>
> Father: Slaves are often lazy, careless and wasteful; because they have no interest in doing better, and we have to maintain them all year. (p. 166)

In *Men of Different Countries* (Cooperstown: Stereotyped, printed and sold by H. & E. Phinney, 1829) American Indians are thusly described:

> Sometimes Indians kill other Indians with the bow and arrow; they fight very much; they do not treat women kindly. Savage men never treat women as well as civilized men treat them. (p. 5)

However, toward the end of the period, the injustices surrounding race prejudice were discussed in some of the books. The basis for dismay over unfair and demeaning treatment of minorities was rarely related to the goals of a new nation; it was usually related to the goals of a Christian religion. Social behavior still was judged principally in terms of religious values rather than democratic values. And the concern for the black and the Indian was to a large extent concern for their conversion. John Ferguson in *Memoir of the Life and Character of Rev. Samuel Hopkins . . .* (Boston: L. W. Kimball, 1830) writes:

Amidst a population, at the period of his settlement in Newport deeply engaged in the African slave trade, the attention of Dr. Hopkins was early directed to the iniquity of cruel injustice of a traffic which makes a difference of color a pretext for enslaving our fellow creatures. Slavery was at that time (1773) general throughout New England. In the town of Newport nearly every family, having the means, was a slaveholding family. The right to deal in slaves was not questioned, and men of all professions, including ministers and Christians, consulted only their interest and convenience respecting this unrighteous degradation of the African race . . . We have said that Dr. Hopkins, soon after his settlement at Newport, conceived the design of educating and qualifying pious Africans to go on as missionaries to their own country.

In the first year of our national independence (1776) he addressed an anonymous pamphlet to the Continental Congress, shewing it to be the interest or the duty of the American States to emancipate the African slaves. (pp. 82-88)

Clear differences in sex characteristics were shown in the books. Boys and men worked hard and achieved in their profession and in the community—all the while avoiding drink, to which they were particularly prone. Girls and women practiced gentility and stayed at home. They had few vices other than vanity.

The Ladder of Learning; to be Ascended Early in the Morning (New Haven: S. Babcock, Sidney's press, 1830) describes a boy's path to strength and achievement:

This is the boy who got up in the morning,
And then set his foot on the Ladder of Learning.

1st Step	Spelling
2nd Step	Reading
3rd Step	Writing
4th Step	Tales
5th Step	Accounts
6th Step	Grammar
7th Step	Truth
8th Step	Kindness
9th Step	Mercy
10th Step	Justice
11th Step	Gratitude
12th Step	Trade

On the other hand, Miss Woodland (*Bear and Forbear: or, The History of Julia Marchmont* (New-York: W. B. Gilley, 94 Broadway, 1827) describes feminine virtues as follows:

> Nothing is more conducive to female happiness, or more certain to insure the affection of those with whom we live, than a yielding forebearing temper. (p. 3)

And in *Mentor, or Dialogues, Between a Parent and Children* a woman's place is clearly limited:

> The peculiar sphere of woman is, in general, domestick life, in the midst of her children and household affairs. (p. 142)

When human actors were present, adult characters alone appeared in almost a third of the books; adults and children together appeared in two-thirds of the books. In few cases did children appear alone. Adults provided important role models. They showed expected social behavior for the future, thus giving some rationale for discipline of children in the present.

In over half of the cases there was evidence of social-class differentiation. A number of the described households included servants, some black slaves and some not. There was, further, considerable discussion of poverty and poorer classes, which were not to be scorned but to be helped. *The Entertaining, Moral, and Religious Repository* (Elizabeth-Town: Printed by Shepard Pollock, for Cornelius Davis. No. 94, Water-Street, New York, 1799) states:

> This story shews us that God despises not laborers on account of their poverty, or negroes on account of their color. . . . (p. 304)

And Ann Taylor Gilbert writes in *Hymns for infant minds* (Boston: S. T. Armstrong, 1810):

> Child of Affluence
> Since I with so many comforts am blest,
> May it be my delight to reduce the distrest.

> Child of Poverty
> Give me at least the crumbs that fall
> From tables richly spread.

> But seeing Lord Thou dost withhold
> The riches some possess,
> Grant me what better is than gold,
> Thy grace and righteousness.

The Week-day Book for Boys and Girls, By the editors of the Popular library (Boston: J. Allen & Co., 1835) warns:

> We are cautioned in Scripture against the too great love of money.
> It is, indeed, a foolish and wicked thing to set your heart on money,
> or on anything in this present world. (p. 58)

Animal characters appeared in 19 percent of the books. In 8 percent animals really represented people in fur who tended to be more negative than human characters in their behavior; in 11 percent of the stories animals behaved as animals in human dominated settings.

God was an important part of over half of the books; a few books also mentioned elves and fairies. God's presence in a book was overwhelming and provided the rationale for behaving the way one should; he was the principal guiding force for this world and for the next.

Main characters continued in this time period to be mostly adults (46 percent of the books), although children were increasing as main characters (44 percent of the books). Animals, God, and inanimate objects made up the remaining principals.

Characters show both positive and negative affect. No attempt is made to hide negative feelings, though extreme negativism is more often attributed to animal than to human actors. On the whole, human actors show complex intellectual and emotional processes. The processes of thought and feeling are spelled out so the child reader will have an understanding of the why and wherefore of proscribed behavior and social values.

In 61 percent of the books the most important need shown is that of strength and achievement. The tables of contents of some books speak specifically to achievement in various areas:

> Dana, Joseph, Comp., *A New American Selection of Lessons, in Reading and Speaking*. Designed for the use of schools. 3d edition, cor. and improved. (Boston: Printed at Exeter by H. Ranlet, For Thomas and Andrews, Jan. 1799).
>
> CONTENTS:
> Directions for Reading and Speaking
> Select Sentences and Maxims
> Necessity of forming Religious Principles in Early Life
> Acquisition of Virtuous Habits
> Happiness and Dignity of Manhood depend on the Conduct of the
>   Youthful Age
> Piety to God
> Modesty and Docility
> Sincerity and Truth
> Benevolence and Humanity
> Courtesy and Engaging Manner
> Temperance in Pleasure

Whatever violates Nature cannot afford Pleasure
Industry and Application
Employment of Time
Order to be observed in Amusements
Idleness avoided by the observation of Order

Cummings, A. I., *The teacher's parting gift; or, Advice to the young* . . . (Fitchburg: S. & G. Shepley, 1816).

INDEX
Introduction
Importance of Education
Self-Culture of the Mind
Study
General Reading
Selection of Books
Observation
The Hour of Thought
Order in Arrangement
Ornaments of the Mind
Friendship
Benevolence
Veracity
Fidelity
Humility
Sincerity
Sympathy
Decision
A Virtuous and Religious character

The need for eternal salvation, for obeying God's will in order to merit everlasting happiness with God, is still important (found in 58 percent of the books). The here and now was geared to the future, not on this earth but in another place, by command of an awesome being. Even alphabets were put to use to carry this message; one was that of Will Whistle in *History of the Birds in the Air* . . . (New Haven: From Sidney's press, 1808):

I	II
A is for a bad boy.	End not the day in sin
Be not you a bad boy.	For it is ill to do so.
Can you do as I bid you.	God has bid us do no sin,
Do not you be an ill boy.	He is bad who can do so.

III

In a bad boy is no joy.
Joy is for him who is not bad.
Ken is to see it far off.
Let no ill way be in you.

IV

Men are too apt to sin.
No one has joy in the pit.
O let me not die in sin.
Put us in Thy way, O God.

V

Q we put by, and go on.
Rod is for him who is bad.
Sin is the way to the pit.
Try to do as you are bid.
Use not the way of bad men.

VI

Vex not God, but do his law.
We are to do the law of God.
X we are not now to use.
You are to do as you are bid.
Z is to be at the end.

The following *New England Primer* (Rutland: Printed by W. Fay, 1820) provides an often-used alphabet:

A

Adam and Eve
Their God did grieve.

B

Thy life to mend
This Book attend.

C

The Cat doth play,
And after slay.

D

A dog will bite
A thief at night.

E

An Eagle's flight
Is out of sight.

F

The idle Fool
Is whipt at school.

G

As runs the Glass
Our life doth pass.

H

Wrought by the Hand
Great works do stand.

J

Job felt the rod,
Yet blest his God.

K

The paper Kite
Is boy's delight.

L

The Lion bold
The Lamb doth hold.

M

The Moon gives light
In time of night.

N

Nightingales sing
In time of spring.

O

The Owl at night
Hoots out of sight.

P

Peter denied
His Lord and cried.

Q

Queens and Kings must
Lie in the dust.

R
The Rose in bloom
Sheds sweet perfume.

S
Samuel annoints
Whom God appoints.

T
Time cuts down all
Both great and small.

U
Urns hold, we see
Coffee and Tea.

W
Whales in the Sea
God's voice obey.

X
Xerxes the great
Shar'd common fate.

Y
Youth should delight
In doing right.

Z
Zaccheus he
Did climb the tree
His Lord to see.

Love, important in 38 percent of the books, was another need—love of parents and children, love of friends and neighbors. Care, respect, and love of others less fortunate was also stressed. If it was not a sin to be poor, it was a sin to fail to help the poor or maligned. Job Plimpton in *The American Spelling Book, or Youth's Instructor . . .* (Dedham, Mass.: Printed by H. Mann, 1807) is very explicit on this score:

Lesson 19—The Good Boy Whose Parents are Rich

He knows that all rich people are not good; and that God gives a great deal of money to some persons, in order that they mas assist those who are poor. (p. 78)

Lesson 20—The Good Boy Whose Parents are Poor

The good boy whose parents are poor, rises very early in the morning; and all day long, does as much as he can, to help his father and mother.

When he goes to school, he walks very quick, or does not lose time on the road.

He says: "I have often been told, and I have read, that it is God who makes some to be poor, and some to be rich; that the rich have many troubles which we know nothing of; and that the poor, if they are but good, may be very happy. Indeed, I think that when I am good, nobody can be happier than I am." (pp. 79-80)

A limited number of books talked of other needs—the need for safety (10 percent), for food (4 percent), and even for play and adventure (4 percent). Play was still largely thought of as unnecessary if not sometimes dangerous.

In 13 percent of the cases there were specific physical or psychological threats to obtaining needs. In 50 percent of the books there were no specific threats, but needs could not be obtained on one's own—one needed the help of other humans or of God to obtain them. In 37 percent of the cases there was no problem in obtaining needs if the person worked at it. Needs were rarely expressed in terms of individual goals; rather, they were expressed in terms of group goals of the concerns and the will of God. For needs were related to a future time period, with delayed gratification of wishes.

The religious institution was even more important in this time period than it had been earlier in helping to satisfy needs. The church was growing, its schools and Sunday school presses were growing. Sixty-four percent of the books discuss its mission, its activities, the behavior it proscribes, and the consequences of inattention to these proscriptions. Samuel Willard in his *Franklin Primer: Containing a New and Useful Selection of Moral Lessons*, 4th ed. (Boston: Printed by J. M. Dunham, 1803) writes:

> Love God for he is good.
> Fear God, for he is just. Pray to God, for all things come from him.
> Fools make a mock at sin, but he that is wise will be good. (p. 17)

In *I Am afraid There is a God!* the presence of the Almighty is certainly clear:

> The dying words of a poor penitent Infidel can never be forgotten,
> "I am afraid there is a God!" (p. 47)

Next to the church in importance among social institutions was the family. Forty-seven percent of the books discussed the roles and responsibilities of family members. The family, of course, was closely linked to the church, for it helped carry out the church's mission of teaching the young. Family government is discussed in *Essays from the Desk of Poor Robert the Scribe* (Doylestown: Printed by Asher Miner, July 1815):

> If your children you'd command,
> Parents, keep a steady hand.

> 1. Never strike a child while you are in anger. Never interfere with your husband or wife in the correction of a child in its presence. The parents must be united, or there is an end to government. Never make light promises to children, of rewards or punishments, but scrupulously *fulfill* what you do promise. Begin early with your children. Break their temper if it is high, while young; it may cost you and them a pang, but it will save you both fifty afterwards; and then be steady in your government. Use the rod sparingly—it is better and easier to command from them love and respect, than their fear. Keep these rules, and my word for it, your children will be a

happiness to you while young, and an honor to you when they grow up. (p. 62)

The school, appearing as a guiding force in 22 percent of the books, was also important, not only because it provided academic skills or social skills but because it provided mechanisms for coping with a life that was fraught with uncertainty and danger. George McElcheran in *The Systematic Spelling Book; Containing the Rudiments of the English Language for the Use of Schools in the U.S.* (Albany: Printed for the author, 1805) writes:

> Education is a sure foundation of tranquility, amidst all the disappointments and torments in life; it is a friend that can never deceive, that is ever present to comfort and assist, whether in adversity or prosperity; a blessing that can never be ravished from us by any casualty, fraud, violence or aggression, but remains with us at all times, circumstances and places, and may be had recourse to when every other earthly comfort fails us. It stamps an indelible mark of pre-eminence upon its possessors, that neither chance, power or fortune can equal in others, that are void of this inestimable blessing.

The family described in the books consisted in almost all cases of a nuclear family of parents and children. In 63 percent of the cases, family decisions were made by parents jointly. In those cases where they were made by either mother or father, it was more often the mother's decision. In 58 percent of the cases both parents spent time with and taught the child; when only one parent did so it was twice as often the mother as the father. Discipline was in over half the cases carried out by both parents. When it was carried out by one parent, that parent was much more likely to be the mother. When mother or father disciplined alone, they more often stressed self-direction than if they disciplined together.

Social responsibility of individuals was primarily to the group, especially the family group, and to God; it was not to the individual alone. Stimulants such as drugs and alcohol were deplored, especially in the church-affiliated presses. In terms of the cognitive relationship between human actors, 37 percent showed only rational elements, 30 percent had both rational and irrational elements, and 33 percent were based largely on a religious belief system where the reason for working hard, for obeying one's parents, and for having honest relationships with others was to obey the will of God.

Affective relationships between actors were never just apart; they were either intimate or both intimate and apart. Goals of individuals were to serve God and to help their fellowman; rarely (2 percent of the cases) were they for self gain. Social stratification was found among the majority of books of this period. By and large, where there was stratification, there was also mobility.

Needs were to be met through conformity to adult, and more importantly, to supernatural norms (90 percent of the books). In only 7 percent of the cases was social change encouraged, and this usually related to a desire for new political structures, unhampered by British controls.

Satisfaction of need occurred in all but four of the two hundred books reviewed for this period. In one case needs went unsatisfied owing to the individual's inadequacies. In the other three cases they went unsatisfied owing to God's displeasure. Success was not often attributed solely to the individual himself. It was usually attributed to God's intervention (36 percent of the cases), to the help of one's family (15 percent of the cases), or to help from God, as well as a variety of other primary group sources (42 percent of the cases).

The main characters, by and large, view themselves and others as competent. The world is still looked at, though, as an uncertain place, with death often present and with many day-to-day problems to be overcome.

Four books have been singled out for detailed focus—Parson Weems's *Life of George Washington* (1808), *Cries of Philadelphia* (1810), *The Glass of Whiskey* (c.1825), a temperance book from the American Sunday School Union, and Goodrich's *First Book of History* (1831). All of these books reflect a growing American culture with distinctive American values and attitudes. It is certainly true that many of these values and attitudes have British origins, but they have been institutionalized in special ways to establish a proud new nation.

The Life of George Washington

Parson Weems gives a detailed account of Washington's early socialization. Described for the reader are a young child's hesitant steps towards goodness and godliness, showing the temptations he has to pass on the way. The incident of the hatchet, and the cherry tree, as described by Weems, is well known. Here is another incident of Washington's youth, involving apples (*The Life of George Washington; With Curious Anecdotes, Equally Honorable to Himself and Exemplary to his Young Countrymen,* 7th ed., greatly improved [Philadelphia, 1808]):

> The first place of education to which George was ever sent, was a little "old field school," kept by one of his father's tenants, named Hobby; an honest, poor old man, who acted in the double character of sexton and schoolmaster. On his skill as a gravedigger, tradition is silent; but for a teacher of youth, his qualifications were certainly of the humbler sort; making what is generally called an A. B. C. schoolmaster. Such was the preceptor who first taught Washington the knowledge of letters! Hobby lived to see his young pupil in all his glory, and rejoiced exceedingly. In his cups—for though a sexton, he would sometimes drink particularly on the General's birth

days—he used to boast that " 'twas he, who, between his knees, had laid the foundation of George Washington's greatness."

But though George was early sent to a schoolmaster, yet he was not on that account neglected by his father. Deeply sensible of the loveliness and worth of which human nature is capable, through the virtues and graces early implanted in the heart, he never for a moment, lost sight of George in those all-important respects.

To assist his son to overcome that selfish spirit, which too often leads children to fret and fight about trifles, was a notable care of Mr. Washington. For this purpose, of all the presents, such as cakes, fruit, &c. he received, he was always desired to give a liberal part to his play-mates. To enable him to do this with more alacrity, his father would remind him of the love which he would thereby gain, and the frequent presents which would in return be made to him; and also would tell of that great and good God, who delights above all things to see children love one another, and will assuredly reward them for acting so amiable a part.

Some idea of Mr. Washington's plan of education in this respect may be collected from the following anecdote, related to me twenty years ago by an aged lady, who was a distant relative, and, when a girl, spent much of her time in the family:

"On a fine morning," said she, "in the fall of 1737, Mr. Washington having little George by the hand, came to the door and asked my cousin Washington and myself to walk with him to the orchard, promising he would show us a fine sight. On arriving at the orchard, we were presented with a fine sight indeed. The whole earth, as far as we could see, was strewed with fruit: and yet the trees were beinding under the weight of apples, which hung in clusters like grapes, and vainly strove to hide their blushing cheeks behind the green leaves. Now, George, said his father, look here, my son! don't you remember when this good cousin of yours brought you that fine large apple last spring, how hardly I could prevail on you to divide with your brothers and sisters; though I promised you that if you would but do it, God Almighty would give you plenty of apples this fall. Poor George could not say a word; but hanging down his head, looked quite confused, while with his little naked toes he scratched in the soft ground. Now look up, my son, continued his father, look up, George! and see there how richly the blessed God has made good my promise to you. Wherever you turn your eyes, you see the trees loaded with fine fruit; many of them indeed breaking down; while the ground is covered with mellow apples, more than you could eat, my son, in all your life time."

George looked in silence on the wide wilderness of fruit. He
marked the busy humming bees, and heard the gay notes of birds;
then lifting his eyes filled with shining mosture, to his father, he
softly said, ''Well, Pa, only forgive me this time; and see if I ever
be so stingy any more.'' (pp. 10-11)

Weems gives much more detail to Washington's adult activities. While the
revolutionary battles are described minutely and with fervor, real victories in
Washington's adult life, as in his childhood, are victories over human frailities.
Concern with duty to God as well as duty to one's fellowman is paramount:

CHAPTER XVI

WASHINGTON'S CHARACTER CONTINUED

HIS PATRIOTISM

In this grand republican virtue, we can with pleasure compare our
Washington with the greatest worthies of ancient or modern times.

The patriotism of the Roman emperor, Alexander, has been celebrated through all ages, because he was never known to give any
place through favour or friendship; but employed those only whom
he believed to be best qualified to serve his country. In our Washington we meet this great and honest emperor again. For, in choosing
men to serve his country, Washington knew no recommendation but
merit—had no favourite but worth. No relations, however near—no
friends, however dear—stood any chance for places under him, provided he knew men better qualified. Respecting such men, he never
troubled himself to enquire, whether they were foreigners or natives,
federalists or democrats. Some of the young officers of his native
state, on hearing that colonel Washington was made commander-in-
chief, were prodigiously pleased, expecting to be made field officers
immediately. But in this they were so utterly mistaken, that some of
them have foolishly said, ''it was a misfortune to be a Virginian.''
Indeed, his great soul was so truly republican, that, during the whole
of his administration, he was never known to advance an individual
of his own name and family.

The British, with good reason, admire and extol admiral Blake as
one of the bravest and best of patriots; because, though he disliked
Oliver Cromwell, yet he fought gallantly under him; and, with his
dying breath, exhorted his men, ''to love their country as a common
mother; and, no matter what hands the government might fall into, to
fight for her like good children.''

Of the same noble spirit was Washington. Often was he called to
obey men greatly his inferiors, and to execute orders which he entirely disapproved. But he was never known to falter. Sensible of the
infinite importance of union and order to the good of his country, he

Ill. 11: Mason Locke Weems. *The Life of George Washington*. Philadelphia: M. Carey and Sons, 1819. [4⅞″ x 2⅞″]

ever yielded a prompt obedience to her delegated will. And, not content with setting us, through life, so fair an example, he leaves us at his death, this blessed advice: "Your government claims your utmost confidence and support. Respect for its authority, compliance with its laws, acquiescence in its measures, are duties enjoined by the fundamental maxims of true liberty. The basis of our political system is the right of the people to make and alter their constitutions of government. But the constitution, which at any time exists, until changed by an explicit and authentic act of the wholepeople, is sacredly obligatory upon all." (pp. 217-218)

The purpose of this book is to instruct in moral and social behavior and also in historical facts. The book is sober and didactic, with the historical figure of George Washington used to reaffirm the religious and social ideals which the author felt were important. Major role models tend to be white, upper-middle class, and male. American Indians and black slaves are evident in the book, but they play minor and subordinate roles in delineating ideal values and behavior.

The primary need expressed throughout the book is the need for adherence to God's will and eternal salvation. Strength, achievement, and self-fulfillment are also strong needs. There is no problem of achieving such needs if one works at it. Religion is basically the most important institution through which one achieves, although political activity is more talked about. Family is also important, and in the family both mother and father participate in taking care of the child—spending time with him and teaching him.

In this book, unlike many others, social change is mentioned. It involves the most far-reaching social upheaval in our land, the birth of this nation. Washington's army was a revolutionary army in the clearest sense of the word.

Satisfaction was obtained in the book—by means of the actor's hard work, help from his family and his compatriots, and, above all, help from God. Washington was extolled as a leader, but he was also pictured as needing help of other humans and of his maker. The world was uncertain, and only by means of such help could one hope to achieve a safe, free environment.

The Cries of Philadelphia

There are more editions of *Cries of London* in the Rare Book Collection than there are editions of cries of American cities, but there are copies of *The Cries of Philadelphia, Cries of New York,* and *The Boston Cries.* Cries were written to amuse; they bespoke the energy and the interests of a growing city. *The Cries of Philadelphia,* ornamented with elegant woodcuts (Philadelphia: Published by Johnson and Warner. John Bouvier, printer, 1810) showed considerable civic pride:

PHILADELPHIA

Is the metropolis of Pennsylvania, and the largest city in the
United States—the number of inhabitants, including the Liberties,
are about 100,000.

It was founded by the great William Penn.—The Streets are generally wide, and cross each other at right angles, the houses are built
chiefly of brick, are three stories high.—The situation of the city is
very favourable both for foreign and inland trade, lying on the west
bank of the river Delaware, and being the only port of entry in the
important state of which it is the capital.

The manufactures of this place are numerous, the market for the
supply of the people is not certainly excelled by any in the world.
(p. 2)

The book shows respect of people and of individual contributions to the public
welfare:

WATCHMAN

"Past twelve o'clock, and a fine moonlight morning!"

To preserve the city in safety from thieves and robbers, a number
of men who are called watchmen, are appointed to travel the streets
from ten o'clock at night till day light; thus the inhabitants repose in
safety, while this useful class of people are guarding their property,
and always prepared to sound an alarm of fire, in time to prevent
much injury.

At many of the corners are small round boxes, called watch
houses.—In these boxes, our faithful guards resort for shelter from
the rain, the snow, or the cold.—This however is only allowed, after
they have travelled over their ward or district several times.—The
first time they go round after the clock strikes, it is their duty to cry
the time, and after midnight, also the sort of weather.—At other
times they pass along quietly, to look out for rogues or to quiet
disorderly passengers.

For all this service, these useful men get only about twelve or
fifteen dollars a month, but expect a gift at Christmas and New
Year's day. They surely deserve it, and we hope all good citizens
will remember them.

FIRE

Fire! Fire! Fire!

This is the most awful alarm heard in our streets, and when it
happens in a dark and gloomy night, it is the more solemn.

BROOMS! BROOMS!

" *Any Brooms or Brushes to-*
day ?"

Come buy a new Brush,
  Or a nice sweeping Broom,
'Tis pleasant indeed
  To have a clean room.

HOT CORN!

" *Here's your nice Hot Corn!*
" *Smoking hot! piping hot!*
" *O what beauties I have got!*"

Here's smoking Hot Corn,
  With salt that is nigh,
Only two pence an ear,—
  O pass me not by!

Ill. 12: *New York Cries, in Rhyme.* New York: Printed and sold by Mahlon
Day, c.1825. [4″ x 3½″]

When a fire is discovered in the night, the watchmen are the first
to sound the alarm—the bells in the different parts of the city increase the unpleasant news, and in a few minutes the general cry of
fire! fire! leaves no one without the opportunity of doing some good.

Indeed on such occasions the people of all ranks assemble, and we
often observe the most delicate persons making great exertions to
serve those in distress.

The use of the hoase, applied to the conduits which convey the
river water thro' the streets, is a means of stopping the progress of
fire, better than the engines, which are still used to advantage in
conjunction with the other.

The Cries of Philadelphia was written to entertain and to reassure. The main
characters interacted in day-to-day activities of their own community, about
which they felt real pride. Persons of upper and lower socioeconomic classes
were shown, and dignity was afforded to both the more and the less well-to-do.
The basic needs of actors was for safety (from fire and social disorder) and for
strength and achievement (through work at various trades). Needs were related
to the group rather than to the individual good; people banded together for
mutual aid.

Ill. 13: *New York Cries, in Rhyme*. New York: Printed and sold by Mahlon Day, c.1825. [4″ x 3½″]

The economic institution was focused upon. It was through work that the individuals in the community related one to another. Relationships were rational, intimate, group-oriented, and nonhierarchical. Needs were directed to the status quo. Satisfaction of needs did occur; there was a certain amount of joy and satisfaction in the countenance of the people and in their cries. People were depicted as controlling their own lives in a burgeoning world.

The Glass of Whiskey

The Sunday school literature in America had its roots in England with the works of Anna Barbauld, Hannah More, Elizabeth Turner, Maria Edgeworth, and Jane and Ann Taylor. The American Sunday School Union took over this literature and published widely. Proponents of the realistic school of writing, the Union was greatly opposed to the adherents of the fairy tale, and violent arguments on both sides will be found in prefaces to books of this period (see American Sunday School Union [1]).

The American Sunday School Union was formed in 1824 through the merger of the resources of various denominations, to make provisions for a confederated system of religious instruction. To execute this program of consolidated religious education nationwide, auxiliary branches of the Union came into existence in almost every state and territory. In 1830 the Union resolved to establish a Sunday school in every neighborhood in the western states that was without one, and in 1833 it adopted a similar resolution with respect to southern states. To do this the Union employed about 350 missionaries, many of whom were students in theological seminaries, who traversed the country revitalizing decaying schools or establishing new ones.

There were two objectives of the Society: to provide the young with oral instruction, and to furnish suitable juvenile reading material to be used both in the schools and at home. The Union published hundreds of volumes for its libraries, as well as an infinite variety of educational works, magazines, and journals. The most common subjects were accounts of conversions, directions for the observance of the Lord's Day, temperance propaganda, stories stressing the duty of charity to the poor and kindness to animals, and warnings against idleness and frivolous play.

The temperance literature was very didactic. The most commonplace occurrences of life or even the ordinary pleasures of childhood were made to serve its purposes. Minor human frailities, such as spending pennies at the candy shop, or holding a spoonful of brandy in the mouth for a toothache, after sweeping condemnations, were used as springboards from which an unwary youth plunged into a drunkard's grave. *The Glass of Whiskey* (Philadelphia: American Sunday-School Union, c.1825) is typical of the temperance Sunday school literature. Published about 1825, it is an unpretentious volume—1⅞ by 2⅞ inches, with a paper cover. Its message, though, is clear and not a little melodramatic:

> There is a bottle. It has something in it which is called whiskey.
> Little, reader, I hope you will never taste any as long as you live. It
> is a poison. So is brandy, so is rum, so is gin, and many other drinks.
> They are called strong drink. They are so strong that they knock
> people down, and kill them. They are sometimes called ardent
> spirits, that is burning spirits. They burn up those who drink them.
>
> Do you see that glass? If you were to take it half full of spirits, it
> would take away your senses.
>
> Do you see that man? His name is Bob Brown. That little boy is
> named Hugh. Bob is giving Hugh some strong drink in a spoon.
> Poor child, he liked the taste of it, for it was sweetened with sugar,
> and had nutmeg on it. But it is poison. When Hugh got bigger, he
> remembered that the taste was pleasant, and he wanted some more.
> Whenever he could get it, he used to drink a little.
>
> Do you think a little would hurt any body? Yes. Because, if any
> one takes a little, he will soon begin to like a little more. Then he
> will take a little every day. And this is the way people get to be

Ill. 14: *The Glass of Whiskey*. Philadelphia: American Sunday-School Union. No 146 Chestnut Street, c.1825. [1½″ x 1″, 1½″ x 1″]

drunkards. Does liquor kill people? I will tell you. I knew a little boy about six years old. He went to a closet where there was a jug of rum. He tasted it. He liked it. He tasted a little more. Then he drank a good deal. At last he became drunk, and fell over and lay there till he died. He was found dead by the jug of rum. (pp. 2-6)

Although the book was a work of fiction, its purpose was to provide moral and social instruction. Its particular lesson concerned the evils of drink, which were discussed in a homelike setting with very human actors. The actors as seen through the illustrations were white males. The main character was a boy whose poor behavior patterns, begun in childhood, resulted in great harm by the time he became an adult. The child-reader is shown the consequences of immoral action over time.

The evils of drink were put in two contexts: offense to God and offense to society. God deplores it. And it leads to social ruin and death as well. Need for eternal salvation and strength were shown and were to be obtained through the religious institution. The family was not in this book; direction came from God and responsibility was to God: ''The Bible says that drunkards shall not inherit the kingdom of God'' (pp. 6-7).

Needs were not attained in this book, because of the characters' refusal to heed God's will. The view of the world was somber, and death was very much present.

The First Book of History

Histories and geographies abounded during this period. There was a genuine interest in enlarging the child's horizons—to show him other peoples and other lands. There was also an interest in giving him knowledge, understanding, and respect for his own country. Samuel Griswold Goodrich was a very prolific exponent of this genre during the sixty-seven years of his life (for additional materials on Goodrich, see Goodrich [2], Roselle [8], and *Horn Book Magazine* [10]). It is estimated that no less than seven million copies of about 120 different titles by Goodrich were sold over a period of thirty years (1827–1857).

The First Book of History is one of his earliest books. The greater portion of the book is devoted to United States history, each of the states being described in terms of its geography, history, culture (trade, religion, relationships of whites to Indians, black slaves). Two chapters are devoted to the Puritans—their character, their purpose in coming to America, the persecutions they suffered. The American Revolution occupies seven chapters, and a history of the country after the revolution, up to the time of Andrew Jackson's presidency, is also provided.

The remaining chapters deal with other parts of America—Greenland and Iceland in North America, Mexico and Guatemala in Central America, and Colombia, Peru, Bolivia, Chili, Patagonia, Brazil, and Guiana in South America, as well as the West Indies. There are etchings throughout the book and at the end are full-page maps of all the areas discussed. Goodrich's descriptions of the states are crammed with information (*The First Book of History* [Boston, Richardson, Lord and Holbrook, 1832]):

CHAP. X
STATE OF CONNECTICUT

1. Connecticut, with the exception of Rhode Island, is the smallest of the New England States; but it has more inhabitants than any of them, except Massachusetts and Maine. The country is very hilly, but it abounds in streams and rivers, and is generally quite fertile.

2. The people are very industrious. A great many of them are

occupied in cultivating the land, and they cultivate it very well. They raise a good many cattle, horses, hogs, sheep, and some grain and kitchen vegetables. A great many of the people are occupied in manufactories, and a considerable number are engaged in commerce. Almost every person in this State is busy about something.

3. Let us suppose that we begin at the eastern part of the State, and travel through it. We will commence our journey at Norwich. This town is situated on the Thames, and we shall see quite a number of vessels there, engaged in carrying on trade with New York, Philadelphia, and Charleston. There are several falls in the river, at Norwich, and these afford fine mill-seats, where there are some very extensive cotton manufactories.

4. The country around Norwich, was once occupied by a celebrated tribe of Indians, called Mohicans. These Mohicans were once at war with some other Indians. One night, several of these Indians had encamped on the top of some high rocks.

5. Their enemies discovered their situation, and secretly encircled them on all sides but one. On that side, was a steep precipice, at the foot of which was the river. When the morning came, the party of Indians first mentioned were about to depart, when they discovered that they were surrounded by their foes.

6. They made a short resistance; but perceiving that they were outnumbered by their enemies, they leaped over the rocks, and were killed by the fall.

7. Having examined Norwich, we will take a boat, and go down the river Thames, to New London. At this place, we shall see a steamboat that goes to New York, and we shall also observe a good many other vessels. Among the vessels, we shall see a large ship fitting out to go to the Pacific Ocean to catch whales.

8. We shall perhaps see another vessel, that has just come back from a whaling voyage, after an absence of three years. If she is not unloaded, we shall find on board of her, about three hundred barrels of whale-oil, and a good deal of whale-bone. The oil is used for burning in lamps, and the whale-bone is for umbrella frames, and many other purposes.

9. Near New London, we shall see two forts; one of them is called Fort Trumbull, and the other Fort Griswold. The latter is situated in Groton, just across the river Thames.

10. I will tell you an odd story of what happened in Groton, near twenty years ago. There was war then, between our country and Great Britain. There were several British ships in sight, and it was expected they would soon make an attack upon the forts. A company of soldiers from Hartford occupied a house in Groton, as their barracks.

11. One night as they were asleep, there was a sudden cry of alarm among the soldiers. They seized their arms, and rushed out of the barracks. The drums were beat, the sentinel fired his gun, and all supposed that the British were now about to make the expected attack. Some of the men declared they could see the enemy landing, and others thought they could hear the roar of cannon in the distance.

12. The officers assembled, and inquired into the matter. They soon discovered, that the British had nothing to do with the alarm. It seems that one of the soldiers, whose name was Tom Stire, while he was sleeping with the rest, fell into a dream. He dreamed that the British were coming, and in his sleep he exclaimed, 'Alarm! alarm! the enemy are coming!' This occasioned the whole disturbance.

13. After we have examined New London, we will set out and go to Hartford. This is a very fine town, situated on Connecticut river. We must visit the Deaf and Dumb Asylum, where we shall see about one hundred deaf and dumb pupils, who are taught to read and write, and who can converse by signs, almost as well as we can by talking. We shall also see at Hartford, place for persons who are insane, called the Retreat. Here they are taken care of, and many of them are cured. Before we leave town, we must go to Washington College, which is a fine institution.

14. After leaving Hartford, we will go to Middletown, which is beautifully situated on Connecticut river. On our way from Hartford, we shall pass through Wethersfield, a pleasant place, where the people raise many thousand bushels of onions, every year. These onions are sent to all parts of the country. Some of them go as far as Charleston, New Orleans, and the West Indies.

15. After leaving Middletown, we shall pass through Durham, where the people make an immense quantity of shoes. At length we shall arrive at New Haven, which is the handsomest town in New England. Here we shall see a large basin, where there are a great many canal boats. These boats go up and down the Farmington canal; they carry up a great deal of merchandise, and bring down the produce of the country.

16. At New Haven we shall also see Yale College. This consists of several brick buildings, in which there are three or four hundred students. We must go into one of these buildings and see the cabinet. This is a collection of beautiful minerals from all parts of the world.

17. It is very interesting to examine this cabinet, for there are stones there, which have been brought from various parts of Europe, Asia, Africa, and America. There are two stone pillars there, which came from the famous Giant's Causeway, in Ireland.

18. There are also some specimens of stones, which fell from the air in Connecticut, about twenty years ago. These stones formed a

part of a vast red meteor, that flew along in the sky, and finally
exploded with a great noise. The stones fell in the town of Weston.

19. If we travel in other parts of Connecticut, we shall find at
Berlin, a great many people busy in manufacturing tin ware. At
Meriden, they make tin and pewter ware. At Bristol, they make
wooden clocks, and very good clocks they are. At Waterbury, they
make buttons; at Danbury, they make hats; at Salisbury, there are
extensive iron-works.

20. In short, the people of Connecticut are very busy and ingenious. Many of them go to the Southern and Western States, and even
as far as Mexico, to sell the articles that are manufactured in this
State. (pp. 22-24)

Goodrich's descriptions of southern states show a different set of physical and
social conditions from the states of the North:

CHAP. XLII

THE FOUR SOUTHERN ATLANTIC STATES

1. I have now given you some account of Virginia, North
Carolina, South Carolina, and Georgia. These four States are in
many respects alike. The eastern portions are generally low, sandy,
and barren. The western portions are hilly and mountainous.

2. Their chief productions are cotton, tobacco, and rice. The
climate is hot, and in summer it is unhealthy, in the low country. The
land is chiefly divided into large plantations. The owners of these are
called planters. They possess a multitude of black slaves, who perform all the labors of the field, and in the house.

3. The slaves are generally well treated; that is, they have
enough to eat, drink, and wear, and are not required to labor beyond
their strength. But yet these poor negroes have no education, they
have no property, no liberty, no right to consult their own wishes, or,
like the rest of mankind, pursue happiness in their own way. They
have little knowledge of religion, and sink into their graves almost as
ignorant of the destiny that awaits them, as the brutes that perish.

4. Beside all this, when a planter dies, his slaves are often sold;
some to one person and some to another. Perchance the wife is taken
by this man, the husband by that, and their children by a third. Thus
the family is separated, and very often they never see each other
again.

5. A gentleman who was in Georgia, two or three years ago,
told me he once witnessed a public sale of negroes there. They were
put up at auction, and many gentlemen came to bid for them. The
slaves consisted of men, women, and children. The bidders ex-

THE

FIRST   BOOK

OF

HISTORY.

FOR CHILDREN AND YOUTH.

BY THE AUTHOR OF PETER PARLEY'S TALES.

WITH SIXTY ENGRAVINGS AND SIXTEEN MAPS.

BOSTON:

RICHARDSON, LORD, AND HOLBROOK.

1832.

Ill. 15: Samuel Griswold Goodrich. *The First Book of History. For Children and Youth.* By the author of Peter Parley's tales. . . . Boston: Richardson, Lord, and Holbrook, 1832. [5½'' x 7''] amined them, turned them round, and made them walk back and forth, as if they had been cattle or horses.

6. At length, the sale was finished. One of the negro women had three children; a daughter about fourteen years old, and two boys about eight or ten years old. It happened that the children were bought by one person, and the mother by another. They were now to be separated, and never expected to see each other more. The gentleman who told me the story said the little boys did not mind the parting much, but the agony of the mother, and the distress of the daughter, were past description.

7. Such are some of the evils of slavery. It is a bad system altogether, and all good people believe that it is wrong. I hope the time will soon come, when there will be no slaves in our country. A benevolent society has been formed for the purpose of setting these negroes free, and for sending them to Africa. They have already established a colony there, consisting entirely of blacks, called Liberia. Several hundred have already gone there; and the colony is likely to prosper. I sincerely hope that the slaves in the United States may be gradually liberated, and that they may enjoy happiness and freedom in the native land of the negro race.

8. I have already told you that the first slaves brought to this country, arrived at Virginia in 1619. For about fifty years before the settlement of this colony, the merchants of England had been engaged in the slave trade. They used to send large ships to the western coast of Africa; these were then loaded with negroes, which were taken to the West Indies, to South America, and various other places, and sold. Sometimes the slaves were bought in Africa, of those who had taken them in war, and sometimes the sailors went ashore, stole men, women, and children, and forced them on board their ships.

9. These poor creatures were crowded into the vessels, and used in the most barbarous manner. Many of them expired for want of fresh air; some became deranged and jumped into the sea. Sometimes mothers died, and their little children perished for want of care; and sometimes the men killed themselves rather than endure the torments they suffered.

10. Such were some of the horrors attending the slave trade. Yet it continued to be carried on, and very soon there were a great many slaves in all the colonies. There were more in the Southern than in the Northern States; but still in Pennsylvania, New York, and New England, there were several thousands.

11. But at length, the people became convinced that slavery was wrong, and, in all the States north of Maryland, it was abolished.

The Southern States still permit it; but I hope they, too, will, ere long, prohibit it. (pp. 81-82)

The purpose of this book was to instruct, to provide historical information about the growth of this nation and also about its diverse peoples and customs. Material was provided in short, matter-of-fact sentences and numbered paragraphs. There were a considerable number of important actors engaged primarily in economic and political activity. Racial characteristics of the individuals were an integral part of the history, and those chapters involving the northern states discussed relationships of Indians with each other and with the white man. Chapters on southern states discussed relationships of blacks and whites and also the institution of slavery—which was deplored. Although children and educational institutions are depicted, most of the characters are adults, since history is made by adults.

Human needs emphasized were strength, achievement, and self-fulfillment. Concern was with the group rather than the individual, and with the development of a better society for all. Political and economic activities were focused on: the battles won, the declaration signed, the forests felled, the farms developed. Relationships between actors were certainly rationalized, and needs were met largely by self-direction and innovation.

The time period discussed was the development of the new world, in which old norms were discarded and new norms were experimented with. Success was obtained by the leading actors in the books, and it was obtained through their own efforts coupled with the help of their fellowman. In general, the world and the people in it were looked on positively. There was work to be done and there were problems to be faced, but there was also hope and strength in the building of this nation.

The four books just discussed continue to preach the Puritan ethic. Obey God's commands. Work hard. Do not fritter time away. The importance of God as the source of all power and wisdom and direction is very clear, so even Parson Weems in discussing America's greatest hero (*The Life of George Washington*) reminds his reader:

Let the poor witling argue all he can,
It is Religion still that makes the man. (p. 174)

But distinctively American values and hopes are beginning to emerge and crystallize. And there is obvious pride in the growth of the United States.

References

1. American Sunday School Union, *First Lessons in the Great Principles of Religion*. Designed to be used in Infant Sabbath Schools and Private Homes. Philadelphia, 1833.

2. Goodrich, Samuel. *Recollections of a Lifetime*. New York: Miller, Orton, 1857.
3. Halsey, Rosalie V. *Forgotten Books of the American Nursery*. Boston: Charles E. Goodspeed, 1911.
4. Johnson, Clifton. *Old-Time Schools and School-Books*. New York: Dover Publications, 1963.
5. Kiefer, Monica M. *American Children Through Their Books, 1700–1835*. Philadelphia: University of Pennsylvania Press, 1948.
6. Meigs, Cornelia L., ed. *A Critical History of Children's Literature*. New York: Macmillan, 1953.
7. Nietz, John A. *Old Textbooks*. Pittsburgh: University of Pittsburgh Press, 1961.
8. Roselle, Daniel. *Samuel Griswold Goodrich, Creator of Peter Parley: A Study of his Life and Works*. Albany: State University of New York Press, 1968.
9. Rosenbach, Abraham S.W. *Early American Children's Books*. Portland, Maine: The Southworth Press, 1933.
10. *The Dawn of Imagination in American Books for Children. Horn Book Magazine* 20(1944):168–175.
11. *Samuel Wood and Sons, Early New York Publishers of Children's Books*. New York: New York Public Library, 1942.

Chapter 4

1836-1875: "He had striven . . . and he had succeeded. He felt proud and happy, and grateful to God. . . ."

Almost three-fourths of the books of this period contain some amount of religious instruction.* Even if the focus of the books is on academic subjects or amusement, God and eternal salvation are also discussed. In a good number of the books they are the primary topic of discussion, as in *Letters to the Children of Pious Parents,* by the author of "parental training" (Boston, Massachusetts: Sunday School Society, 1850):

> Your first and highest obligations are to God. He is the author of your being, and the source of all your blessings. . . .
> But while this is freely admitted, and urged, you owe to your parents as the instruments of divine goodness, a debt of gratitude which you can never pay. How much they have suffered for you! How much have they done for you! What anxious days and sleepless nights have they passed, deeply pondering your circumstances, your character, and your necessities, planning for your welfare, praying for your preservation from surrounding dangers, for the renewal of your nature and the salvation of your soul. What self-denial and sacrifices have they endured for your benefit.

Some books not only encourage the reader to engage in pious behavior himself, they encourage him to act in a missionary capacity, advocating pious behavior in others. An often published book is *The Gospel Kite* (Boston: Sunday School Society, 1845) about a child missionary who constructs a big kite. The child ties a Bible on it, then sends the kite aloft, hoping it will land near a poor heathen in need of conversion. The child reader is then shown how he can accomplish the same goal by giving money to the Sunday School Society to send books to libraries of the undeveloped American West. Ten to twenty-five dollars worth of books could be sent in each "kite," the Sunday School Society providing the string that allows it to fly.

*For further analyses of books of this period, see Cruse [6], Darling [7], Jordan [10], Meigs [13], the *Horn Book Magazine* [20], and *A Mid-century Child and her Books* [21].

In *The Boys Keepsake* (Philadelphia: American Sunday School Union, 1845) the purpose of the Sunday School press is forcefully described:

> The happiest man is he who lives to make others happy. It is important, however, that we should know what it is that makes others truly happy, or we cannot tell whether what we do for them is for their good or not. A father often forbids his children some enjoyments which would make them very happy for the present, because he sees that it would lead to much unhappiness afterwards.
>
> But there is one thing we may always safely do, and be very sure that it will increase the happiness of the world—and that is, to spread the knowledge of heavenly truth; and this the American Sunday School Union tries to do every day.
>
> Such books as the present are designed to encourage a love of reading, and to lead our young friends to seek for the larger and still more instructive volumes—hundreds of which they will find in the Society's catalogue.

In addition to religious instruction, an important purpose of books of the period is instruction in social behavior; over half of the books focus on this goal, and one of the social behaviors most often addressed is that of drinking. In *Andrew Douglass* (New York: National Temperance Society and Publication House, 1868) the temptation and the duty with regard to abstinence are addressed:

> The tavern was, unfortunately, close at hand; so he went there, and the first drop of brandy that had passed his lips for many years was taken eagerly, and did its work, as the first step in a wrong course generally does. (p. 71)

> The strong conviction that it was his duty to try to save others from the ruin that had so nearly been his own sad fate, impelled Andrew again to exert his influence through the neighborhood; and, as a consequence, the temperance meeting held within many miles of his home was sure to be well attended, if it was known that among the speakers would be Andrew Douglass, the Lame Blacksmith. (pp. 231-232)

Although most of the discussion about proper social behavior refers to proper social behavior of the white Protestant, minority persons are sometimes focused upon. When minorities appear in the books, such instruction is seen to be more difficult because of their uncivilized life style. Julia Wright, in *The Indian's Friend* (Philadelphia: Presbyterian Publications Committee, c.1869), discusses such education among the Indians:

The Indians were very wild and very poor, fond of whiskey and their heathenish ways. . . .

Do you think the Indians were glad to see him (Christian missionary), and loved him because he had come so far to do them good? Oh no. They seemed to hate him; Satan stirred their hearts up to hate him because he wanted them to put away their false gods and their whiskey.

David hoped and prayed. He built a school-house, and got a teacher for it. When the Indians were ill, he was to them doctor and nurse. He followed them, telling them of Jesus, and with tears in his eyes begging them to worship the only true God, and Christ his son. (pp. 41-42)

How kind of God to send the Indians such a friend as David Brainerd! God had never forgotten the Indian race. His tender mercy is over all his works, and again and again good men had it put in their hearts to go and tell the Indians of a Saviour. (p. 53)

You know preaching to the Indians was not quite like preaching to other people, for the Indians were ignorant, and did not even know how to take care of themselves. Mr. Brainerd had to tell them how to plant their crops, build their houses, mend their fences, and all such things. (pp. 56-57)

The third most frequent purpose of books of this period is instruction in school subjects; such is the purpose of 19 percent of the books. ABC's are still prevalent, as in *A Pleasing Toy for Children* (Concord, N. H.: R. Merrill, 1843):

The Alphabet Versified

With ABC, Join EFG,
And HIK and U,
And SRL, and X as well,
And MNP and Q;
Then O and T, and WD,
And V and Y and Z,
And lastly say, the lonely J
Completes the company. (pp. 6-7)

There are many series of beginner readers, including those by Lyman Cobb, William Angell, David Bates Tower, and, of course, William Holmes McGuffey. The *New England Primer* is still being published, as are the works of Noah Webster. Some distinctively southern readers appear, such as Mrs. M. B.

Moore's series: *Dixie Primer, The First Dixie Reader, The Geographical Reader, for the Dixie Children,* printed in Raleigh, North Carolina, by Branson, Farrar and Company, in 1863. Most readers, as in the following McGuffey example, are concerned with religious and social as well as academic instruction (*McGuffey's Second Eclectic Reader* [Cincinnati: American Book Company, 1879]):

LESSON I

news′pā per	cōld	ôr′der	seēm	through
stŏck′ings	chăt	stō′ry	light	Hăr′ry
bránch′es	kĭss	bûrns	Mrs.	e vĕnts′
an óther′er	Mr.	stōōl	lămp	mĕnds_

Evening at Home

1. It is winter. The cold wind whistles through the branches of the trees.

2. Mr. Brown has done his day's work, and his children, Harry and Kate, have come home from school. They learned their lessons well to-day, and both feel happy.

3. Tea is over. Mrs. Brown has put the little sitting room in order. The fire burns brightly. One lamp gives light enough for all. One the stool is a basket of fine apples. They seem to say, ''Won't you have one?''

4. Harry and Kate read a story in a new book. The father reads his newspaper, and the mother mends Harry's stockings.

5. By and by, they will tell one another what they have been reading about, and will have a chat over the events of the day.

6. Harry and Kate's bedtime will come first. I think I see them kiss their dear father and mother a sweet good night.

7. Do you not wish that every boy and girl could have a home like this? (pp. 11-12)

Histories and geographies are also plentiful. Toward the latter part of this period, they deal not only with the American Revolution but also with the American Civil War, where powerful internal struggles are at work to bring American ideals and reality closer together.

A book of the period which had important impact on history is fiction rather than nonfiction: Harriet Beecher Stowe's *Uncle Tom's Cabin,* first published in 1852. Stowe's book is not really addressed to children, but young readers took it over and several children's editions were published. The book led to deep public controversy prior to the start of the Civil War.

There is, especially in the latter part of this period, an increase in books whose purpose is solely to amuse (17 percent of the books between 1856-75). Nursery-rhyme books, with larger format and colored illustrations, became more frequent. Clement Clarke Moore's beloved *A Visit from St. Nicholas* went through several editions. (The book was first written in 1822 but not published under his name until 1844; the first edition in the Rare Book collection is 1855.) There are editions of Grimm and Anderson and Aesop. Hawthorne's *A Wonder-book for Girls and Boys* (Boston: Ticknor, Reed and Fields) was first published in 1852.

Other books to amuse, and sometimes to instruct, include adolescent novels. Novels for girls stress family relationships. Louisa May Alcott and her books on the March family, beginning with *Little Women,* Martha Farquharson and her *Elsie Dinsmore* books, Rebecca Clarke and her *Little Prudy* series are prime examples. Novels for boys stress adventure. William T. Adams, Horatio Alger, and Elijah Kellogg wrote fast-paced stories showing boys who were very mobile, geographically and socially.

In this period New York emerged as an important locale for publishing; 32 percent of the books were published there. Boston and Philadelphia were also important, 28 percent of the books being published in Boston and 27 percent in Philadelphia. Religious publishing houses flourished. In addition to the American Sunday School Union Press (Philadelphia), there were many other active church presses, such as those of the Massachusetts Sunday School Society (Boston), the American Baptist Publication Society (Philadelphia), the Presbyterian Board of Publication (Philadelphia), the General Protestant Epis-copal Sunday School Union and Church Book Society (New York), the Sunday School Union (New York), the Board of Publication, Reformed Church of America (New York), and the American Tract Society (New York).

Book authors during these years were more often male than female. Few books were now written by the clergy (7 percent), and many were written by educators in order to enhance curriculum or, in the case of some novelists, to escape from it.

Sixty-three percent of the books of the period are fiction, 13 percent are a combination of fiction and nonfiction, and 24 percent are nonfiction only. Series books as a popular genre came into being; they carried the same cast of characters through adventure after adventure. Usually such books had age- and sex-casting, being directed toward the preteen-aged girl or boy. Jacob Abbott was a prolific author of series books for each sex:

> *Cousin Lucy Among the Mountains,* Boston: B. B. Mussey, 1843
> *Cousin Lucy at Play,* Boston: B. B. Mussey, 1842
> *Cousin Lucy at Study,* Boston: B. B. Mussey, 1842
> *Cousin Lucy on the Seashore,* Boston: B. B. Mussey, 1843
> *Cousin Lucy's Conversations,* Boston: B. B. Mussey, 1842
> *Rollo at Play,* Boston: T. H. Carter, 1838
> *Rollo at School,* Boston: T. H. Carter, 1839
> *Rollo at Work,* Philadelphia: Hogan and Thompson, 1845
> *The Rollo Code of Morals,* Boston: Crocker and Brewster, 1841

He was chubby and plump—a right jolly old elf;

And I laughed when I saw him in spite of myself.

A wink of his eye, and a twist of his head,

Soon gave me to know I had nothing to dread.

He spoke not a word, but went straight to his work,

And filled all the stockings; then turned with a jerk,

And laying his finger aside of his nose,

And giving a nod, up the chimney he rose.

He sprang to his sleigh, to his team gave a whistle,

And away they all flew like the down of a thistle;

But I heard him exclaim, ere he drove out of sight,

"Merry Christmas to all, and to all a good night!"

Ill. 16: Clement Clarke Moore, *A Visit from St. Nicholas.* Illustrated from drawings by F.O.C. Darley. New York: J. G. Gregory, 1862. [8'' x 10½'']

Rollo in Geneva, Boston: Brown, Taggard and Chase, 1857
Rollo in Holland, Boston: Brown, Taggard and Chase, 1857
Rollo in London, Boston: W. J. Reynolds and Co., 1855
Rollo in Naples, Boston: Brown, Taggard and Chase, 1858
Rollo in Paris, Boston: W. J. Reynolds and Co., 1854
Rollo in Rome, Boston: Brown, Taggard and Chase, 1858.

Book settings are almost all reality-oriented; fantasy occurs in only 4 percent of the cases. The settings are also matter-of-fact, humor occurring in 3 percent of the cases. Most of the settings are in rural areas. When settings are looked at in terms of relationship to major characters in the book, in 64 percent of the cases they constitute their home or their community, in 11 percent they constitute a far-away place, and in 25 percent they involve a combination of both.

Book characters at this time are primarily human beings who interact with each other in very human situations. Primary group situations are the most frequent, described in two-thirds of the cases. In one-third of the cases, usually in adventure stories for boys, both primary and secondary groups are described. There is considerable emphasis on the interdependence of people and on the obligation of those more fortunate to help those less fortunate, as in *Uncle John's Second Book* (New York: D. Appleton and company, 1860):

> We should be kind to the poor; for God is very kind to us, and he commands us to be kind to the poor. Besides, we may be as poor as this old, blind man; and if we are not kind to him, can we expect that anyone will be kind to us? (p. 19)

Mrs. A. K. Dunning, in *Ralph Waring's Money* (Philadelphia: American Sunday School Union, c.1874), writes:

> Charge them that are rich in this world, that they be not high-minded, nor trust in uncertain riches, but in the living God, who giveth us all things richly to enjoy;
> That they do good, that they be rich in good works, ready to distribute, willing to communicate;
> Laying up in store for themselves a good foundation against the time to come, that they may lay hold on eternal life. . . . (p. 30)

Minority characters appear more frequently now than before—in 17 percent of the books. When they appear, they almost invariably have inferior status, as in Paul Cobden's *Take a Peep* (Boston: Lee and Shepard, publishers. New York: Lee, Shepard and Dillingham, 1874):

> But don't you suppose I knows dat wite is a prettier color dan black? Of course I does. I don't complain ob de Lord; wouldn't say noting against him for de whole ob dis yer world. (p. 10)

Rarely are minorities portrayed with dignity and compassion as in Aunt Mary's
The Rose (New York: Sheldon & Co., 1863):

> There was a noble little boy
> They called him "Virginny Jack;"
> His eyes were bright—his dark hair curled,
> But ah! his skin was black!
>
> Jack and his Mother once were slaves
> Hard toiling in the sun;
> They hoed tobacco in the field
> Till the long task was done.
>
> But when their master died, he made
> His suffering people free;
> And then no kings or queens on earth
> Could half so happy be.
> . . . .
>
> "Mother," he cried with bursting heart,
> "To school I took my ball,
> At recess lent it to a boy,
> Who raised a shout and call
>
> "For all to bring their bats and have
> A short but merry game;
> And though the ball was mine, they stared
> In wonder when *I* came.
>
> "I struck it once, and far enough
> Beyond their bats it flew;
> When one cried out, "You nigger boy,
> We will not play with you."
>
> (His Mother responds:)
> "The good Book says, 'He loveth those,
> Whose hearts to him are given;'
> And black or white, twill be the same
> With those who get to heaven.
>
> "And when those wicked children laugh,
> Or call a cruel name,
> 'Tis on your Maker, not on *you*
> They cast the scorn and blame."

Indians are depicted less frequently in the books than blacks, but when they
appear, they are usually shown to have inferior capabilities.

Other status differences investigated include sex, age, and social class.

Although status differences are seldom shown between males and females, male characters in general are allowed to do much more than female characters. Boys are pictured in exciting and adventuresome situations, girls are pictured in the home. In terms of age groupings, most of the books contain both adult and child characters. There is considerable increase in adolescent characters during the period with the rise of series books for boys and girls; one fourth of the books feature adolescent characters. About half of the books show social-class differences.

Characters other than human are also frequent in the books. Animals appear in a third of the cases, and when they appear they generally appear as domesticated animals rather than as people in fur. God also appears as a character in two-thirds of the cases. Elves and fairies appear in 1 percent of the cases.

Main characters of the books are adults in 42 percent of the cases, children in 37 percent of the cases, adolescents in 15 percent of the cases. In the remaining books animals or supernatural beings are main characters.

The characters in the books are usually complex. They display positive and negative emotion. They show appropriate reaction to stress. And except in rare cases, such as that little prig Elsie Dinsmore, their natures are neither all good nor all bad, but a combination of both good and bad traits.

Within this period the psychological need of characters most often expressed is for eternal salvation. The need is found in 73 percent of the books, a higher proportion than found in any other period in our country's history. The Sunday School message comes across in both Sunday School and other presses. Daniel Baker, in his discourses for children (*Daniel Baker's Talk to Little Children* [Philadelphia: Presbyterian board of publication, c.1856] writes:

"My little boy, don't you know that you have a soul to be saved?"

What a good little girl is————
She is her Mother's rose
but sweetest rose isn't as
sweet as a good little girl
who loves and obeys Mother and
makes her happy.

What a good little boy is————
his Father's jewel
loves and obeys Father and
makes him happy.

"Oh, What a blessed thing
it is when we come to die,
to have nothing to do but
to breathe our last, and
peacefully fall asleep
in the arms of a loving Saviour!" (p. 60)

The Reverend H. Andrews, in *Voices From the Old Elm, or, Uncle Henry's Talks With the Little Folks* (New-York: Carlton & Porter, c.1857), also talks of death and the hereafter:

> Henry was gathering the roses of his eighth summer when his kind father died; and scarce had the early frosts of autumn tinged the brightness of the forests, when his loving Mother, committing her darlings to the care of Heaven, lay down to sleep beside her husband's grave.
>
> Sad, indeed, were the hearts of the orphans, as they returned from the lonely graveyard to their still more lonely and desolate home. They took the old, worn Bible from the stand at the head of their Mother's bed, and found the precious promises which their parents had so often read to them. (pp. 16-17)

The second most frequently expressed need, appearing in 70 percent of the books, is for love. Love of parent and child is the most often spoken of, although in Victorian novels for girls romantic love is also featured. Love of parent for child is shown in *The Widow's Jewels,* by a lady (Boston: Waite Peirce, & Co., 1844):

> When a wealthy Roman lady was visiting a noble friend of hers, she opened before her the rich casket of jewels which she possessed. There lay soft, pure pearls, rosy rubies, and glowing diamonds, blending their light in brilliant harmony and profusion. Their owner looked proudly up to her friend, and asked what she could show to rival them. Without wishing or attempting similar display, she calmly waived the subject until her children were returned from school. Then drawing them towards her with eyes beaming with love and gratitude, said, *"These are my Jewels."*

Love of child for parent is expressed by Jane Taylor in *Original Poems, for Infant Minds* (Philadelphia: H. F. Anners, 1840):

MY MOTHER

Who fed me from her gentle breast,
And hush'd me in her arms to rest,
And on my cheek sweet kisses press'd? (p. 58)

MY FATHER

Who took me from my mother's arms,
And, smiling at her soft alarms,
Show'd me the world and nature's charms? (p. 60)

Strength and achievement are needs mentioned in 66 percent of the books, primarily in two kinds: biographies of famous persons and novels about enterprising young men. Samuel Griswold Goodrich's *The Life of Franklin,* (Philadelphia: Thomas Cowperthwait and Company, 1848) describes Franklin's youthful school and work achievements as follows:

He continued at the grammar school, however, only about a year, though he had risen to the head of his class, and promised to be a very fine scholar. His father was burthened with a numerous family, and could not carry him through a course of college education. He accordingly changed his first purpose, and sent Benjamin to a school for writing and arithmetic, kept by Mr. George Brownwell.

This master was quite skilful in his profession, being mild and kind to his scholars, but very successful in teaching them. Benjamin learned to write a good hand in a short time, but he could not manage arithmetic so easily. At ten years of age he was taken from school to help his father in the business of a tallow-chandler; and was employed in cutting the wick for the candles, going errands, and tending the shop.

Benjamin disliked the trade, and had a strong inclination to go to sea; but his father opposed his wishes in this respect, and determined to keep him at home. The house in which he lived happened to be near the water, and Benjamin was always playing with boats, and swimming. When sailing with other boys, he was usually the leader, and he confesses that he sometimes led them into difficulties.

There was a salt marsh which bounded part of the mill-pond, on the edge of which the boys used to stand to fish for minnows. They had trampled it so much, however, as to make it a mere quagmire. Franklin proposed to his friends to build a wharf there, for them to stand upon; and showed them a large heap of stones, which were intended for a new house near the marsh, and would answer their purpose exactly.

Accordingly, that evening, when the workmen were gone home, he assembled a number of his playfellows, and they worked diligently, like so many emmets, sometimes two or three to a stone, till they had brought them all to make their little wharf. On the next morning, the workmen were surprised on missing the stones. The authors of the removal were detected, complained of, and punished by their parents. Franklin attempted to show the usefulness of their work; but his father took that occasion to convince him, that that which was not truly honest could not be truly useful.

Benjamin continued employed in the business of his father about two years, that is, till he was twelve years old. His brother John, who had also been brought up to the trade, had left his father, married, and set up for himself in Rhode Island. There was now every appearance that Benjamin was destined to become a tallow-chandler. As his dislike to the trade continued, his father was afraid that, if he did not put Benjamin to one that was more agreeable, he would run away, and to sea, as an elder brother of his had done. In consequence of this apprehension, he used to take him to walk, to see joiners, bricklayers, turners and braziers at their work, that he might observe his inclination, and fix it on some trade or profession that would keep him on land.

His father at length determined on the cutler's trade, and placed him for some days on trial with his cousin Samuel, who was bred to that trade in London, and had just established himself in Boston. It was then usual to ask a sum of money for receiving an apprentice, and the cutler charged so much for taking Benjamin, that his father was displeased, and put him to his old business again.

From his infancy Benjamin had been passionately fond of reading; and all the money that he could get was laid out in purchasing books. He was very fond of voyages and travels. The dangers and adventures of sailors in the different parts of the world, and stories of the strange people and customs they met with, he would always read with delight.

The first books that he was able to buy were the works of a famous old English writer, named John Bunyan. These he afterwards sold, in order to purchase some volumes of Historical Collections. His father's library consisted principally of works on divinity, most of which he read at an early age. Beside these, there was a book by De Foe, the author of *Robinson Crusoe;* and another called *An Essay to do Good,* by Dr. Mather, an old New England divine.

This fondness for books at length determined his father to bring him up as a printer, though he had already one son in that employment. In 1717, this son returned from England with a press and letters to set up his business in Boston. Benjamin liked this trade much better than that of his father, but still had a desire to go to sea. To prevent this step, his father was impatient to have him bound apprentice to his brother, and at length persuaded him to consent to it.

He was to serve as apprentice till he was twenty-one years of age, and during the last year was to be allowed the wages of a journeyman. (pp. 12-15)

A fourth need, expressed in a significant number of books (11 percent), is that for play and adventure. By the 1870's a real change is evident in the acceptance of play and adventure as legitimate and worthwhile. For younger children, there were books of rhymes and games. For older children, especially boys, there were tales of faraway places and wondrous opportunities. Richard Meade Bache depicts the desire to roam as a common feeling of adolescent boys (*The Young Wrecker of the Florida Reef* [Philadelphia: James S. Claxton, 1866]):

> Without having any distaste for business generally, or for my father's business in particular, I grew up with that indefinable longing that is common to many boys—a desire to roam. A vague feeling constantly beset me that I must ramble somewhere in the world. . . . It was not long before I imparted these feelings to my father, and begged him to let me go upon a voyage of some sort; but I found him opposed to it, and I thought him obdurate. He represented to me, that my wish was nothing but a senseless craving for excitement, and that if it were manfully resisted, it could be subdued, and that it was my duty to conquer it. All this he said to me, talking as many a father has done to his son, and will do fruitlessly to the end of time. . . .
> (pp. 14-15)

Few of the books present physical or psychological threats to achievement of needs. For the most part problems in solving needs revolve about the person's inability to achieve on his own. He needs help, help from God and his family and his friends. Most of the needs relate to the glory of God or the good of others as well as oneself. The good of others is focused upon even when the need involved is economic achievement; for when one does achieve in worldly goods one is supposed to share them with others less fortunate. Two-thirds of the books involve life after death as well as life on earth; there is a need for good works now to merit salvation in the hereafter.

Of the institutions which are involved in satisfying needs, the religious institution is foremost, mentioned in 75 percent of the books. In *The Sabbath School Annual* [for 1846], ed. Mrs. M. H. Adams (Boston: J. M. Usher, 1846) the child is told:

> Little children learn to pray! Learn to pray in silence—in your thoughts! Learn to pray in soft and holy words! Learn to pray aloud! Pray in secret—pray by yourself—pray with your brother, your sister—pray before your father, your mother, your teacher! Yea, pray all the days of your youth, that when in stature you become men and women, you can offer an audible prayer at the family altar, in the Sabbath School, the holy conference, at the sick bed, in the hour of affliction, at the home of death! (pp. 167-168)

The institution of the family is referred to almost as frequently, in 74 percent of the books. Family responsibilities and roles are spelled out in detail, frequent mention being made of the duty of parents to discipline. Two kinds of parents are depicted, those who discipline firmly and relate proper behavior to Bible teachings, and those who are permissive, allowing children to do as they please, even permitting them to ridicule their parents.

But tenderness and a little fun are also shown to be important in the parent-child relationship, as in *Bertie and His Best Things* (Philadelphia: Presbyterian board of publication, c.1865):

> It was the bright twilight of a winter's day, and Bertie was in his favourite place in his papa's study. His papa was a minister of the gospel; and, like others of his calling, he was most of the time very busy there with his papers and books. But he always liked to have his little son with him; and, when he was not more than usually engaged, he did not mind if Bertie did occasionally make a little too much noise with his wooden horses and wagons, or even cry, "pop pop" very loudly, as he pretended to fire off his minnie cannon. Sometimes he quite enjoyed a game of romps with Bertie himself; and many a merry frolic they had together, as with Neptune, the pet spaniel, they rolled over and over on the soft carpet. (pp. 3-4)

Relationships between husbands and wives are likewise discussed. Wives are, above all, to be good natured in the presence of their husbands. Mary Jane Hildeburn, in *Dr. Leslie's Boys* (Philadelphia: Presbyterian publication committee, c.1868), describes an admirable pastor's wife:

> His wife was in all respects a suitable companion, being active, intelligent, cheerful and warm-hearted. She was never gloomy, nor was she given to looking upon the dark side of things. . . . (p. 12)

And husbands, for their part, are at all costs to avoid drinking at the public bar, which brings ruin to the whole family. In *Sloth and Thrift, or, The Causes and Correctives of Social Inequality* (Philadelphia: American Sunday School Union, c.1847) such a downfall is described:

> [A]nd now, when Mosely at evening found his home so cheerless, he fled from his duty wife and crying baby, to the public bar-room, or the grocery, where he found his liquor; and he learned to linger at such places, until the late hours which drove him home, unfilled him for early rising and the next day's labour. (p. 51)

The typical household described in the books consists of the nuclear family of parents and children. Grandparents come to visit, but they do not live in. Family decisions are usually made jointly by husband and wife; in instances where they are made by one or the other, they are as likely to be made by husband as by wife. Concomitantly, the parents usually take care of and discipline the child together; when only one takes responsibility of discipline, it is as often the father as the mother.

Other social institutions are of considerably less importance in this period than are church and family. Economic institutions appear in 28 percent of the books, particularly in books for boys which show them how they may attain fame and fortune through hard work. Other books, though, caution about the use of fortune, which should be employed to help others rather than to indulge onself. In *The rich Gentleman and his Two Sons* (Middletown: C. K. Pelton, printer, 1838) the reader is told:

> Consider, my son, that God made all men equal, but sin has introduced into our world poverty, disease and death. Some are made rich by unlawful gains which is very displeasing to their Creator; but they flourish for awhile like the green bay tree; they tyrannize over the poor and needy, and trample them beneath their feet; they have riches but not by right and the fear of God is not in them. There are others that are left rich by their ancestors, and never know the pinching hand of want, and if such are enlightened with the spirit of benevolence, and the duty they owe to the Supreme Being, they become fathers to the poor and thus fulfill His will. (pp. 8-9)

Likewise, in *The Passing Bell; or, "He Died Rich"* (American Sunday School Union, c. 1848), the reader is admonished:

> Riches are uncertain things. You may soon be deprived of them. If you should come to poverty, it will be a sweet solace to you to have the testimony of conscience that while you had property, you faithfully and liberally devoted it to the service of God and the claims of benevolence. Job, in adversity, was cheered at the thought of having done good while it was in his power. (p. 35)

Leisure-time activities appear in 20 percent of the books. Some delightful toy books, riddle books, and Mother Goose books were published during this time, with larger and larger illustrations. Leisure was usually placed, though, in a wider context of doing one's duty first or playing second, as in *Mama's Lessons for her Little Boys and Girls* (Providence: Geo. P. Daniels, 1843)

> Toys are for a boy who has done his work. He must do his work, and then he may have his toys. (p. 3)

Education and the importance of learning is mentioned in 17 percent of the books. Mrs. Frances Elizabeth Barrow, in *Pop-guns: One Serious and One Funny* (New York: Sheldon and co., 1864), writes about the purpose of her books:

> To be sure I have given a funny title to the books, and shall try to tell *some* funny stories; but beneath this fun I want you to feel that I am also trying to show you how the cultivation of high and generous

> qualities, and noble and right principles, is the only way by which
> you may reap real and steadfast happiness—The only way to use the
> love and respect of all around you. (pp. 21-22)

In *Uncle John's Second Book* (New York: D. Appleton and company, 1860)
the importance of education is made clear:

> "Oh father I wish I knew everything in the world, said little Mary
> Sale . . ."

> "I am glad to see you wish to learn. If you really wish to improve,
> you will always find someone ready and willing to tell you every-
> thing you may wish to know, and can know." (p.142)

Political institutions appear least often, in 16 percent of the books. But
biographies of this country's founders were still being produced at the time and
were quite popular. Histories describe political events, especially of the
American Revolution and the Civil War. Since most books were published in
the North, the northern view of the Civil War, as a victory for the North and for
the country, is given. Slavery is condemned, although black dialects and
characterizations of blacks as inferior remain.

Stressed in these books is the importance of social responsibility. Such
responsibility includes concern for family and community and cognizance of
God's will. It also includes, in one-fourth of the books, abstinence from
alcohol. Numerous stories portray husbands and fathers no longer able to
provide for their wives and children due to the effects of drunkenness.

Relationships between characters in the story are, in the majority of cases,
rational, relating to the larger public good. In a substantial number of books a
strong religious belief system is also important in regulating behavior. People
behave in a certain way because of respect for and obligations to others and
because of obligation to God.

Relationships are usually intimate. Except in some political and economic
settings, people are on a first-name basis and show positive affect to one
another.

Goals relate to the good of all rather than to one's own good. One must be
pious to please God rather than just to avoid hell. One makes money to share
with those in need rather than just to enjoy alone.

In almost half of the books there is social stratification, but there is also
considerable social mobility. Through hard work the poor could expect to
become rich. In Horatio Alger's stories and others of the genre, the poor not
only could but should show diligence and prudence so as to rise to the top for the
good of all.

Needs are met in the great majority of cases by conformity to adult and
supernatural norms. The proscriptions for the young are laid out clearly and
concisely, self-direction being infrequently encouraged (in 13 percent of the

books). Even less encouraged was social change. The present order was deemed adequate and true, and there is scant questioning of the status quo.

In all but 2 percent of the cases satisfactions are obtained, usually through the help of the individual's God and family. Persons feel good about themselves but are mindful of all they owe to the supernatural and to their elders. They think well of others. The world is viewed, though, as an uncertain place, one in which there are many problems and pitfalls. Persons are obliged, then, to work hard and trust in the Lord. *Letters to the Children of Pious Parents* states:

> How rapturous the songs when parents and children, an unbroken
> circle, shall stand before the throne of God, wearing the golden
> crown and bearing the palms of victory. (p. 90)

In *The children's Speaker and Anniversary Gem,* by Mrs. E. E. Boyd and Emma M. Johnston (Philadelphia: J. P. Skelly and Co., 1872), Mrs. Boyd writes:

VERSE FOR A LITTLE GIRL

> I am the very least of all
> The little ones ya see;
> But what would be the world without
> Even a child like me?
> I want to be a blessing, to
> My home and all I love.
> And when I die, I want to be
> God's little one above. (p. 11)

TO BE SPOKEN BY A LITTLE LIGHT-HAIRED BOY:

> I'm a very little fellow,
> And my hair is very yellow;
> I've learned to laugh, I've learned
> to play,
> But, best of all, I've learned to pray. (p. 12)

Death is present in 70 percent of the books. In *Light and Support for the Dark Valley* (Philadelphia: Presbyterian board of publication, c.1851) the reader is reminded:

> Our times are in the hand of God. All that we certainly know of
> death is its inevitable occurrence. There is no discharge in this war.
> (p. 55)

Daniel Baker, in *Daniel Baker's Talk to Little Children,* writes:

> Oh, What a blessed thing
> it is when we come to die,

to have nothing to do but
to breathe our last, and
peacefully fall asleep
in the arms of a loving Saviour! (p. 60)

Again four works have been singled out for detailed analysis: Jacob Abbott's *Rollo at Work* (1845), William Taylor Adams' *The Boat Club* (1855), Louisa May Alcott's *Little Women* (1868), and Horatio Alger's *Strive and Succeed* (1872). These novels were written primarily for adolescents, who are addressed significantly for the first time during this period. All the books stress Puritan values of diligence, restraint, self-reliance. Role models are clear, and the rewards of proper behavior quite inviting.

Rollo at Work

James Jacob Abbott lived from 1803 to 1879. Born in Hallowell, Maine, of a strict Calvinist family, he was sent at the age of seventeen to Andover Theological Seminary and after graduation was ordained a minister. He did not accept pastoral work at once, but from 1825 to 1829 filled the chair of mathematics at Amherst College.

For some years Abbott was headmaster of Mount Vernon, a girl's school which he founded. Here his theories of education, embodied later in his books for children, were expressed. He moved to his last home in Farmington, Maine, in 1839. It was in this mountain home that he found the surroundings and the characters of his Rollo books, the charm of which lies in his descriptions of the outdoor life of a young New England boy.

Despite his service as a minister, there is surprisingly little direct religion in Abbott's 200-plus volumes. (There are over 300 editions in the Rare Book Room of the Library of Congress.) But there is a religion of duty found therein, the very essence of faith in New England. For more details of the man and his work, the reader is directed to Abbott [1], Abbott [2], and Weber [19].

The Rollo books feature an engaging, if unthinking young boy, often in very familiar surroundings of home, hillside, and school. He is most often shown with his parents and other adults, whose overriding concern is, quite simply, to socialize him. The following passage from *Rollo at Work; or The Way for a Boy to Learn to be Industrious*, 5th ed. (Philadelphia: Hogan & Thompson, 1845) shows how his elders go about instructing in proper social behavior:

RIDES

Rollo often used to ride out with his father and mother. When he was quite a small boy, he did not know how to manage so as to get frequent rides. He used to keep talking, himself, a great deal, and interrupting his father and mother, when they wanted to talk; and if he was tired he would complain, and ask them, again and again, when they should get home. Then he was often thirsty, and would tease his father and mother for water, in places where there was no water to be got, and then fret because he was obliged to wait a little while. In consequence of this, his father and mother did not take him very often. When they wanted a quiet, still, pleasant ride, they had to leave Rollo behind. A great many children act just as Rollo did, and thus deprive themselves of a great many very pleasant rides.

Rollo observed, however, that his uncle almost always took Lucy with him when he went to ride. And one day, when he was playing in the yard where Jonas was at work setting out trees, he saw his uncle riding by, with another person in the chaise, and Lucy sitting between them on a little low seat. Lucy smiled and nodded as she went by; and when she had gone, Rollo said,

"There goes Lucy, taking a ride. Uncle almost always takes her, when he goes anywhere. I wonder why father does not take me as often."

"I know why," said Jonas.

"What is the reason?" said Rollo.

"Because you are troublesome, and Lucy is not. If I was a boy like you, I should manage so as almost always to ride with my father."

"Why, what should you do?" said Rollo.

"Why, in the first place, I should never find fault with my seat. I should sit exactly where they put me, without any complaint. Then I should not talk much, and I should never interrupt them when they were talking. If I saw anything on the road that I wanted to ask about, I should wait until I had a good opportunity to do it without disturbing their conversation; and then, if I wanted anything to eat or drink, I should not ask for it, unless I was in a place where they could easily get it for me. Thus I should not be any trouble to them, and so they would let me go almost always."

Rollo was silent. He began to recollect how much trouble he had given his parents, when riding with them, without thinking of it at the time. He did not say anything to Jonas about it, but he secretly resolved to try Jonas's experiment the very next time he went to ride.

He did so, and in a very short time his father and mother both perceived that there was, somehow or other, a great change in his manners. He had ceased to be troublesome, and had become quite a pleasant travelling companion. And the effect was exactly as Jonas had foretold. His father and mother liked very much to have such a still, pleasant little boy sitting between them; and at last they began

almost to think they could not have a pleasant ride themselves,
unless Rollo was with them. (pp. 35-38)

Besides proper behavior towards others, the child must be taught proper
behavior towards work. Work always came before play. Children were
tempted to skip the former in favor of the latter, and a good deal of effort
must be devoted to instilling perseverance, a desire for hard work, and steadfastness in the small New England boy-cum-man:

THE OLD NAILS

The next morning, after breakfast, Rollo's father told him he was
ready for him to go to his work. He took a small basket in his hand,
and led Rollo out into the barn, and told him to wait there a few
minutes, and he would bring him something to do.

Rollo sat down on a little bundle of straw, wondering what his
work was going to be.

Presently his father came back, bringing in his hands a box full of
old nails, which he got out of an old store-room, in a corner of the
barn. He brought it along, and set it down on the barn floor.

"Why, father," said Rollo, "what am I going to do with those old
nails?"

"You are going to sort them. Here are a great many kinds, all
together. I want them all picked over—those that are alike put by
themselves. I will tell you exactly how to do it."

Rollo put his hand into the box, and began to pick up some of the
nails, and look them over, while his father was speaking; but his
father told him to put them down, and not begin until he had got all
his directions.

"You must listen," said he, "and understand the directions now,
for I cannot tell you twice."

He then took a little wisp of straw, and brushed away a clean place
upon the barn floor, and then poured down the nails upon it.

"O, how many nails!" said Rollo.

His father then took up a handful of them, and showed Rollo that
there were several differnet sizes; and he placed them down upon the
floor in little heaps, each size by itself. Those that were crooked
also he laid away in a separate pile.

"Now, Rollo," said he, "I want you to go to work sorting these
nails, steadily and industriously, until they are all done. There are
not more than three or four kinds of nails, and you can do them pretty
fast if you work steadily, and do not get to playing with them. If you
find any pieces of iron, or anything else that you do not know what
to do with, lay them aside, and go on with the nails. Do you understand it all?"

IT IS NEVER RIGHT TO STOP BY THE WAY.—Page 9.

Ill. 17: Jacob Abbott. *Rollo at School*. New York, Sheldon and Company, Publishers, 1868. [3½'' x 6'']

THE ORGAN GRINDER.—Page 112.

Ill. 18: Jacob Abbott. *Rollo at School*. New York, Sheldon and Company, Publishers, 1868. [3½″ x 6″]

Rollo said he did, and so his father left him, and went into the house. Rollo sat down upon the clean barn floor, and began his task.

"I don't think this is any great thing," said he; "I can do this easily enough;" and he took up some of the nails, and began to arrange them as his father had directed.

But Rollo did not perceive what the real difficulty in his task was. It was, indeed, very easy to see what nails were large, and what were small, and what were of middle size, and to put them in their proper heaps. There was nothing very hard in that. The difficulty was, that, after having sorted a few, it would become tedious and tiresome work, doing it there all alone in the barn—picking out old nails, with nobody to help him, and nobody to talk to, and nothing to see, but those little heaps of rusty iron on the floor.

This, I say, was the real trouble; and Rollo's father knew, when he set his little boy about it, that he would soon get very tired of it, and, not being accustomed to anything but play, would not persevere.

And so it was. Rollo sorted out a few, and then he began to think that it was rather tiresome to be there all alone; and he thought it would be a good plan for him to go and ask his father to let him go and get his cousin James to come and help him. (pp. 45-48)

The purpose of this book is to instruct in social values related to needs of a small rural community. Settings are reality oriented and matter-of-fact, located in and around the home.

The actors are primarily family members, with white, middle-class backgrounds. They show affection and concern for one another and responsibility to others as well.

The principal needs expressed are, first, for strength and achievement, for getting a job done, and, second, for love, for significant relationships with others. There is in the book some need for play, but there is also an awareness that too much play is probably unhealthy. There are no problems in solving needs if the person really works at it. Needs relate to group rather than to individual welfare and often to a future time on earth when the individual child must assume adult roles.

Needs are satisfied through the social institutions of family, work, and leisure. In terms of family, parents are in the home, and in this book the father/son relationship is particularly strong. The father spends time with the child and disciplines him. Social responsibility is focused principally on family but also on community needs. Relationships are rational and intimate. Conformity to adult norms is strongly encouraged, with the orientation being towards maintenance of the status quo. Satisfaction of needs is attained through hard work and family support. Views of self and of the world are thus largely positive.

The Boat Club

William Taylor Adams (pseudonym, Oliver Optic) was one of a number of authors who wrote adventure stories for boys during this period. Charles A. Fosdick (pseudonym, Harry Castlemon) is also representative of this genre, as is Elijah Kellogg. Adams (1822–1897) was a New England school teacher who, from age 50, wrote 116 full-length books, while continuing to hold a school principalship. He also edited magazines for children: *Oliver Optic's Magazine for Boys and Girls, Our Little Ones,* and *Student and Schoolmate.* There are over 200 editions of his works in the Rare Book Room of the Library of Congress. Adams' series of books on travel and adventure include the following:

Army and Navy Stories	Yacht Club Series
"Boat Club" Series	The Onward and Upward Series
Lake Shore Series	Young America Abroad Series
Soldier Boy Series	Riverdale Stories
Sailor Boy Series	Flora Lee Story Books
Starry Flag Series	The Great Western Series
The Way of the World	Our Boys' and Girls' Offering
The Household Library	Our Boys' and Girls' Souvenir
Woodville Stories	

Adams was principally interested in providing adventurous fun for boys, but he was also interested in providing them lessons in geography and science. And he was interested in the development of the male character. A good example of Adams' concerns is found in *The Boat Club.* Its all-male cast has some rollicking good times, but in a very respectable way, as shown in the following selection (Boston: Brown, Besin and Company, 1855):

CHAPTER 12. THE "THUNDERBOLT"

The appearance of the club in uniform was unique and pleasing, and each of the members was "every inch a sailor." Uncle Ben was delighted with the change. "They looked so much more shipshape than in their shore togs."

"Come, Uncle Ben, we are all ready," said Frank.

"I arn't goin' woth you this time."

"You must go without him to-day, Frank," added Captain Sedley. "Uncle Ben must take the things over to the island for the collation."

"Are we to go alone?"

"Certainly."

"Hurrah!" cried Charles, who always used this word to express his gratification.

"But boys, you must preserve good discipline. According to the constitution you must all obey the coxswain. And, Frank, be very careful, don't get aground on the rocks at the north shore, and if you go down the river, don't go too near the dam."

"I will not, father," replied Frank, who was fully impressed by the responsibility of his position as commander of the Zephyr. "Take your places in the boat. Tony, number them."

The doors which gave egress from the boathouse to the lake were thrown open by Uncle Ben.

"Now, back her steady," continued Frank, standing up in the stern sheets. "Don't let her rub, Tony. Steady; one hard push; now she goes;" and the Zephyr shot out into the lake.

"The flags, Frank," said Charles.

"Ay, ay; Tony hoist yours;" and at the same time, Frank raised the American flag at the stern.

"Ready; now for the oars. Up!"

"Down."

"Ready."

"Pull."

Frank felt like a prince as the Zephyr darted away.

"Where are you going, Frank?" asked Charles.

"I don't know; anywhere that the club wish to go." (pp. 144-145)

In this book the young men experiment with adult roles through club activities. Work is involved, and the political process is invoked with a serious democratic election:

CHAPTER 20. CONCLUSION

The first two weeks of the organization of the boat club passed away, and the members were assembled in Zephyr Hall to elect a coxswain. According to the constitution, Frank's term of office had expired.

"Whom do you intend to vote for, Fred?" asked Charles Hardy, who appeared to be very anxious about the election.

"I don't know; I haven't decided yet," replied Fred Harper. "You know what Captain Sedley said the other day about it."

"Yes, but if I have got to vote, I want to get my mind made up. I don't see what harm there can be in talking about it a little."

"He said he did not want any electioneering about the officer—'log rolling,' my father calls it."

"Of course not," replied Charles, demurely.

"The best fellow ought to get the office," said Fred, slyly.

"Of course, but who is the best fellow? That's the question. We ought to talk it over among ourselves a little."

"What good would that do?"

"Each fellow would know whom the others were going to vote for."

"That would not help him to ascertain who would make the best coxswain."

"But it would help towards making a choice."

"There will be a choice fast enough." (pp. 241-242)

The purpose of the book, as Adams himself states, is "to combine healthy moral lessons with a sufficient amount of exciting interest to render the story attractive to the young" (pp. 5-6). The book in this respect is similar to Jacob Abbott's *Rollo* books, which also aim at ensuring character as well as providing amusement for young persons.

The locale of the story is rural New England. It is away from the home of the individual characters, on a lake. It is far enough away from their families for the child characters to experiment with decision-making on their own.

The characters are well-to-do, white, middle-class boys. Their social involvement is with peer groups. The needs expressed are for strength and achievement as well as for play and adventure. There are no real problems in solving needs; the boys simply have to heed their adult mentors and work at it. Human needs are seen in a group rather than an individual context, the interdependence and responsibility of individuals being stressed.

The primary institution involved in satisfying need is one of leisure. Leisure activity is well organized and controlled, involving rules and regulations and even uniforms. The orientation, needless to say, is to the status quo. Success is in the end obtained, through hard work and through following the advice of one's elders. The characters in the book, then, are able to view themselves, and the world in general, favorably.

Little Women

Many realistic stories for adolescent girls were written in this time period by talented and prolific female authors whose major concern was the American family. Martha Finley (1828–1909), who wrote under the name of Farquharson, published a series of books about a young Victorian lady of impeccable virtue, the *Elsie Dinsmore* series. These books begin with Elsie as a child, carry her through childhood, girlhood, wifehood, motherhood, and widowhood (see Brown [5]). Rebecca Clarke (1833–1906) began a series of books for younger girl readers, *The Little Prudy* series, in which Little Prudy turns out to be just as moral as Elsie.

The most famous female novelist of the period, though, was Louisa May Alcott (1832–1888). Born in Germantown, Pennsylvania, the daughter of

Amos Bronson Alcott, the philosopher and educator, and Abba May Alcott, described as a brilliant and practical New Englander, Louisa was one of four sisters. Her father insisted upon a strict family life with simple meatless meals. He often took into their meagre household destitute homeless people. There were closeness and warmth in that household despite poverty, disruptions from many moves, mostly in and around the Boston area; and various other adversities. For further readings on Louisa May Alcott and on the Alcott family, see Alcott [3], Gulliver [8], *Horn Book Magazine* [9], McCuskey [*12*], Meigs [14], Sayler [15], Sanborn [16], Stern [17], and *More Books* [22].

Alcott had often thought of writing a book about her own family ("the pathetic family" as she sometimes called it) and in 1867 set about composing *Little Women*, published in 1868, with illustrations by her younger sister, May Alcott. It was an immediate success and is still one of the most popular and widely read books ever written for girls in the English language. Based on many real-life incidents concerning Louisa herself, her sisters, and her parents, the book has sentiment, humor, and romantic appeal.

There were sequels about the March family. *An Old-Fashioned Girl*, based on Louisa's own experiences of earning her living, came in 1870, and in 1871 came *Little Men*, about the later years of the now famous family. *Eight Cousins* and its sequel, *Rose in Bloom*, tell of the extended March family connections. The last of the books on the Marches, *Jo's Boys*, appeared in 1886. There are other books, but it is really on *Little Women* that Alcott's fame rests; its universal appeal is attested by the fact that it has been translated into more than twenty languages.

The intimacy of life among the Alcotts is shared with the reader in *Little Women*. And Jo, the most irresistible and vivid of the four adolescent March girls, is in many ways a portrait of Louisa May Alcott herself (*Little Women; or, Meg, Jo, Beth, and Amy* [Boston: Roberts Brothers, 1868]):

> "You are old enough to leave off boyish tricks, and behave better, Josephine. It didn't matter so much when you were a little girl; but now you are so tall, and turn up your hair, you should remember that you are a young lady."
>
> "I ain't! and if turning up my hair makes me one, I'll wear it in two tails till I'm twenty," cried Jo, pulling off her net, and shaking down a chestnut mane. "I hate to think I've got to grow up and be Miss March, and wear long gowns, and look as prim as a China-aster. It's bad enough to be a girl, any way, when I like boys' games, and work, and manners. I can't get over my disappointment in not being a boy, and it's worse than ever now, for I'm dying to go and fight with papa, and I can only stay at home and knit like a poky old woman;" and Jo shook the blue army-sock till the needles rattled like castanets, and her ball bounded across the room.

''Poor Jo; it's too bad! But it can't be helped, so you must try to be
contented with making your name boyish, and playing brother to us
girls,'' said Beth, stroking the rough head at her knee with a hand
that all the dish washing and dusting in the world could not make
ungentle in its touch. (pp. 10-11)

The joys and sorrows, the daily occurrences, and the celebrations of the March
family are portrayed with clarity and warmth. This Christmas scene, with
father away at war, is an example:

''Where is mother?'' asked Meg, as she and Jo ran down to thank
her for their gifts, half an hour later.
''Goodness only knows. Some poor creeter come a-beggin', and
your ma went straight off to see what was needed. There never was
such a woman for givin' away vittles and drink, clothes and firin','
replied Hannah, who had lived with the family since Meg was born,
and was considered by them all more as a friend than a servant.
''She will be back soon, I guess; so do your cakes, and have
everything ready,'' said Meg, looking over the presents which were
collected in a basket and kept under the sofa, ready to be produced at

AMY AND LAURIE.

'' I'm all ready for the secrets.'' said Laurie, looking up with a decided expression of interest in his eyes. — PAGE 239.

Ill. 19: Louisa May Alcott. *Little Women: or, Meg, Jo, Beth and Amy.*
Illustrated by May Alcott. Boston: Roberts Brothers, 1869. [9'' x 6¾'']

the proper time. "Why, where is Amy's bottle of Cologne?" she added, as the little flask did not appear.

"She took it out a minute ago, and went off with it to put a ribbon on it, or some such notion," replied Jo, dancing about the room to take the first stiffness off the new army-slippers.

"How nice my handkerchiefs look, don't they? Hannah washed and ironed them for me, and I marked them all myself," said Beth, looking proudly at the somewhat uneven letters which had cost her such labor.

"Bless the child, she's gone and put 'Mother' on them instead of 'M.March;' how funny!" cried Jo, taking up one.

"Isn't it right? I thought it was better to do it so, because Meg's initials are 'M.M.,' and I don't want any one to use these but Marmee," said Beth, looking troubled.

"It's all right, dear, and a very pretty idea; quite sensible, too, for no one can ever mistake now. It will please her very much, I know," said Meg, with a frown for Jo, and a smile for Beth.

"There's mother; hide the basket, quick!" cried Jo, as a door slammed, and steps sounded in the hall.

Amy came in hastily, and looked rather abashed when she saw her sisters all waiting for her.

"Where have you been, and what are you hiding behind you?" asked Meg, surprised to see, by her hood and cloak, that lazy Amy had been out so early.

"Don't laugh at me, Jo, I didn't mean any one should know till the time came. I only meant to change the little bottle for a big one, and I gave all my money to get it, and I'm truly trying not to be selfish any more."

As she spoke, Amy showed the handsome flask which replaced the cheap one; and looked so earnest and humble in her little effort to forget herself, that Meg hugged her on the spot, and Jo pronounced her "a trump," while Beth ran to the window, and picked her finest rose to ornament the stately bottle.

"You see, I felt ashamed of my present, after reading and talking about being good this morning, so I ran round the corner and changed it the minute I was up; and I'm so glad, for mine is the handsomest now."

Another bang of the street-door sent the basket under the sofa, and the girls to the table eager for breakfast.

"Merry Christmas, Marmee! Lots of them! Thank you for our books; we read some, and mean to every day," they cried, in chorus. (pp. 24-26)

The main purpose of *Little Women* is amusement, and yet it is also a statement of human values and beliefs. The telling is reality-oriented and matter-of-fact, placed in the semirural area around Boston like the one where the Alcotts themselves lived. The setting is home.

The characters in the story are very human. They are primarily members of one family—white, upper-middle-class Protestant in background. They believe in industriousness, good works, and piety. They also believe in reading and in discussion of ideas. Portrayal of human behavior is detailed and complex, and a range of human emotions is shown.

The human need presented most strongly in the book is the need for love and tenderness and support of other human beings. Parental love and romantic love are both important; also important is love of neighbor and love of the poor and the handicapped. Another need expressed forcefully by both boys and girls in the book is the need for strength and achievement. Jo March wants a professional career, but the career does not take her out of the home. Nor does it take her out of a traditional role for women: teaching. A need for play, for time to enjoy life through reading, through conversation, through visits to the shore, is also present in the books.

Needs of characters are satisfied primarily through the institution of the family. The March family is an intact nuclear family, although extended family members also appear. The mother and father are in the home, except of necessity, and they care deeply for their children. Even when the father is away at war his presence is very much felt in the home. The parents make decisions together and spend considerable time with the children. Their discipline is by example.

Other social institutions are also shown. Economic institutions, with opportunities for women as well as for men, are important. Leisure, in the form of family birthdays and anniversaries and holiday trips, is enjoyed. Religion is essential because it provides the foundation for values and behavior; it is a religion of charity and love as well as of piety and restraint. Education is also valued, not only because it equips individuals for a profession, but, more significantly, because it enables them to obtain understanding and wisdom.

Within social institutions, needs are approached through rational, intimate, and group-oriented social relationships. They are approached by self-direction in circumscribed areas. For the orientation is not to social change but to the improvement of already good social networks, particularly family networks.

Satisfaction of needs occurs as a result of the efforts of the individual characters helped by the efforts of their family. The characters view themselves positively, realizing their achievements, and also humbly, realizing the importance of group ties in these attainments. They see the world positively, viewing the life cycle of birth, early development, maturity, and death as one continuous whole.

Strive and Succeed

Horatio Alger (1832–1899) was the most popular author in the United States in the last thirty years of the nineteenth century. He wrote over 100 books, with the total sales probably over thirty million copies.

Alger was born in Revere, Massachusetts, the son of a Unitarian clergyman, was educated at Harvard, and then attended the Harvard Divinity School. He was ordained minister of the Unitarian Church in Brewster, Massachusetts, in 1864. Two years later he resigned from the church and moved to New York, where he became associated with the management of the Newsboys' Lodging House, a home for foundlings and runaway boys.

Alger had published several earlier works, but in the atmosphere of the lodging house he began the effort that would make him famous—the construction of stories of poor boys who rose from rags to riches. Beginning with *Ragged Dick* (1867), the Alger hero fired the imagination of two generations of American youth. With the exception of the western frontiersman, no other myth figure has exerted so powerful an influence on American culture. Perseverance and hard work were the avenues to economic success for Alger boys, just as love and courage were the avenues to personal satisfaction for Alcott girls. For additional materials on Alger, see Allen [4], Mayes [11], and Tebbel [18].

In *Strive and Succeed* the adolescent male hero is named Walter Conrad. The story opens shortly after Walter has learned of his father's death and his own fall in fortune (*Strive and Succeed; or, The progress of Walter Conrad*, [Boston: Loring, c.1872]):

> Walter Conrad, then, not quite a year since, had received, when at boarding school, the unexpected intelligence of his father's serious illness. On reaching home, he found his parent dead. Subsequently he learned that his father had bought shares to the extent of a hundred thousand dollars in the Great Metropolitan Mining Company, and through the failure of this company had probably lost everything. This intelligence had doubtless hastened his death. Walter was, of course, obliged to leave school, and accepted temporarily an invitation from Mr. Jacob Drummond, of Stapleton, a remote kinsman, to visit him. In extending the invitation Mr. Drummond was under the illusion that Walter was the heir to a large property. On learning the truth, his manner was changed completely, and Walter, finding himself no longer welcome as a guest, proposed to enter Mr. Drummond's store as a clerk. Being a strong and capable boy, he was readily received on board wages. The board, however, proved to be very poor, and his position was made more disagreeable by

Joshua Drummond, three years older than himself, who, finding he could get nothing out of him, took a dislike to him. Walter finally left Mr. Drummond's employ, and, led by his love of adventure, accepted an offer to travel as a book agent in Ohio. Here he was successful, though he met with one serious adventure, involving him in some danger, but was finally led to abandon the business at the request of Clement Shaw, his father's executor, for the following reason:

The head of the Great Metropolitan Mining Company, through whom his father had been led to invest his entire fortune in it, was a man named James Wall, a specious and plausible man, through whose mismanagement it was believed it had failed. He was strongly suspected of conspiring to make a fortune out of it at the expense of the other stockholders. He had written to Mr. Shaw, offering the sum of two thousand dollars for the thousand shares now held by Walter, an offer which the executor did not feel inclined to accept until he knew that it was made in good faith. He, therefore, wrote to Walter to change his name, and go on to Portville, the home of Mr. Wall, and there use all his shrewdness to discover what he could of the position of the mining company, and Mr. Wall's designs in relation thereto. It may be added that after selling the balance of the estate Walter was found entitled to five hundred dollars. He had, besides, cleared eighty-seven dollars net profit on his sales as book agent. (pp. 10-12)

At his guardian's request, Walter does go to investigate the possibility of foul play at the mining company. He ascertains that foul play is underfoot and that the mine is about to reopen in full with the anticipation of considerable profit. Walter then accosts the head of the company and demands a fair price for his share:

"I have already written to Mr. Clement Shaw—your guardian, is he not?—offering three thousand dollars for your shares. We may lose by it, but the money will go into good hands. I hope you are empowered to accept the offer."

"General Wall," said Walter, firmly, "don't you consider the shares worth more?"

"Well," said he, after a pause, "have you any offer to make?"

"I will sell the shares for sixty thousand dollars."

"You must be crazy," said the general, in excitement.

"I have no fears on that subject," said our hero coolly. "But I may as well tell you, General Wall, that I am entirely acquainted with your plan for obtaining complete control of the stock. I know you have succeeded in buying up most of it at little or nothing, and

that you will probably realize a fortune out of it. But my eyes are
open. They were opened three weeks since, when I overheard, at the
Portville House, a conversation between the landlord and an agent of
yours, who gave full details of the conspiracy into which you had
entered to defraud the original owners of stock. I learned that you
had succeeded with all except myself. The result of this revelation
was, that I determined to visit the mines, and see for myself. I spent
three days there, and I have returned to tell you that you may have
the stock for sixty thousand dollars, or I will keep it. I know it is
worth more than I ask, but I live in the East, and I prefer to have my
money invested there.''

General Wall had risen, and was pacing the room in some agita-
tion.

"The revelation you have made has taken me by surprise,
Mr.—Conrad. I will think over what you have said, and call upon
you at the hotel to-morrow.''

"Very well, sir. . . .''

Negotiation was protracted for some days. At length General Wall
acceded to Walter's terms, and agreed to purchase the stock at the
price named—sixty thousand dollars! ten thousand down, and the
balance payable monthly. Walter instantly telegraphed the good
news to Mr. Shaw, his faithful friend, and received his heartiest
congratulations. (pp. 349-352)

When the business was completed, our hero started for the East. With his
inheritance Walter dutifully returns to school to study law. His intelligence,
hard work, and pluck have enabled him to overcome danger and poverty. He
thanks God. And he uses his money not only for his own educational benefit
but for the educational benefit of others as well.

The purpose of this book is both to provide an entertaining story for the
adolescent boy, one he can identify with personally, and to instruct him in
social values. The values in question relate to the Protestant ethic—hard work,
self-denial, praise to God.

The setting of the book is away from the home of the main character.
Economic mobility requires geographic mobility and hence ties to home
become less important; an adventuresome, aggressive spirit becomes more
important.

In his economic activities, the main character interacts primarily with secondary groups. These are strangers with whom he is at loggerheads. The persons
involved are white, middle-class, mostly male. They include adolescents and
adults, the adolescents quickly taking on adult roles. Class differences are
found among characters but also found is considerable room for social mobility. The main character is an adolescent of impeccable virtue and cheerfulness.

Ill. 20: Horatio Alger. *The Young Salesman*. Philadelphia: The John C. Winston Company. Nineteenth Century. [4⅞'' x 7½'']

He is a positive person, with clear intellectual strengths and concern for the underdog (as contrasted with the *underhanded*).

The needs expressed by characters in the books are primarily for strength and achievement. Sometimes real threats to satisfaction of needs are found, but the individual always overcomes them. These needs are primarily focused on the individual, although when the individual becomes successful he demonstrates compassion and generosity towards others. Needs relate to the future, but it is an immediate future, because economic success comes quickly once one adopts the right kind of behavior.

The major social institution involved in satisfying needs is economic. The boy hero takes on adult roles and makes his own way up the ladder of success. Relationships between individuals are largely rational, apart, individual, and hierarchially oriented. Needs are met both by self-direction and by conformity to adult norms. Creativity is desired for the purpose of changing a person's position in the society, not for the purpose of changing the society itself.

Success in achieving needs and goals comes about largely through the individual's own efforts. He strikes out on his own, and he makes it. He is entitled to and does feel good about himself and about a world of opportunity and prosperity for those who really TRY.

With the advent of books for adolescents during the period, such as those by Adams, Alcott, and Alger, comes a focus on this life as well as the next, on amusement as well as on instruction. The main characters are in transition from childhood to adulthood. Their needs are for earthly things—for love, play and adventure, strength and achievement. These things are acquired for girls in the family, for boys in the market place.

Individuals achieve their goals more as a result of their own effort now, but they do not fail to remember that their success is ultimately due to God's pleasure. They thank God for their favorable circumstances. As Alger says of Walter Conrad:

> He had striven under difficult circumstances, and he had succeeded.
> He felt proud and happy, and grateful to God for having so ordered
> events as to lead to this good fortune. (p. 352)

References

1. Abbott, Jacob. *Gentle Measures for the Training of the Young.* New York: Harpers, 1872.
2. Abbott, Jacob. *The Young Christian, with a Memoir of Jacob Abbott by his Son.* New York: Harpers, 1851.
3. Alcott, Louisa May. *Louisa May Alcott: Her Life, Letters and Journals.* Ed. Ednah D. Cheney. Boston: Little, Brown, 1928.

4. Allen, Frederick. "Horatio Alger, Jr.," *Saturday Review of Literature*
18(1938):3–4, 16–17.

5. Brown, Janet E. *The Saga of Elsie Dinsmore*. University of Buffalo Studies,
Volume 17, July 1945; Volume 3, No. 4 of Monographs in English.

6. Cruse, Amy. *The Victorians and their Reading*. Boston: Houghton Mifflin,
1935.

7. Darling, Richard. "Children's Books Following the Civil War." In *Books in
America's Past, Essays Honoring Rudolph H. Gjelsness*. Ed. David Kaser.
Charlottesville, Virginia: University Press of Virginia, 1966, pp. 63–84.

8. Gulliver, Lucille, comp. *Louisa May Alcott: A Bibliography*. Boston: Little,
Brown, 1932.

9. *Horn Book Magazine*. "Centenary of Little Women, 1868–1968." Boston: Horn
Book, 1968.

10. Jordan, Alice M. *From Rollo to Tom Sawyer and Other Papers*. Boston: Horn
Book, 1948.

11. Mayes, Herbert R. *Alger, A Biography Without a Hero*. New York: Macy-
Masius, 1928.

12. McCuskey, Dorothy. *Bronson Alcott, Teacher*. New York: Macmillan, 1940.

13. Meigs, Cornelia L., ed. *A Critical History of Children's Literature*. New York:
Macmillan, 1953.

14. Meigs, Cornelia L. *Invincible Louisa*. Boston: Little, Brown, 1933.

15. Salyer, Sandford. *Marmee, the Mother of Little Women*. Norman, Oklahoma:
Oklahoma University Press, 1949.

16. Sanborn, F. B., and Harris, W. T. A. *Bronson Alcott: His Life and Philosophy*.
Two volumes. Boston: Ticknor Brothers, 1893.

17. Stern, Madeleine. *Louisa May Alcott*. Norman, Oklahoma University
Press, 1950.

18. Tebbel, John W. *From Rags to Riches: Horatio Alger, Jr., and the American
Dream*. New York: Macmillan, 1963.

19. Weber, Carl J. A. *A Bibliography of Jacob Abbott*. Waterville, Maine: Colby
College Press, 1948.

20. "The Dawn of Imagination in American Books for Children." *Horn Book
Magazine* 20(1944):168–175.

21. *A Mid-Century Child and her Books*. New York: Macmillan, 1926.

22. "The Witch's Cauldron to the Family Hearth, Louisa May Alcott's Literary
Development, 1848–1868." *More Books* 18 (October 1943): 363–380.

Chapter 5

1876-1915: "I'm so glad to be at home again!"

During the period 1876 through 1915 significant changes occurred in the focus of books for children. In the first half of the period books of religious instruction were the most frequent type (found in 41 percent of the sample). By the second half of the time period such books had declined in frequency to 17 percent and would decline further in the future. On the other hand, books of amusement rose from 33 percent of the total sample in the first half of the period to 42 percent in the second half. In all periods thereafter books of amusement would be the most frequently found and would encompass well over 50 percent of the Rare Books sample.*

Religious instruction in the books was now less tied to formal relationships with God and more concerned with social relationships to others. Glory and honor to God were linked to responsibilities to country and to family, as in E. M. Hamilton's *Billy's Motto* (Boston: Congregational Sunday School and Publishing Society, c.1894):

> "Who made you?"
>
> "God."
>
> "What did he make you for?"
>
> "To love and obey Him; to love my fellowmen, and to grow up into a good citizen."
>
> "What is your motto?"
>
> "God and my country," Billy would answer with loyal earnestness.
> (p. 11)

Mrs. A. K. Dunning in *Broken Pitchers* (Philadelphia: Presbyterian Board of Publication, c.1887) writes of the importance of family ties in the Christian life:

> "I have learned much during the past year," said Grace. "I have learned that self-indulgence does not bring happiness, that the path

*For other materials on books of the period, see Arbuthnot [2], Darling [5], and Meigs [9].

There was an old woman who lived in a shoe,
She had so many children, she didn't know
what to do.
She gave them some broth, without any
bread,
She whipped them all round, and sent them
to bed.

Ill. 21: *Mother Goose's Nursery Rhymes, a Collection of Alphabets, Rhymes, Tales, and Jingles.* New York: McLoughlin Brothers, c.1886. [6½'' x 9''] of duty is the path of beauty, and I have also learned to appreciate my home. . . .

"I trust that I have made a beginning of the Christian life," said Grace. "Everyday I ask God to help me to do right, and it seems to me that he does help me; for things that once seemed very hard to me now seem easy." (p. 264-265)

Religious behavior and social behavior were most closely linked to the temperance movement, where God's will is made very clear, as in L. Penney's *Little Drops of Water* (New York: National Temperance Society and Publication House, 1886):

WATER BRIGHT THE STRONGEST DRINK

Cold water is the strongest drink,
Cold water, pure and free;
God knew just what was best, I think,
For you, my friends, and me.

The horse drinks only water dear,
And he is strong, I'm sure;
The camel in the desert drear,
How much he can endure!

Birds o'er many and many a league
Of land and stormy sea,
And scarcely seem to know fatigue—
How strong they all must be

Where do they get their strength, I pray?
Not from the fiery stuff
Men drink, and call so good today;
I call it bad enough.

They get it from the water bright,
God gives with lavish hand
To leap and sparkle in the light,
And bless each clime and land. (pp. 5-6)

In addition to Sunday school and temperance literature, another source of religiosocial didacticism is found in books which describe the activities of community youth groups, such as Boy Scouts and Camp Fire Girls. George Eggleston, in *Captain Sam: or, The Boy Scouts of 1814* (New York: G. Putnam's sons, 1876) writes of the boy's need for guidance:

Many persons suppose—and I have known even college profes-
sors who made the mistake—that a boy's mind is like a meal-bag,

which will just hold so much and needs filling. They fill it as they would fill the meal-bag, for the sake of the meal and without a thought of the bag. In fact a boy's mind is more like the boy himself. It will not do to try to make a man out of him by stuffing meat and bread down his throat. The meat and bread fill him very quickly, but he isn't fully grown when he is full. To make a man of him we must give him food in proper quantities, and let it help him to grow, and the things you learn in school are chiefly valuable as food for the mind. (pp. 33-34)

Responsibility and steadfastness for girls is not forgotten, but it is related to the home, as in Marion Davidson's series of books on Camp Fire Girls.

Another purpose of books in this period was, of course, academic instruction. The primers and spellers at this time were more appealing in content and in format than before. There are several delightful editions of Mother Goose with large and colorful illustrations from this era.

Also available are many geographies and histories of this country and of other countries. In the books on America, accounts of both the Civil War and expansion into the West are detailed. The winning of the West is also the subject of a number of novels for young boys, in which the struggles between cowboys and Indians appear over and over and over again.

A few of the later books in this period (3 percent) do stress understanding of peoples and cultures. One such, *Lolami, the Little Cliffdweller,* by Clara Kern Bayliss (Bloomington, Illinois: Public School Publishing Company, 1908), is a sympathetic study of the ancient civilization of cliffdwellers of New Mexico and Arizona. Another book, *An Army Boy in Mexico,* by Charles Evans Kilbourne (Phildelphia: The Pennsylvania Publishing Company, 1914), focuses on the unjust enslavement of a Yaqui Indian tribe.

One of the earliest books of amusement during this period is undoubtedly one of the most entertaining books in the history of American children's literature. Its most famous passage describes a pedestrian job—the whitewashing of a picket fence. Because of poor behavior, the hero, one Tom Sawyer, has been deprived of his Saturday freedom and required to do some work around the house. Tom is not only concerned with losing a perfectly beautiful holiday but with losing face with his friends. His solution to the latter, harder loss, is as follows (Samuel Clemens, *The Adventures of Tom Sawyer* [1876]):

> "Hello, old chap, you got to work, hey?"
>
> Tom wheeled suddenly and said:
>
> "Why, it's you, Ben! I warn't noticing."
>
> "Say—I'm going in a-swimming, I am. Don't you wish you could? But of course you'd druther work—wouldn't you? Course you would!"
>
> Tom contemplated the boy a bit, and said:

"What do you call work?"

"Why, ain't *that* work?"

Tom resumed his whitewashing, and answered carelessly:

"Well, maybe it is, and maybe it ain't. All I know is, it suits Tom Sawyer."

"Oh come, now, you don't mean to let on that you like it?"

The brush continued to move.

"Like it? Well, I don't see why I oughtn't to like it. Does a boy get a chance to whitewash a fence every day?"

That put the thing in a new light. Ben stopped nibbling his apple. Tom swept his brush daintily back and forth—stepped back to note the effect again—Ben watching every move and getting more and more interested, more and more absorbed. Presently he said:

"Say, Tom, let me whitewash a little."

Tom considered, was about to consent; but he altered his mind:

"No-no-I reckon it wouldn't hardly do, Ben. You see, Aunt Polly's awful particular about this fence—right here on the street, you know—but if it was the back fence I wouldn't mind and she wouldn't. Yes, she's awful particular about this fence; it's got to be done very careful; I reckon there ain't one boy in a thousand, maybe two thousand, that can do it the way it's got to be done."

"No—is that so? Oh come, now—lemme just try. Only just a little—I'd let you, if you was me, Tom."

"Ben, I'd like to, honest Injun; but Aunt Polly—well, Jim wanted to do it, but she wouldn't let him; Sid wanted to do it, and she wouldn't let Sid. Now don't you see how I'm fixed? If you was to tackle this fence and anything was to happen to it—"

"Oh, shucks, I'll be just as careful. Now lemme try. Say—I'll give you the core of my apple."

"Well, here—No, Ben, now don't. I'm afeared—"

"I'll give you all of it!"

Tom gave up the brush with reluctance in his face, but alacrity in his heart. And while the late steamer Big Missouri worked and sweated in the sun, the retired artist sat on a barrel in the shade close by, dangled his legs, munched his apple, and planned the slaughter of more innocents. There was no lack of material; boys happened along every little while; they came to jeer, but remained to whitewash. By the time Ben was fagged out, Tom had traded the next chance to Billy Fisher for a kite, in good repair; and when he played out, Johnny Miller bought in for a dead rat and a string to swing it with—and so on, and so on, hour after hour. And when the middle of the afternoon came, from being a poor poverty-stricken boy in the morning, Tom was literally rolling in wealth. He had besides the things before mentioned, twelve marbles, part of a jew's-harp, a piece of blue bottle glass to look through, a spool cannon, a key that wouldn't unlock anything, a fragment of chalk, a glass stopper of a decanter, a tin soldier, a couple of tadpoles, six firecrackers, a kitten with only one eye, a brass doorknob, a dog collar—but no dog—the handle of a knife, four pieces of orange peel, and a dilapidated old window sash.

He had had a nice, good, idle time all the while—plenty of company—and the fence had three coats of whitewash on it! If he hadn't run out of whitewash, he would have bankrupted every boy in the village.

Tom said to himself that it was not such a hollow world, after all. He had discovered a great law of human action, without knowing it—namely, that in order to make a man or a boy covet a thing, it is only necessary to make the thing difficult to attain. If he had been a great and wise philosopher, like the writer of this book, he would now have comprehended that Work consists of whatever a body is *obliged* to do and that Play consists of whatever a body is not obliged to do. (pp. 17-20)

Approximately half of the authors of books of this period are men, and approximately half are women. Very few of the authors are ministers any longer (2 percent of the sample), and henceforth the clergy will provide only a handful of writers in this sample.

In terms of publishing houses, New York and Boston remain the centers of publishing with 35 percent of the books in the sample published in New York and 37 percent published in Boston. Philadelphia is the locus for 12 percent of the books, and Chicago and other North Central cities are the locus of 12 percent. Thirteen percent of the publishers are church presses.

Most of the works of the period are fiction (80 percent), 10 percent being nonfiction and 10 percent a combination of fiction and nonfiction. The style is mostly prose. During this time, fantasy begins to take hold. Lewis Carroll's *Alice in Wonderland,* published in England in 1865, had an important effect on American writers. *The Wizard of Oz* didn't arrive until 1900, but it had several sequels as well as a number of imitators in the next decade. For younger children, Palmer Cox's *Brownies* offered a continued source of entertainment. Brownies, like fairies and goblins, were imaginary sprites who delighted in harmless pranks and helpful deeds. Their activity was carried out at night while ordinary mortals slept; they never allowed themselves to be seen by humans. Most of the fantasy books were matter-of-fact; there was a slight increase in humor during the period, especially because of the works of Mark Twain.

Settings are more urbanized now (21 percent of the books) just as the country is becoming more urbanized. Settings are still largely the home and neighborhood of the principal characters, but in 19 percent of the cases—over twice as many as in any preceding period—they are elsewhere. Series such as the Lippincott's Trail Blazer Series, dedicated to "The American Boy and this wonderful land which is his in which to grow and prosper," enlarged horizons with titles such as:

Gold Seekers of 49
Buffalo Bill and The Overland Trail
On the Plains with Custer
With Carson and Fremont
Captain John Smith
Daniel Boone
David Crockett

The actors in the books of the period are primarily humans. Few books focus on supernatural beings or animals. In two-thirds of the cases, social involvement is with the family or other primary groups. In books for adolescent boys, though, secondary groups become important as the young male separates out easily and quickly from the home to make his way into the cold world.

Minority actors are found in one-fourth of the books of the period. There are, by and large, still clear status differentials between whites and minorities. May Kingston's *Black Cindy* (Boston: Congregational Sunday School and Publishing Society, c.1888) offer a typical example:

Cynthia Burn was the little girl's real name; but God made her so black that her master called her a black cinder, and then Cindy. Her home was in the South, at the time when little black children were owned by rich men, just as horses and cows, oxen and sheep are owned now.

You will be surprised when I tell you what Cindy had for a dolly. It was a sweet one. Can you guess? A sweet potato with a bit of bright print pinned around it for a dress! Poor little Cindy! She had no one to give her a better dolly. Mammy had always been a slave, and if she had known how to dress a doll, never had the time. . . .

After a while a good lady went where Cindy lived and started a Sunday School.

Cindy came, but the first day she showed she was still in SLAVERY.

And the very worst kind too—SLAVERY TO SIN. . . . (pp. 39-44)

Men and women appear in the books without strong status differential between them. But the opportunities offered them are different, as shown in this discussion by a brother and sister presented in William Osborn Stoddard's *Crowded out of Crofield; or The Boy who Made his Way* (New York: D. Appleton and Company, 1890):

"If they take away every cent I get, I'm going to the city, some time."

"I'd go, too, if I were a boy," she said. "I've got to stay at home and wash dishes and sweep. You can go right out and make your fortune. I've read of lots of boys that went away from home and worked their way up. Some of 'em got to be president."

"Some girls amount to something, too," said Jack. "You've been through the Academy." (p. 35)

Adolescents appear in 40 percent of the books of this time period. The issue of social class and economic mobility comes up most often in stories for adolescents, where boys are offered ample opportunity to rise from rags to riches. Girls, however, have the choice of home life or teaching or the factory. The factory is certainly not a way to fame and fortune, as Virginia W. Johnson in *Katy's Christmas* (New York: Cassell and Company, 1885) points out:

Katie was 12 years old, and her aunt considered it only right that she should earn something for herself, as there were many mouths to feed in the cottage.

The little girl was sent to the factory, to begin at the lowest round of the ladder, which she would climb as the years rolled on, until she could control one of the looms of the upper story, like the older girls, guiding the whirling shuttles with nimble fingers, to weave bright-colored cloth. (pp. 9-10)

Animals appear in one-third of the books, generally as animals rather than as people in fur. When they appear as people in fur, they tend to have negative traits, traits which authors hesitate to ascribe to human characters. In terms of other than natural characters, there are god-like figures in 44 percent of the books. Other forms of supernatural beings—appearing now in 7 percent of the books—are Santa Clauses, elves, and fairies.

In this period, twice as many books have child and adolescent main characters as have adult main characters, a marked reversal from earlier trends. Instead of a focus on the adult that will be, the focus is now on the child that is. Almost one-fourth of the main characters are adolescents, and their transition from childhood to adulthood constitutes the basic plots. Adulthood for white males is pictured as a state of limitless opportunities; adulthood for the remainder of the population is more problematic.

Characters show both emotional and intellectual activities. They show, for the most part, positive affect, with an emphasis on successful achievement of immediate goals on earth. How they go about achieving goals is shown with clarity and specificity.

Needs in this time period are not nearly as often related to the hereafter as before; for the first time the need for eternal salvation is found in less than half the books; it is present in only one-third. Eternal salvation is usually related to social behavior, to conformity to society's norms for the good of the group. And high on the list of society's norms in temperance as shown in Isabelle Alden's *Two Boys*, by Pansy [pseud.] (Boston: D. Lothrop and Company, publishers, c. 1886):

> "My mother doesn't believe in cider; she says it's young alcohol;
> and she doesn't want me to have anything to do with Mr. alcohol
> whether he is young or old."

The most important need discussed is that for love, present in three fourths of the books of the period. Love for and kindness to one's fellow man as well as love for family is highlighted in books for the young child. Romantic love is often depicted in novels for adolescents. There are not many instances, however, of such intense feeling as found in Edward Sylvester Ellis's *The Eye of the Sun* (Chicago: Rand, McNally and Company, 1897):

> "No, Varnum, you must not—really you must not."
> But he did. The weakly struggling form was drawn nearer and his
> ardent lips touched hers with the fervor born of young love's
> dream—that bliss which in all its exquisite and sacred fullness is
> tasted but once in this life by mortal man or woman.
> "Dearest Muriel, you will not say to me nay."
> And she did not.
>
> THE END (p. 299)

Need for play and adventure is evident in 32 percent of the books. In addition to stories of fun and suspense for older children, there were books of games and of moving pictures for younger children. Josephine Pollard, in *Plays and Games for Little Folks* (New York: c.1889), describes the game of Yankee Doodle:

> Two of the players stand holding up their hands so as to form a
> bridge for the rest to pass under, 1 by 1. All sing.
> At the last word the bridgeholders bring their arms down on the
> shoulders of the one who happens to be passing at that time, and keep
> him a prisoner. The captive is then asked whether he will be English
> or American, and according to his decision is placed behind the
> Englishman or American. Thus the game proceeds until all have, 1
> by 1, been caught, and have chosen the country they will fight for.
> Then comes the tug of war, and that side wins which succeeds in
> pulling the other out of its position. (p. 1)

An activity involving play and adventure which appears in several books of the period is that of running away. It is seen as a natural need; natural too is the child's ending up back home safe and sound, as shown in *Worthington's Annual; A Series of Interesting Stories; Biographies; etc.* (New York: R. Worthington, 1884):

RUNNING AWAY

Two little, bright little, gay little men,
One named Tommy, and the other named Ben,
One of them 9, and one of them 10.

Both together, one summer day,
Tired of study, and tired of play,
Made up their minds to run away.

Running as fast as ever they could,
Down the lane in the big green wood,
Soon they were off and gone for good.

Weary at last they sank on the ground,
Where at the close of day they were found,
Wrapped in a slumber sweet and sound.

Broke the next morning, bright and red,
Finding the runaways home in bed.
"How did we ever get here?" they said.

The need for self esteem is evidenced in 64 percent of the books, a slightly higher proportion than that found in previous years. Individuals, particularly male individuals, are supposed to work hard and long; success, it is felt, will come naturally. William Taylor Adams in his many books for boys discusses such success in character after character, as in *Isles of the Sea; or, Young American Homeward Bound* (Boston: Lothrop, Lee and Shepard Company, 1905):

> Of the story, Mr. Tom Spears is the central figure, or at least one
> of the most prominent characters. Possibly he may be deemed a
> rather eccentric character for one under age; but, as the author has so
> often expressed himself before, it does not so much matter what else
> a young man may be, if he only has high aims, and a resolute
> purpose, to carry out his ideal of what is noble, good and true. Tom
> is a high-toned young man, as are all the other characters with whom
> the young reader is at all likely to sympathize, and in whose fortunes
> he is most certain to be interested. (p. 5)

In *Dew Drops and Diamonds, a Rare Collection of Stories in Prose and Verse for Boys and Girls* (Chicago and New York: W. B. Conkey, Company, c.1898), the adolescent is reminded that success comes early, so he must start to work immediately:

THE AGE OF WORK

From the age of 20 to 35 to 40 is a period of great efficiency and activity. Politicians, orators, warriors and artists are then formed, and some of their greatest triumphs gained. Alexander, Hannibal and Napoleon had made themselves known by some of their most extraordinary military achievements before they were 30. William Pitt was prime minister of England at 25, and as a statesman and debator in the House of Commons sustained himself from that day onward against such men as Fox and Burke.

In almost half of the books of the period there are no special problems presented in solving needs. The individual should meet the challenge; he is urged to get in there and perform. An example of this approach is found in Mrs. A. K. Dunning's *Broken Pitchers* (Philadelphia: Presbyterian Board of Publication, c.1887):

> God exempts nobody from work. A sense of responsibility is a brace to manhood and a developer of power; and because God wants work and responsibility to react heathfully on men, he wants them to work with a hearty, joyous spirit. When the joy and the enthusiasm have gone out of work, something is wrong. (pp. 3-4)

In 32 percent of the books, though, it is acknowledged that individuals must help each other in the pursuance of needs because they are not competent to achieve them alone. Edward Everett Hale's stirring poem *For Fifty Years* (Boston: Roberts Brothers, 1893) is a good example of the emphasis on teamwork:

PUT IT THROUGH!

Come Freeman of the land,
Come meet the last demand—
Here's a piece of work in hand,
    Put it through!

Here's a log across the way,
We have stumbled on all day;
Here's a ploughshare in the clay,—
    Put it through!

Here's a country that's half free,
And it waits for you and me
To say what its fate shall be;
    Put it through! (p. 85)

Even though needs for play and adventure, for self-esteem, are found in a high proportion of these books, the concern usually extends to other human beings as well as one's self. For example, while a boy is supposed to compete, to strive for economic gain, once he attains it he is supposed to use such gain to assist others less fortunate.

This time period marks the first in which needs are primarily related to the present (in 57 percent of the books). Previously they were more related to the future. Needs of love and joy for children, of achievement for adolescents are sought now. And one sees the individual character attaining it now; even such a difficult-to-achieve goal as financial success is obtainable very quickly.

The most important social institution involved in satisfying needs is the family (shown in 81 percent of the books). Ideal relationships between spouses are defined, as in J. Thomas Wharton's *A Latter-Day Saint. Being the Story of the Conversion of Ethel Jones* (New York: Henry Holt and Company, 1884):

> And what, then are the duties of married women? . . .
>
> If women are no longer the handmaids they are the partner of their husbands; they enter into contracts with them; they owe duties to them and through them to society, which they must pay. For we all must contract to assist each other; if we did not owe to each other toleration, support and protection, modern society would tumble to pieces. Society must exist; if you imperil its existence by refusing to agree to its requirements, it will crush you.
>
> Girls, be careful! Do not be led away by your desires for racketing amusements and careless enjoyment. You cannot take your lives in your own hands and defy society! You cannot live according to your own sweet wills! (pp. 194-196)

And ideal relationships between parents and children are often sharply defined, as in L. Maria Pratt's *Jo and his Balloons* (Boston: D. Lothrop and company, c.1880):

> Disobedience to his parents, Sabbath-breaking, bad company, drunkenness,—these were the sins that have brought him to ruin and that are bringing down thousands of boys and young men every year. Children! Obey your parents; Remember the Lord's day; shun evil companions; Look not on the wine when it is red; if you would escape such a fate as this. (p. 98)

Several books of this time describe cases of child abuse, which is more often carried out by alcoholic parents. In Amy Blanchard's *Twenty Little Maidens* (Philadelphia: J. B. Lippincott, Company, 1893) the story is told of a little girl whose mother dies, whose father remarries, and whose stepmother beats her. The father drinks all the time, and the child is sent begging. When she doesn't bring home anything, she is thrown out of the house by the angry parents:

"You would not be merry either," returned the little girl, "if your father had kicked you out into the street, and if you were cold, and hungry, and sore all over." (pp. 7-8)

The family household in most of the books still consists of the nuclear family group of parent and child. Decisions about family affairs are made jointly by husband and wife. In two-thirds of the cases the mother and father take care of the children and discipline them; in one-third ot the cases the mother alone holds major responsibility for child care. Interaction between parent and child is considerable in the family setting, and both know their place: the parent to speak and to teach, the child to listen and to learn.

The social institution next in importance during this time period is leisure. In 52 percent of the books attention is paid to the context of having fun. There are a goodly number of nonsense books and books of rhymes and games.

The religious institution is discussed in considerably fewer books of this time (36 percent), but it remains an important and powerful force in human interaction. It spawned a number of social movements, such as the temperance movement, which called for religious fervor, group solidarity, and, of course, abstinence. Frances Willard, in an introduction to a temperance book of the period, *The Voice of the Home; or, How Roy Went West, and How he Came Home Again* (New York: National Temperance Society and Publication House, 1882), extols the work of the author, Mrs. Sarepta Henry, in carrying on the cause:

No epoch fails of its Chronicler; and the books of Mrs. Henry, since the Crusade, preserve the finest essence not only of the Pentecostal movement, but of the Women's Christian Temperance Union, its lineal successor.

Imbued with the spirit of this work from the beginning, calling the women of her own city (Rockford, Ill.) to arms, that memorable writer of 1874, thence forward an indefatigable temperance evangelist, and now superintendent of this department for out National Women's Christian Temperance Union, Mrs. Henry is uniquely qualified to do this work, for she speaks whereof she knows. (p. 5)

Economic institutions appear in 27 percent of the books, mostly in novels for adolescent boys by Horatio Alger, Edward S. Ellis, and others, which explain over and over just how to achieve upward mobility in the large organization. In some instances these books discuss the roles of big business and the union, as in Ellis' *The Young Conductor or Winning his Way* (New York: The Merriam Company, c.1895). In that book is described the effort of railroad association members to call a strike. The book's hero, Dick Farrallen, is chairman of the association and is against the strike. When voting takes place on the strike issue, Farrallen casts the deciding vote against the strike. He explains:

> "154 of you may not thank me for my action tonight, but you will do so before the winter is over."
>
> And so they did. When thousands of idle men tramped the country from end to end, vainly seeking employment; when the factories, mills, and workshops were still and the voice of industry was hushed; when the multitudes of men, women, and children in the cities had to be fed daily to prevent them from perishing of starvation; when gaunt want stalked through the land, and it looked as if a fatal blight had fallen upon all things—then the toilers on the A & R Railway looked upon Dick Farrallen as their best friend, for he had saved them from the results of their own foolishness. (p. 245)

Responsibility of characters is mainly to family, significant others, and God. For the first time period, though, a significant number of books (13 percent) relate the responsibility of characters only to themselves. One of the ways responsibility is carried out for both the individual and the group is through temperance. Temperance is thought to be an important key to success and an important source of failure; it is focused on in 20 percent of the books.

The cognitive relationship between actors has changed somewhat during the period. In more than half the cases rational bases for individual pursuits are presented, related to social needs rather than religious proscription. Earthly situations rather than heavenly ones are focused upon, as in Harvey Scribner's, *A Messenger from Santa Claus and Other Christmas Stories* (Toledo, Ohio: Franklin Printing and Engraving Company, c.1904):

> "You grew rich rapidly; years ago you were reported very wealthy, but you were never satisfied. The more you acquired the more you wanted, until your entire life was absorbed in the one object. You lived in your countinghouse, and the short intervals that you passed with your family might as well have been spent elsewhere, for your mind was still in your business. For 40 years you have shut out the blue sky, the starry night, social intercourse with your family and friends, and with worry and anxiety as your companions, have constantly pressed on to one goal and the acquisition of wealth as the security of happiness, and at the end of that time, broken, wrecked in health, dyspeptic, you return to your own home." (pp. 23-24)

Relationships are both intimate and apart. In the latter part of this period more attention is paid to formal apart relationships between persons, especially in regard to economic activity (60 percent of the books). Goal orientations of individuals continue to involve group as well as individual needs and the spectre of an Almighty God.

In those books where there is social stratification among people, there is usually also social mobility. Upward mobility results from hard work and prudence. Downward mobility results from inopportune stock market drops or the individual's own predeliction to alcohol.

Needs are met primarily by means of conformity to norms (in 82 percent of the books). Concomitantly, there is little encouragement for self-direction and social change, although occasionally the latter is brought up.

Satisfaction of needs is almost always obtained. Satisfaction usually occurs through the individual's own efforts, supported by the help of other people close to him and by the help of his God. In a larger proportion of books than before, however, satisfaction occurs through the individual's own efforts alone (16 percent of the books). Similarly, the main actor's view of himself and of other people is more positive now than previously. The world is seen as friendlier, even though the person is obliged to work hard.

In 56 percent of the books, death and the hereafter are present. A person is to consider his relationship with other humans on earth in the context of his relationship with God in the next life, as seen in Harvey Scribner's *A Messenger from Santa Claus, and Other Christmas Stories* (Toledo, Ohio: Franklin Printing and Engraving Company, c.1904):

> "Do you know who I am and how much I am worth?"
>
> "Yes, you are old Moneybags, you have made a half million dollars in your life and you have got every dollar of it. It is on the credit side of your ledger, but when you get into the other world you will find that it is charged up to you on the other side. You owe heaven $500,000 which will not be distributed into the proper channels until long after you are dead, and then you will not get credit for it." (pp. 13-14)

Four books are highlighted for this period. The first, Harriet Lothrop's *Five Little Peppers and How They Grew*, was published in serial form in the magazine *Wide Awake* in 1878 and in book form in 1881. It is a story of closely knit family life, in the mold of female Victorian writers beginning with Louisa May Alcott. The second book, Samuel Langhorne Clemens' *The Adventures of Huckleberry Finn*, was published in 1884. A book for and about children, many still consider it to be America's best novel. Third is L. Frank Baum's famous fantasy, *The Wizard of Oz*, first published in 1900 and followed by numerous sequels. *The Wizard* is still a major book event and a major stage and screen event as well. Finally, there is one of Edward Sylvester Ellis' one hundred or so dime novels, *The Boy Patrol Around the Council Fire* (published in 1913). Ellis' adventure stories were widely read by several generations of boys.

The Five Little Peppers and How They Grew

Harriet Mulford Lothrop (pseudonym Margaret Sidney) lived from 1844 to

1924. She was born in New Haven, Connecticut, the daughter of Sidney Mason Stone, one of that city's first architects. She graduated from Grove Hall School in New Haven and began to contribute to the magazine, *Wide Awake*, in 1878. Two years later this magazine began the serial publication of *Five Little Peppers and How They Grew*, of which more than two million copies had been sold at the time of her death. In 1881 the author married Daniel Lothrop, the publisher, who had been very interested in her early works and whose firm, D. Lothrop and Company, was publishing her books. From 1882 until Mr. Lothrop's death ten years later, they lived at "Wayside," Hawthorne's old home in Concord.

The Five Little Peppers and How They Grew focuses in a gentle, intimate fashion on everyday life in a large family. Its original success led to sequels: *The Five Little Peppers Midway*, *The Five Little Peppers Grown-Up*, *Phronsie Pepper*, and several other books dealing with the Pepper family. Mrs. Lothrop wrote other stories for children but the *Pepper* books were the most loved.

The Five Little Peppers and How They Grew is about idyllic family life in genteel poverty. Everyone loves one another and helps one another. It is different from many other Victorian novels in that the main characters are not members of the comfortable middle class. They must deal with the hard day-to-day realities of economic uncertainty and want:

> It was just on the edge of twilight; and the little Peppers, all except Ben, the oldest of the flock, were enjoying a "breathing spell," as their mother called it, which meant some quiet work suitable for the hour. All the "breathing spell" they could remember however, poor things; for times were always hard with them nowadays; and since the father died, when Phronsie was a baby, Mrs. Pepper had had hard work to scrape together money enough to put bread into her children's mouths, and to pay the rent of the little brown house.
>
> But she had met life too bravely to be beaten down now. So with a stout heart and a cheery face, she had worked away day after day at making coats, and tailoring and mending of all descriptions; and she had seen with pride that couldn't be concealed, her noisy, happy brood growing up around her, and filling her heart with comfort, and making the little brown house fairly ring with jollity and fun.
>
> "Poor things!" she would say to herself, "they haven't had any bringing up; they've just scrambled up!" And then she would set her lips together tightly, and fly at her work faster than ever. "I must get schooling for them some way, but I don't see how!"
>
> Once or twice she had thought, "Now the time is coming!" but it never did: for winter shut in very cold, and it took so much more to feed and warm them, that the money went faster than ever. And

then, when the way seemed clear again, the store changed hands, so that for a long time she failed to get her usual supply of sacks and coats to make; and that made sad havoc in the quarters and half-dollars laid up as her nest egg. But—''Well, it'll come some time,'' she would say to herself; ''because it must!'' And so at it again she would fly, brisker than ever.

''To help mother,'' was the great ambition of all the children, older and younger; but in Polly's and Ben's souls, the desire grew so overwhelmingly great as to absorb all lesser thoughts. Many and vast were their secret plans, by which they were to astonish her at some future day, which they would only confide—as they did everything else—to one another. For this brother and sister were everything to each other, and stood loyally together through ''thick and thin.''

Polly was ten, and Ben one year older; and the younger three of the ''Five Little Peppers,'' as they were always called, looked up to them with the intensest admiration and love. What they failed to do, couldn't very well be done by any one! (pp. 8-9)

From this book one learns something of the social support systems for families, particularly indigent families of the period. There were no large

"MOTHER'S RICH ENOUGH."

Ill. 22: Harriet Mulford Lothrop. *Five Little Peppers and How They Grew*, by Margaret Sidney (pseud.). Boston: D. Lothrop and Company, 1881. [5'' x 3'']

public-welfare agencies or social-service programs or free clinics. A prominent character in the book is "Grandma Bascom," who was not really the children's grandmother at all. Yet, she was addressed as "Grandma" by the Peppers and other persons in the village as a matter of courtesy, because she was the one people turned to for advice and comfort. As for medical help, the village doctor came when there was any sort of a problem, and he could be responsive to more than just health needs:

> "It's Phronsie," said the mother, "and I don't know what the matter is with her; you'll have to go for the doctor, Polly, and just as fast as you can."
>
> Polly still stood, holding the bowl, and staring with all her might. Phronsie sick!
>
> "Don't wake her," said Mrs. Pepper.
>
> Poor Polly couldn't have stirred to save her life, for a minute; then she said—"Where shall I go?"
>
> "Oh, run to Dr. Fisher's; and don't be gone long."
>
> Polly set down the bowl of butter, and sped on the wings of the wind for the doctor. Something dreadful was the matter, she felt, for never had a physician been summoned to the hearty Pepper family since she could remember, only when the father died. Fear lent speed to her feet; and soon the doctor came, and bent over poor little Phronsie, who still lay in her mother's arms, in a burning fever.
>
> "It's measles," he pronounced, "that's all; no cause for alarm; you ever had it?" he asked, turning suddenly around on Polly, who was watching with wide-open eyes for the verdict.
>
> "No, sir," answered Polly, not knowing in the least what "measles" was.
>
> "What shall we do!" said Mrs. Pepper; "there haven't any of them had it."
>
> The doctor was over by the little old table under the window, mixing up some black-looking stuff in a tumbler, and he didn't hear her.
>
> "There," he said, putting a spoonful into Phronsie's mouth, "she'll get along well enough; only keep her out of the cold." Then he pulled out a big silver watch. He was a little thin man, and the watch was immense. Polly for her life couldn't keep her eyes off from it; if Ben could only have one so fine!
>
> "Polly," whispered Mrs. Pepper, "run and get my purse; it's in the top bureau drawer."
>
> "Yes'm," said Polly, taking her eyes off, by a violent wrench, from the fascinating watch; and she ran quickly and got the little old stocking-leg, where the hard earnings that staid long enough to be

put anywhere, always found refuge. She put it into her mother's lap, and watched while Mrs. Pepper counted out slowly one dollar in small pieces.

"Here sir," said Mrs. Pepper, holding them out towards the doctor; "and thank you for coming."

"Hey!" said the little man, spinning round; "that dollar's the Lord's!"

Mrs. Pepper looked bewildered, and still sat holding it out.

"And the Lord has given it to you to take care of these children with; see that you do it." And without another word he was gone.

"Wasn't he good, mammy?" asked Polly, after the first surprise was over.

"I'm sure he was," said Mrs. Pepper. "Well, tie it up again, Polly, tie it up tight; we shall want it, I'm sure," sighing at her little sick girl. (pp. 63-65)

The primary purpose of the book is amusement, but instruction in morals is also important, as seen in the helping networks discussed through the book. Family members help one another, and their help is paralleled by the help community members offer to one another. It is not shameful to be poor or sick, but it is shameful not to assist the poor or the sick. A work of fiction, the book is reality-oriented with little humor. The locale is essentially rural and focused on the home and its day-to-day rhythms.

The social involvement of human characters is with family and other primary groups. The main characters include the five little Peppers and their overworked mother. They interact with one another in a very positive fashion, without jealousies, tantrums, fights between children—all is peace and serenity.

The basic need shown is for love. Most of the other needs—for salvation, for safety, for strength and achievement—are also present. There are no problems in solving needs; one just has to work long and hard at them. Needs always concern others as well as oneself, and they relate to the present time period. It is the ordinary activities that are stressed.

The major institution available to characters in satisfying needs is the family. The family is the center of life, and while there are other institutions which interact with it (economic and religious and educational), such interaction is minimal. In the Pepper family the father is dead, so the mother becomes the sole provider of care; her devotion to duty and good humor at all times is quite remarkable. Focused upon is not only the mother's care of the children but also the children's care and concern about the mother within the family constellation.

Characters in the book are rational and intimate, oriented to the group rather than to the individual. There is both social stratification and social mobility—in the end the impoverished Peppers are taken in by wealthy relatives. Needs are met primarily through conformity to adult norms, though from time to time (as in coping with an old broken-down stove) the children do seem to show a great deal of ingenuity. There is no real orientation to change; life is essentially too ideal for change to be desired.

Satisfaction of needs is obtained primarily through the family. Family members have some doubts from time to time as to whether they are fulfilling their duty towards one another, but, by and large, they feel good about themselves and about those around them. Their views of the world are largely positive; trials and tribulations and even death are present but are not overwhelming.

The Adventures of Huckleberry Finn

At the same time that books of romantic home life were being written for girls, books of adventure were being written for boys. Samuel Langhorne Clemens wrote *The Adventures of Tom Sawyer* in 1871 and *The Adventures of Huckleberry Finn* in 1884. Based on the author's recollection of boyhood in Missouri, the two books combine imagination, brave deeds, realism, and high humor.

Clemens (1835–1910) was born in Florida, Missouri, the son of the Justice of the Peace. His father died when he was twelve, and he became a printer's apprentice, working for two local newspapers. He began his writing career on the *Hannibal Journal*, following which he worked as a journeyman printer and traveled through various parts of the United States. In 1857 he became an apprentice river pilot on Mississippi steamboats, and in 1859 he secured a pilot's license. His famous pseudonym, Mark Twain, derives from the words signifying *two fathoms*, called out by river pilots on the Mississippi when taking soundings. Further details on the man and his work can be found in Allen [1], Clemens [4], De Voto [6], Howells [8], Twain [10], and Wecter [11].

Huckleberry Finn is the story of the son of the local drunkard, told in brilliant southern, first-person dialect. The book describes the exploits of Huck, a runaway white child, and Jim, a runaway black slave, as they float down the Mississippi on a raft together. *Huckleberry Finn* approaches institutions as they have not been approached before. Traditional descriptions of political, family, economic, religious, educational, and leisure-time activities and groups are not to be seen. Instead, the main characters live by their wits, surviving on a day-to-day basis by hook or by crook; they do not want organized social support systems.

The ensuing description of the relationship between Huck and his father in *The Adventures of Huckleberry Finn* (New York: Charles L. Webster and

Company, 1885) differs markedly from the idealized relationships which we have discussed before:

CHAPTER V

I had shut the door to. Then I turned around, and there he was. I used to be scared of him all the time, he tanned me so much. I reckoned I was scared now, too; but in a minute I see I was mistaken. That is, after the first jolt, as you may say, when my breath sort of hitched—he being so unexpected; but right away after, I see I warn't scared of him worth bothering about.

He was most fifty, and he looked it. His hair was long and tangled and greasy, and hung down, and you could see his eyes shining through like he was behind vines. It was all black, no gray; so was his long, mixed-up whiskers. There warn't no color in his face, where his face showed; it was white; not like another man's white, but a white to make a body sick, a white to make a body's flesh crawl—a tree-toad white, a fish-belly white. As for his clothes—just rags, that was all. He had one ankle resting on 'tother knee; the boot on that foot was busted, and two of his toes stuck through, and he worked them now and then. His hat was laying on the floor; an old black slouch with the top caved in, like a lid.

I stood a-looking at him; he set there a-looking at me, with his chair tilted back a little. I set the candle down. I noticed the window was up; so he had clumb in by the shed. He kept a-looking me all over. By-and-by he says:

"Starchy clothes—very. You think you're a good deal of a big-bug, don't you?"

"Maybe I am, maybe I ain't," I says.

"Don't you give me none o' your lip," says he. "You've put on considerable many frills since I been away. I'll take you down a peg before I get done with you. You're educated, too, they say; can read and write. You think you're better'n your father, now don't you, because he can't? I'll take it out of you. Who told you you might meddle with such hifalut'n foolishness, hey?—who told you you could?"

"The widow. She told me."

"The widow, hey?—and who told the widow she could put in her shovel about a thing that ain't none of her business?"

"Nobody never told her."

"Well, I'll learn her how to meddle. And looky here—you drop that school, you hear? I'll learn people to bring up a boy to put on airs over his own father and let on to be better'n what he is. You lemme catch you fooling around that school again, you hear? Your mother couldn't read, and she couldn't write, nuther, before she died. None of the family couldn't, before they died. I can't; and here you're a-swelling yourself up like this. I ain't the man to stand it—you hear? Say—lemme hear you read.''

I took up a book and begun something about General Washington and the wars. When I'd read about a half a minute, he fetched the book a whack with his hand and knocked it across the house. He says:

''It's so. You can do it. I had my doubts when you told me. Now looky here; you stop that putting on frills. I won't have it. I'll lay for you, my smarty; and if I catch you about that school I'll tan you good. First you know you'll get religion, too. I never see such a son.'' (pp. 39-40)

An unreal life is presented in *Huckleberry Finn*—a life of splendid adventure and of spine-tingling uncertainty. It is a life void of formal group affiliation, though it acknowledges friendship of one or two people at a time. It focuses on the individual himself and his own pursuits.

Huck Finn does his own thing actively rather than passively. He creates his own society, with his own view of right and wrong, success and failure. It is right, in Huck's view, to escape from his father's abuse; it is also right, in his view, to ignore the anxieties over his disappearance of Judge Thatcher, Aunt Sally, and others trying to help him. Huck feels successful if he outwits imposters and frauds. He also feels successful if he outwits anyone who wishes to socialize him.

His life on a raft on the Mississippi sounds simply marvelous:

CHAPTER XII

Must a been close onto one o'clock when we got below the island at last, and the raft did seem to go mighty slow. If a boat was to come along, we was going to take to the canoe and break for the Illinois shore; and it was well a boat didn't come, for we hadn't ever thought to put the gun into the canoe, or a fishing-line or anything to eat. We was in ruther too much of a sweat to think of so many things. It warn't good judgment to put *everything* on the raft.

If the men went to the island, I just expect they found the camp fire I built, and watched it all night for Jim to come. Anyways, they stayed away from us, and if my building the fire never fooled them it warn't no fault of mine. I played it as low-down on them as I could.

When the first streak of day begun to show, we tied up to a tow-head in a big bend on the Illinois side, and hacked off cotton-wood branches with the hatchet and covered up the raft with them so

HUCKLEBERRY FINN.

Ill. 23: Samuel Langhorne Clemens. *The Adventures of Huckleberry Finn*, by Mark Twain (pseud.), illustrated by E.W. Kemble. New York: Charles L. Webster and Company, 1885. [4¾″ x 6½″]

she looked like there had been a cave-in in the bank there. A tow-head is a sand-bar that has cotton-woods on it as thick as harrow-teeth.

We had mountains on the Missouri shore and heavy timber on the Illinois side, and the channel was down the Missouri shore at that place, so we warn't afraid of anybody running across us. We laid there all day and watched the rafts and steamboats spin down the Missouri shore, and up-bound steamboats fight the big river in the middle. I told Jim all about the time I had jabbering with that woman; and Jim said she was a smart one, and if she was to start after us herself she wouldn't set down and watch a camp fire—no, sir, she'd fetch a dog. Well, then, I said, why couldn't she tell her husband to fetch a dog? Jim said he bet she did think of it by the time the men was ready to start, and he believed they must a gone up town to get a dog and so they lost all that time, or else we wouldn't be here on a tow-head sixteen or seventeen mile below the village—no, indeedy, we would be in that same old town again. So I said I didn't care what was the reason they didn't get us as long as they didn't.

When it was beginning to come on dark, we poked our heads out of the cottonwood thicket and looked up, and down, and across; nothing in sight; so Jim took up some of the top planks of the raft and built a snug wigwam to get under in blazing weather and rainy, and to keep the things dry. Jim made a floor for the wigwam, and raised it a foot or more above the level of the raft, so now the blankets and all the traps was out of the reach of steamboat waves. Right in the middle of the wigwam we made a layer of dirt about five or six inches deep with a frame around it for to hold it to its place; this was to build a fire on in sloppy weather or chilly; the wigwam would keep it from being seen. We made an extra steering oar, too, because one of the others might get broke, on a snag or something. We fixed up a short forked stick to hang the old lantern on; because we must always light the lantern whenever we see a steamboat coming down stream, to keep from getting run over; but we wouldn't have to light it for upstream boats unless we see we was in what they call a "crossing;" for the river was pretty high yet, very low banks being still a little under water; so up-bound boats didn't always run the channel, but hunted easy water. (pp. 93-94)

The life of adventure is indeed so satisfying that at the end of the book Huck makes an important decision about his future:

I reckon I got to light out for the Territory ahead of the rest, because Aunt Sally she's going to adopt me and sivilize me and I can't stand it. I been there before. (p. 366)

The purpose of the book is to entertain; there is certainly no desire to instruct. But an interest is shown in providing insight about human beings and human relationships, as in the deep friendship and respect between the white boy with potential middle-class ties, Huck, and the black runaway slave, Jim.

The story is fiction, though told in the first person as if it were cold fact. It is the sort of fantasy that every boy, and in this day and age every girl, can empathize with completely. As a matter of fact, adult readers empathize just as well.

The setting is rural and as far away from the home setting of the main characters as possible. The characters include humans and animals. Some of the humans claim supernatural powers, but the evidence of such is doubtful. Human involvement is primarily between Huck and Jim. They do have face-to-face encounters with other individuals from time to time, some being more agreeable than others.

The runaway slave, Jim, is very important in the book. He is depicted as a unique and valuable individual. There are some negative remarks made about his race, and there is some condescension to southern, black dialect in evidence, but on the whole, Jim's attributes far outweigh his deficiencies.

Persons of all ages are shown, but the principal focus is on the adolescent male. Females come off far worse than blacks in caricature. Individuals have negative and positive affect, more often negative, and intellectual processes are brilliantly described. Rarely in a book are human foibles dissected as well.

The human needs focused upon are, first of all, play and adventure, and also achievement. Achievement, however, is defined in terms of Huck's own adolescent values, not in terms of conventional adult values. Building a floatable raft, surviving in the wilderness—these are the strength and achievement needs he is concerned with. There are certainly problems to be faced in solving needs—problems such as mastering the devious currents of the river, avoiding abuse by an enraged parent, and escaping interference by other well-meaning adults. Needs relate primarily to Huck himself, but there is genuine concern and compassion for a best friend. The time involved is the present; no need to dwell on the past or speculate over the future.

All the major social institutions are mentioned in the book, but the one which is paramount is leisure, a leisure which is not time-bound or tradition-bound and in which possibilities are unlimited. The institution of the family comes up from time to time, and the ideal nuclear family constellation is understood as important to some people (mostly adult) but irrelevant to others (mostly children).

Huck's responsibility is to himself. His relationships with other humans are highly rational; they are intimate or apart, depending on the situation. His needs are met entirely by self-direction. But Huck Finn's general orientation is not to change the whole world, only to change his little corner of it.

And he does achieve satisfactions through his own wiles, certainly not through the help of his family or other interested parties, most of whom he does not trust. His view of himself is a good one, but he is not conceited. His view of people in general is summed up in the philosophy of live and let live. His view of the world, though, is that it is uncertain at best; danger and even death are sometime in view; and worse, adults are almost always in view, and they usually spell trouble.

The Wonderful Wizard of Oz

L. Frank Baum was a man of very diverse talents. Born in Chittenango, New York, in 1856, he first worked as a newspaper reporter in New York City, then managed several theaters. He also acted and wrote for the theater. Leaving the theater in his late twenties, he devoted himself to raising poultry; his first published book was a textbook on chickens: *The Book of Hamburgs* (1886). Subsequently, he engaged in the manufacture of a new brand of axle-grease *(Baum's Castorine)*, ran a general store *(Baum's Bazaar)*, edited a weekly newspaper, became a crockery salesman, and founded a national association of shop window-dressers! In 1897 he combined with a young, almost unknown, artist named Maxfield Parrish to publish his first children's book, *Mother Goose in Prose*. In 1900 he published *The Wonderful Wizard of Oz*, illustrated by his artist friend, William Wallace Denslow. The book became an instant success and is considered today to be America's favorite fantasy.

Baum wrote other children's stories but is best known for the Oz books, which include *Ozma of Oz* (1906), *Dorothy and the Wizard in Oz* (1908), *The Road to Oz* (1909), *The Emerald City of Oz* (1910), *The Patchwork Girl of Oz* (1913), *Tik-Tok of Oz* (1914), *The Scarecrow of Oz* (1915), *Rinkitink in Oz* (1916), *The Lost Princess of Oz* (1917), *The Tin Woodman of Oz* (1918), *The Magic of Oz* (1919), and *Glinda of Oz* (1920) (see Gardner [7] for more details on Baum and Oz). In 1902 he returned to the theater to write the book and lyrics for a musical comedy based on *The Wizard*, which was a success in Chicago and in New York. *The Wizard* has been made into a movie several times, the best-known production being the 1939 color musical starring Judy Garland.

Baum died in Hollywood, where he had spent his last years, in 1919. Since his death, twenty-six further Oz books have been published by others; Ruth Plumly Thompson, John R. Neil (one of his illustrators), Jack Snow, Rachel Cosgrove, and Colonel Frank Baum (Baum's son). The series ended in 1951; between them the forty Oz books have sold an estimated ten million copies throughout the world.

The Wizard of Oz is about life at home and life away from home. It is about real and about very unreal persons (such as Dorothy, a Tin Woodman, a Scarecrow, a Cowardly Lion, a Wizard, good and bad witches, and Munchkins). But, real or unreal, all persons have very human feelings. In Chapter 6, the Cowardly Lion discusses some of his:

"What makes you a coward?" asked Dorothy, looking at the great beast in wonder, for he was as big as a small horse.

"It's a mystery," replied the Lion. "I suppose I was born that way. All the other animals in the forest naturally expect me to be brave, for the Lion is everywhere thought to be the King of Beasts. I learned that if I roared very loudly every living thing was frightened and got out of my way. Whenever I've met a man I've been awfully scared; but I just roared at him, and he has always run away as fast as he could go. If the elephants and the tigers and the bears had ever tried to fight me, I should have run myself—I'm such a coward; but just as soon as they hear me roar they all try to get away from me, and of course I let them go."

"But that isn't right. The King of Beasts shouldn't be a coward," said the Scarecrow.

"I know it," returned the Lion, wiping a tear from his eye with the tip of his tail; "it is my great sorrow, and makes my life very unhappy. But whenever there is danger my heart begins to beat fast."

"Perhaps you have heart disease," said the Tin Woodman.

"It may be," said the Lion. (pp. 68-69)

The Wizard touches on all our own fantasies, those we create about ourselves and about our world. How good it would be to be different, more adventuresome, more brilliant than we really are! In Chapter 15, concerned with the real identity of Oz, The Terrible, perhaps the most appealing character is the Wizard himself:

"I thought Oz was a great Head," said Dorothy.

"I thought Oz was a lovely Lady," said the Scarecrow.

"And I thought Oz was a terrible Beast," said the Tin Woodman.

"And I thought Oz was a Ball of Fire," exclaimed the Lion.

"No; you are all wrong," said the little man meekly. "I have been making believe."

"Making believe!" cried Dorothy. "are you not a great Wizard?"

"Hush, my dear," he said; "don't speak so loud, or you will be overheard—and I should be ruined. I'm supposed to be a great Wizard."

"And aren't you?" she asked.

"Not a bit of it, my dear; I'm just a common man."

"You're more than that," said the Scarecrow, in a grieved tone; "you're a humbug."

"Exactly so!" declared the little man, rubbing his hands together as if it pleased him; "I am a humbug."

Ill. 24: Lyman Frank Baum. *The Wonderful Wizard of Oz*, with pictures by
W. W. Denslow. Chicago and New York: G. M. Hill Company, 1900.
[6¼'' x 9¼'']

Ill. 25: Lyman Frank Baum. *The Wonderful Wizard of Oz,* with pictures by
W.W. Denslow. Chicago and New York, G.M. Hill Company, 1900. [6¼″
x 9½″]

> "But this is terrible," said the Tin Woodman; "how shall I ever get my heart?"
>
> "Or I my courage?" asked the Lion.
>
> "Or I my brains?" wailed the Scarecrow, wiping the tears from his eyes with his coat-sleeve.
>
> "My dear friends," said Oz, "I pray you not to speak of these little things. Think of me and the trouble I'm in at being found out."
> (pp. 184-185)

Fantasies, of course, have to have an ending. And in this one the little girl returns, after some very exciting travels, to her drab home in the Kansas prairies. She has sought a return home ever since the cyclone carried her away, in the opening pages of the book, to the land of the Munchkins. Here is her reaction to her return:

> Aunt Em had just come out of the house to water the cabbages when she looked up and saw Dorothy running toward her.
>
> "My darling child!" she cried, folding the little girl in her arms and covering her face with kisses; "where in the world did you come from?"
>
> "From the Land of Oz," said Dorothy gravely. "And here is Toto, too. And oh, Aunt Em! I'm so glad to be at home again!"

THE END (p. 261)

The purpose of *The Wizard* is amusement. Baum states in the introduction to a later edition that he wanted to write a fairy story which was "solely to please children of today. It aspires to be a modernized fairy tale, in which the wonderment and joy are retained, and the heartaches and nightmares are left out."

The fantasy is presented matter-of-factly. It includes a number of plain rural scenes and a very elaborate Emerald City, home of Oz. Most of the locations are far away from Dorothy's home, although throughout her journey down the yellow brick road she talks of wanting to return.

Human, animal, and all kinds of superhuman actors are present. Some of the individuals are clearly good and others clearly bad, but most seem to behave somewhere in between. The main character is a child, removed from her family by an act of nature, who meets with all kinds of beings and all kinds of adventures. She shows a lot of affect and good common sense in her time of peril.

The basic human need expressed is for love and acceptance. Dorothy wants to go home to her family which loves her. The Tin Woodman wants a heart to relate to others. Another need expressed is for strength and achievement. The Scarecrow wants brains, the Lion courage, and the Wizard fame. There are myriad problems in solving needs, both physical and psychological, all fantastic. Human needs relate to the present rather than to a past or future time.

The social institutions involved in solving needs are hardly the usual ones. They do involve organizational systems, controlled by witches or wizards or other extraordinary leaders. Their logic varies from system to system; the readers must think fast to keep up. Relationships can be intimate, as between family members, and distant, as between individual person and Wizard. Goals are generally individual goals. Social stratification is present, but it is difficult to tell who has more prestige, a good witch or a bad witch or a poor wizard! Needs are met both by self-direction and by conformity to norms—Wizard norms.

Satisfaction of needs occurs through the individual's own efforts and through magic. Dorothy's view of herself is good, and her view of others is respectful. The world is seen as uncertain, filled with cyclones and unpredictable beings. It also, though, has wonder and excitement in large measure.

The Boy Patrol Around the Council Fire

Edward Sylvester Ellis was born in Geneva, Ohio, in 1840. He was, for a while, a school teacher, and then he began to write stories for adolescents. In 1860 he published *Seth Jones, or The Captives of the Frontier,* which sold nearly a half million copies in its first six months and continued to sell steadily for many years. It was described by literary critics as "the perfect dime novel" and ensured Ellis' reputation as a popular writer of boys' adventure stories. (A bibliography of dime novels is provided by Bragin [3].) Ellis specialized in stories about American Indians, cowboys, bearhunters, and trappers, all set in the American West. He had several series of books: The Flying Boys Series, The Launch Boys Series, The Deerfoot Series, The Log Cabin Series, The Wyoming Series, The Boy Patrol Series. Ellis used seven different pseudonyms in addition to his own name. In later years he wrote a six-volume illustrated *History of the United States* (1896), which was sold on a large subscription plan all over the country. He died in 1916, having written close to one hundred stories.

The Boy Patrol Around the Council Fire, from The Boy Patrol Series, concerns the summer-vacation experiences of three Boy Scout Patrols (Stag Patrol, Blazing Arrow Patrol, and Eagle Patrol) on the shore of Gosling Lake, in Southern Maine. The patrols had some ordinary experiences while canoeing and roaming in the woods. They also had high adventures, in which they were able to display the bravery and wisdom of Boy Scouts, as in this passage from *The Boy Patrol Around the Council Fire* (Philadelphia: John C. Winston, Company, 1913):

Mike Murphy's ready wit did not desert him at the moment when, as may be said, he discovered he was caught between two fires. One of the tramps was standing on the ground in front or below him, while the second was approaching from the rear or only a few paces farther off. And Hoke Butler, who should have been instant to rush to the help of his friend, was nowhere in sight.

"I say, docther, why don't ye hurry up?" shouted Mike, as if calling over the head of the grinning hobo, whose eyes were fixed upon him with a dangerous expression, as if he had decided to even up matters for previous humiliations.

The peremptory manner of the lad produced its effect, and Saxy Hutt paused and looked up at him. A scratching, rattling noise caused Mike to turn his head. Biggs was furiously climbing the logs on the other side. Grasping the topmost one, he dived over, sprawling upon his hands and knees, instantly leaping to his feet, and making off at the speed he had shown in his former flight. He evidently believed in the near approach of the man whom he dreaded.

Mike swung around on his perch, so that his feet hung outside, and gazed calmly down upon the repulsive face.

"The top of the morning to ye, Saxy," greeted the lad; "I hope ye are well."

"Huh! yer needn't try that bluff on us," growled the scamp; "it won't work; thar ain't no doctor round these parts and I wouldn't care a hang if there was. I owe you one, younker, and I'm going to take it out of your hide."

To tell the truth, Mike was pleased to hear this declaration. Biggs, whom he regarded as the worst of the couple, had taken himself off and need not be considered further, so that it was one against one, and the youngster had a firm grip on his shillaleh. With a fair field and no favor Mike was content to let the best man win. (pp. 147-148)

Boy Scouts, of course, are well known for their service to the public. There are several incidents in the book which show how they serve admirably, as in this passage on the search for a kidnapped child. In the end, of course, the child is found and returned safe and sound to the arms of her ever grateful mother:

A FORTUNATE MEETING

Scout Master Hall was right when he said Alvin Landon and Chester Haynes would not waste a minute in carrying out the task he had given them. They were determined to secure the arrest of the men who it was believed had kidnapped the little daughter of Doctor

Spellman, before they could leave that section. In addition, they aimed to get the help of George Burton and his bloodhound.

This last was far more important than the other, and would insure the discovery of the fate of the child. If Zip was allowed to take the scent within twenty-four hours after she left home—and possibly a little later—he would never lose it.

It was four miles over the rough broken trace to the highway, and then two more of smoother traveling would bring them to the straggling town of Bovil, where they hoped to secure telephonic communication with Boothbay Harbor and other near by towns. If that could be done, they could reach Samoset Hotel, on Mouse Island, by the same means. It would be like young Burton to start at once. He could be taken quickly across to Boothbay in a motorboat, where he knew the right course to follow, since he had been over it with Zip. He would have to ascend the Sheepscot and walk three miles to reach Bovil, but if a midnight start was made, he ought to reach the village at daylight and soon after.

It was between eleven and twelve o'clock that Alvin and Chester came in sight of the score of buildings which make up the village of Bovil. When they passed through it on their way to Gosling Lake, they paid so slight attention that they could not recall whether it had an inn. Vastly to their delight, however, they came upon the old-fashioned structure near the center of the place, and it was the only one in which a light was burning. (pp. 280-281)

And with more amazement than before, the procession of pursuers saw Zip follow the path across the clearing to the door of the cabin, where he stopped, threw up his nose and bayed. It was noticed that he had reached the end of the trail.

Ruth Spellman was inside the log structure.

In a twinkling the whole company was grouped around the front of the building.

"Why don't you go in?" demanded the Doctor, pressing impatiently forward.

"You forget the latchstring is inside," reminded Scout Master Hall.

"What difference does that make? Is this a time to hesitate? Let's break in the door! Make room for me and I'll do it!"

Mike Murphy, Alvin Landon and Chester Haynes ran to the little window a few paces beyond the door and peered through the panes.

"Sunbeam is there!" shouted Mike, "and nothing is the matter with her!"

Before he could explain further, there was a crash. The impact of

Doctor Spellman's powerful shoulder carried the staple which held the latch from its fastenings and the door swung inward. Through it swarmed the Boy Scouts, the physician and his wife in the lead.

In the front of the broad fireplace, where the embers had long died, sat Uncle Elk in his rocking chair, silent, motionless and with head bowed. Seated on his knees, with her curls half hiding her pretty face and resting against his massive chest, was Ruth Spellman, sleeping as sweetly as if on her cot at home.

With a glad cry, the mother rushed forward and flung her arms about the child, sobbing with joy.

"O my darling! Thank heaven you are found!" and she smothered the bewildered one with kisses and caresses. (pp. 302-303)

The purpose of *The Boy Patrol* is twofold: amusement and instruction in proper social behavior. The fictional style moves swiftly, with just enough danger and suspense to keep pages turning. The setting is rural, away from the homes of the adolescent characters, but in an environment—as protected as the home—a Boy Scout camp.

Human beings are focused upon, and interaction is most often with primary-group members. The individuals are all white, but there is one important character here in terms of human diversity: the character of a senile man, whose behavior is described with clarity, sympathy, and understanding. The conditions of old age are not often focused upon in children's books of any period, and this book handles them well. Positive and negative affect are shown among characters, with the Boy Scouts having generally positive and other persons often negative emotions. In the case of the elderly man, though, the complexities of thought processes and emotions of a person living in the past are particularly well brought forth.

The basic needs shown are for strength and achievement and for play and adventure. Even though the background situation is one of leisure, there is an underlying concern with the values of responsibility and work. Boy Scouts are supposed to do good deeds, and they have to find them to do even in the midst of summer fun. There are physical threats to solving needs, but they are not very great; one knows there will be a happy ending. Concern is with others rather than with oneself alone and with the present rather than with the past or the future.

The principal social organization discussed is the Boy Scouts, an institution with ties to education, religion, and family. Social responsibility is always to the group, and interrelationships are rational and intimate, largely nonhierarchical. Behavior involves conformity to adult norms and orientation to the status quo.

Satisfaction of needs comes from group action. The main characters view themselves positively but feel that all people require help from others. For the world is uncertain; death is present and so are other lesser trials—there is safety in numbers.

In the four books just described there are far fewer mentions of man's relationship to the Almighty and far more of man's relationship to his fellow man. In both *The Adventures of Huckleberry Finn* and *The Wonderful Wizard of Oz* nontraditional social institutions and life styles are presented very appealingly for the reader's consideration. The purpose of these books is amusement rather than instruction. Some describe high adventure. One provides amazing fantasies. But at the end of the literary excursion, the reader is more often than not led back to safety and encouraged to feel as Dorothy does in *The Wonderful Wizard of Oz:* "I'm so glad to be at home again!" (p. 261).

References

1. Allen, Jerry. *The Adventures of Mark Twain*. Boston: Little, Brown, 1954.
2. Arbuthnot, May Hill. *Children and Books*. Chicago: Scott, Foresman and Company, 1947.
3. Bragin, Charles. *Dime Novels, 1860–1964: A Bibliography*. Brooklyn, New York, 1964.
4. Clemens, Sara. *My Father, Mark Twain*. New York: Harper, 1931.
5. Darling, Richard L. "Children's Books Following the Civil War." In *Books in America's Past, Essays Honoring Rudolph H. Gjelsness*, ed. David Kaser. Charlottesville, Virginia: University Press of Virginia, 1966.
6. De Voto, Bernard. *Mark Twain at Work*. Cambridge, Massachusetts: Harvard University Press, 1944.
7. Gardner, Martin, and Nye, Russell B. *The Wizard of Oz and Who He Was*. East Lansing: Michigan State University Press, 1957.
8. Howells, William Dean. *My Mark Twain*. New York: Harper, 1910.
9. Meigs, Cornelia, ed. *A Critical History of Children's Literature*. New York: Macmillan, 1953.
10. Twain, Mark. *Mark Twain's Autobiography*. Ed. Albert Bigelow Paine. New York: Harper, 1924.
11. Wecter, Dixon. *Sam Clemens of Hannibal*. Boston: Houghton Mifflin, 1952.

Chapter 6

1916-1955: "You have been my friend. . . . That in itself is a tremendous thing."

Significant technological advances in the first half of the twentieth century affected book publishing and provided the public with other new and important forms of mass communication as well. Advances in the color-printing process allowed the picture book to become larger, more brilliant, and more affordable. Advances in visual communications brought first movies in the neighborhood and then television in the living room. With television in more and more living rooms, a major concern among parents and educators became the amount of time children watched TV and the types of programs they watched. Movies and television and books have been interrelated from the start, for movies and TV not only compete with books for children's attention, they use books as part of program fare (the annual television presentation of the MGM movie, *The Wizard of Oz*, being perhaps the most familiar example). Likewise, movie and TV materials are translated into books (*Mickey Mouse, Captain Kangaroo, Sesame Street* series).

Looking at books of this period, one finds for the first time religious instruction to be of little import (evident in only 2 percent of the sample). When religious instruction is presented in these books, it is presented in terms of social requirements of understanding and kindness. In *Christmas* (1940), a story set in Europe during World War II, Eleanor Roosevelt writes of the need to take into account the beliefs of other people and behave towards others with love and peace and gentleness.

Instruction in social behavior is also of much less importance than in previous periods, found in 9 percent of the sample books. Various social behaviors—some involving other persons, some involving strengthening of one's own abilities—are advocated. Elizabeth Herbert Childs' *The fun of Saving Up: Thrift Bank Book* (1921) advocates economic sobriety.

Books of instruction for the young, such as primers and ABC's, account for 3 percent of the sample. Texts relate to the child's own world now more than ever before, featuring day-to-day activities and concerns, shown in Helen Sewell's *ABC for Everyday* (1939) which starts off with *A* for awake, *B* for buttons, *C* for cereal, and *D* for dog.

Books of instruction on scientific matters (10 percent of the sample) continue to be built with care and detail. They are presented for younger age groups now, a number of publishing houses producing easy-to-read science series as well as more advanced books for the older child.

Books written for the purpose of providing understanding of the human being, of human societies, grew in number, especially in the latter half of the period (they comprised 22 percent of the books from 1935 to 1955). These books included stories about the growth of families, such as those of Laura Ingalls Wilder, and stories about the development of regions of the United States, such as those of Lois Lenski. These books also included stories of ideal social relationships and of ideal world views. A book still popular today is Munro Leaf's *The Story of Ferdinand* (New York: The Viking Press, 1936), which advocates peace and love and flowers rather than aggression. Prior to the publication of this book, the American people had gone through the horrors of World War I; subsequently, they went through World War II, the Korean War, and the Vietnam War. It is not surprising that Ferdinand remains a favorite:

> Once upon a time in Spain there was a little bull and his name was Ferdinand.
>
> All the other little bulls he lived with would run and jump and butt their heads together, but not Ferdinand. He liked to just sit quietly and smell the flowers.
>
> He had a favorite spot out in the pasture under a cork tree. It was his favorite tree and he would sit in its shade all day and smell the flowers.
>
> Sometimes his Mother, who was a cow, would worry about him. She was afraid he would be lonesome all by himself.
>
> "Why don't you run and play with the other little bulls and skip and butt your head?" she would say.
>
> But Ferdinand would shake his head. "I like it better here where I can just sit quietly and smell the flowers."
>
> His Mother saw that he was not lonesome, and because she was an understanding Mother, even though she was a cow, she let him just sit there and be happy.

Most of the books in the sample from this period, though, were not didactic in any way, shape, or form. Instead, their sole purpose was entertainment, and they provided it in a variety of forms—from picture books and pop-up books for the very young to mystery novels and science fiction for adolescents (for a literary review of books of the period, see Meigs [6]).

Picture books became larger and more brilliant in color. Among the picture book authors-artists of this period who gave generously of their talents to children were Ingri and Edgar d'Aulaire, Robert Lawson, Robert McCloskey,

Ill. 26: Munro Leaf. *The Story of Ferdinand*. Illustrated by Robert Lawson. New York: The Viking Press, 1936. [6⅞″ x 8⅛″]

Maud and Miska Petersham, Lois Lenski, William Pène du Bois, Leo Politi, and Roger Duvoisin. Walt Disney's Mickey Mouse emerged on film in 1928 and appeared on the Rare Books list of 1933. Dr. Seuss produced the first of his picture books, *And to Think that I Saw it on Mulberry Street* in 1937. Maurice Sendak first appeared as an illustrator in 1952. Picture books most often featured the familiar, simply and humorously, as does Ruth Krauss' *A Hole is to Dig: A First Book of Definitions*, illustrated by Maurice Sendak (1952). Krauss' words to be defined include mashed potatoes (to afford everyone enough), hands (to hold), and arms (to hug with).

There were many editions of *The Night Before Christmas* printed during

Ill. 27: Maud and Miska Petersham. *The Rooster Crows: A Book of American Rhymes and Jingles*. New York: The Macmillan Company, 1945. [7¾'' x 10¼'']

this period, as well as issues of *Mother Goose* and issues of Aesop, Anderson, and Grimm. There were numerous books published about dolls who had real feelings (John Gruelle's *Raggedy Ann* books) and numerous books about animals who talked (Hugh Lofting's *Dr. Dolittle* series).

For older children, entertaining "series" books proliferated during this time. Prominent examples were the seventeen different series created by Edward Stratemeyer and his daughter, Harriet Adams. Titles included *Nancy Drew*, *The Hardy Boys*, *The Bobbsey Twins*, *Rover Boys*, and *Tom Swift*, and the books carried the same cast of characters through adventure after adventure. They had age and sex casting, some directed to the teen-aged boy and some to the teen-aged girl. (See Praeger [7] and *Fortune Magazine* [12] for further discussion of the Stratemeyer literary empire.)

In this time period, 51 percent of the books were written by male authors, 38 percent by female authors, and 3 percent jointly by male and female authors; 8 percent of the books had unknown authors. Only one of the authors had an identifiable ministerial background; the majority were professional educators or writers.

New York City had by this time established itself as the undisputed capital of publishing: 74 percent of the books of the sample were published there. Five percent of the books were published in Boston and 6 percent in Philadelphia, cities which had been much more important in previous years. Other northeast and north central cities had modest publication outputs (14 percent).

In this period a considerably higher proportion of books are fictional (81 percent). American folklore is a frequent fictional form of the time, with stories of Paul Bunyan, Daniel Boone, Johnny Appleseed, John Henry, and other folk heroes much in evidence.

Most of the books of the period were prose, and their content was reality-oriented. There was considerably more humor shown in this period than in earlier periods. Humor was present in 17 percent of the books and was particularly evident among books for young children. James Johnson Sweeney's *Three Young Rats, and Other Rhymes* (1946) discusses the fact that little boys are made of slugs and snails and puppy dogs' tails. Walt Disney's *Walt Disney's Circus* (1944) describes a school without rules in which nobody pays attention and all the students talk at once.

The locale of stories is still largely rural, even as the country becomes more and more urbanized. When locale is related to main character, half of the situations involve his home and environs, but half involve scenes away from home. Travel and exploration are considered important components of life, as in E. B. White's *Stuart Little* (New York: Harper and Brothers, 1945) where both man and mouse, in a brief encounter, discuss adventures:

> "Which direction are you headed?" he asked.
> "North," said Stuart.

"North is nice," said the repairman. "I've always enjoyed going
north. Of course, south-west is a fine direction, too."

"Yes, I suppose it is," said Stuart, thoughtfully.

"And there's east," continued the repairman. "I once had an
interesting experience on an easterly course . . ."

Stuart rose from the ditch, climbed into his car, and started up the
road that led toward the north. The sun was just coming up over the
hills on his right. As he peered ahead into the great land that
stretched before him, the way seemed long. But the sky was bright,
and he somehow felt he was headed in the right direction. (pp.
128-131)

Characters in books of this period were, in 24 percent of the cases, only
human beings, in 50 percent they included humans and animals, and in 17
percent of the cases humans and supernatural beings or inanimate objects. In 9
percent of the books animals alone were characters. Social involvement of
human characters in the books is largely with family members. In one-third of
the books the involvement is almost exclusively within the family, as day-to-
day activities in the home are focused upon. In another third of the books the
family and other primary groups are included, with peer groups of some
importance. And in the remaining third of the books the family, other primary
groups and secondary groups are all involved in interaction.

Many kinds of families are shown—families of an earlier as well as a later
time in America's history, black and white American families, and families of
other nationalities. The family is shown as a source of comfort and joy, and
sometimes also as a necessary bother; parents have to be around because little
children cannot exist without them.

The proportion of books describing minorities declined during the period to
12 percent. However, in those books where whites and minorities appear
together, there are proportionately more which give the minority member equal
status and dignity with white characters (in seven of eighteen books). Racial
stereotypes are still evident, as in Inez Hogan's *Nicodemus and the Houn' Dog*
(1933) which describes a black child as lazy and irresponsible. But the worth
and strength of minority peoples is also shown, as in Harold Felton's *John
Henry and His Hammer* (New York: Alfred A. Knopf, 1950):

They say that John Henry's spirit still moves in the Big Bend
Tunnel, and that his spirit moves in all of the tunnels in the land of
his birth, and that his spirit protects the trains and the people who use
the tunnels. They say that it is a kindly, helpful spirit, and a determined one, and strong.

The spirit is sometimes heard, but never seen for the tunnels are
black and John Henry was black. (p. 80)

Females appear as frequently as do males in the books, with equal status. However, the activities girls perform are less intellectual and less exciting than those of boys. C. J. Maginley, in *Make and Ride It* (New York: Harcourt Brace, 1949), encourages boys to make tractors, jeeps, chore wagons, bike trailers, and racers, using imagination and skill. Margaret Rawlings, on the other hand, in her book, *The Secret River* (New York: Scribner, 1955), has girls making much less exciting items:

"Mother dear, may I make some pink paper roses?"
"Of course, my child."
Her mother was very considerate and did not ask questions unless she had to.

A considerable number of books still focus on adult characters (28 percent), adult role models explicitly setting standards of behavior. In these books the child is given a clear idea of where he should land in terms of his future. The majority of books, though, concern children and adults interacting with one another, and the child is allowed to be a child.

As in previous periods, social-class differences among actors are addressed in approximately one-third of the books. The rich are admonished to help the poor, especially the widowed and orphaned, and the poor are admonished to work diligently to better their station. The majority of books, though, ignore these distinctions in favor of a stereotype of equality or of a preoccupation with entertainment, where class is irrelevant.

Most often than before, when animals are shown, they are shown as animals but talking, often with hilarious results. In 30 percent of the books they are shown as people in fur, usually with negative social characteristics.

God appears as an actor in considerably fewer books during this period (14 percent). Santa claus and other good spirits appear in 8 percent, and bad spirits—demons and such—appear in 2 percent of the books. In Charles Kingsley's *The Heroes: Greek Fairy Tales* (1954) God as a character remains strong, the fount of all wisdom and courage.

During this period the main characters in books are changing. In 40 percent of the sample the main character is the child, who is paid attention to and treated with respect. Adolescents comprise main characters in 7 percent, adults in 22 percent, and animals in 21 percent of the books. Remaining books feature supernatural beings or inanimate objects of one sort or another.

Affect among characters is usually appropriate. Temper tantrums, jealousies, and fears are described. But described even more are feelings of tenderness and interdependence, as in Minny Ayers' *The Quest of the Golden Key* (1919), where the golden key is depicted as love for one's fellow man.

Individual characters in the books interact in complicated fashion, and intellectual and emotional processes are detailed so that the reader knows not only what the character has done but also why he did it. Such clarity occurs in books for the very young as well as books for the older child.

The human needs of characters shown in books of this period differ from those shown in earlier periods. The first major difference was in the lessened emphasis on the need for eternal salvation; it appeared in only 6 percent of the books. Physical needs, as in times previous, appeared rarely, in 2 percent of the books. The need for safety increased in importance, appearing in 23 percent of the books: threats of war and global destruction were of concern, especially in times of world conflict. Lucy Perkins' *The Belgian Twins* (1917), set in Europe in World War I, shows anxiety about war, pestilence, and sudden death.

The need for love among characters continued in importance (in 70 percent of the books). A wonderful expression of mother love, as well-liked now as when first published, is by the author of several Rare Books entries, Margaret Wise Brown. Brown's *The Runaway Bunny* (1942) begins with a little bunny who wants to run away. His mother tells him that if he does run away, she will run after him. He threatens to become a fish in a trout stream and swim away from her. She replies that if he does this, she will become a fisherman and fish for him. On they go with such fantasies until the little bunny decides he would just as soon stay home after all.

The need for play and adventure was expressed often in this time period, in 44 percent of the books. A marvelous example of playful fantasy is found in Dr. Seuss's *And to Think that I saw it on Mulberry Street* (1937). The book concerns a young boy who has been admonished by his father to pay attention to what he sees coming home from school on Mulberry Street and to report back on his experience. The young boy attempts to comply; in fact, he does much more than just comply—he invents a zebra and a blue and gold chariot and a charioteer and all sorts of other wonderful sights on Mulberry Street!

The need for strength and achievement, particularly for boy characters, is also very important during this period, as shown in 58 percent of the books. Physical and mental rigor and purposeful activity is recommended even in alphabet books. An example is *The Alphabet Book* (1917) in which *T* stands for taking exercise to make one's muscles grow.

The need for prestige is found in only 5 percent of the books. Concern with pomp and circumstance have never been a major focus in American books for children. But the need for self-actualization increases in the period to 12 percent of the books: reaching one's own potential, enlarging one's own horizons, is seen as important.

In two-thirds of the books, the attainment of needs is not problematical. In one-third of the books, attainment is problematical, usually because of physical threats from the outside. Two world wars and a massive economic depression occurred during the period, and while direct references to them occurred infrequently, allusions to catastrophies were there.

In 74 percent of the books the human needs of characters relate to other persons and their well-being as well as to the characters themselves. In 10 percent of the books they are limited to the individual characters, and in the remainder of the books they relate only to the welfare of God or other persons. Much more than previously, needs are focused on the present. The here and now is important, particularly with reference to child characters. Children are allowed to concentrate on being children; they are not forced to think of their future in this life or the next.

The major social institution to which characters turn for satisfying needs is once again the family. Family life is shown not only as it exists at this time period, but as it existed in the past. James Daugherty, in *Daniel Boone* (New York: The Viking Press, 1939), writes of the different roles of men and women during the lifetime of a legendary folk hero of the eighteenth century:

> Boys learned the easy way to swing an ax all day long, hold an ox-drawn plow on a straight furrow, mend a harness, and hitch a horse, all with a sure swift skill and easy grace. The quick and deadly manual of loading, sighting, and firing a rifle became an automatic action. . . .
>
> Girls were nimble-fingered with wool and warp on the clanking-timbered looms that made the warm stout homespun cloth of their go-to-meeting clothes. Butter, soap, and sugarmaking, cooking on an open fireplace or baking in outdoor ovens, swingling flax, and carding wool, and the molding of candles and bullets were some of the courses in which they soon qualified with high honors. They were happy making their own world, busy with making and mending or caring for the gentle or rambunctious farm animals that were almost members of the household. They provided in wise ways for the needs of tomorrow. (p. 12)

Modern family relationships are shown in Virginia Lee Burton's *The Little House* (Boston: Houghton Mifflin, 1942). The little house once stood proudly in the country, home to a family that felt close and secure:

> Once upon a time there was a Little House way out in the country. She was a pretty Little House and she was strong and well built. The man who built her so well said, "This Little House shall never be sold for gold or silver and she will live to see our great-great grandchildren's great-great-grandchildren living in her." (p. 1)

But in time the city crowded around the little house until it stood in completely alien territory of big buildings. Finally, the house as well as family tradition are preserved as the great-great-grandchildren carry the house out of the city into a receptive environment:

> They tried the Little House here, and they tried her there. Finally

they saw a little hill in the middle of a field . . . and apple trees growing around. "There," said the great-great-granddaughter, "that's just the place."

"Yes, it is," said the Little House to herself.

A cellar was dug on top of the hill and slowly they moved the House from the road to the hill. The windows and shutters were fixed and once again they painted her a lovely shade of pink. (pp. 37–38)

The human family is still the nuclear family of parent and child, with parents most often makind decisions jointly about the family's welfare. When decisions are made by one parent alone, it is twice as likely to be the mother as the father. Parents usually care for the child together; when only one parent performs child care, it is again twice as likely to be the mother. The amount of time spent by parents with the child is substantial, and there tends to be superordinate/subordinate status involved; parent and child know their places. Discipline of the child tends to be conducted jointly by parents, the mother being the more likely disciplinarian when only one parent is involved.

Another important social facet to which characters turn for satisfaction of needs is leisure, which is focused upon more now than previously (in 65 percent of the books). There were many popular series books about preadolescent and adolescent life. Girls and boys solved mysteries, climbed mountains, discovered buried treasure. They also played at home and in their neighborhood with family and friends. Eleanor Estes' books about the Pye children relate to day-to-day pleasures, as in *Ginger Pye* (New York: Harcourt, Brace, and World, 1951):

Would Gracie-the-Cat be jealous if the Pyes got another pet—a dog? That was what Jerry Pye wanted to know and what he was dreaming about as he sat with Rachel, his sister, on their little upstairs veranda. Gracie had belonged to the family for eleven years. This was longer than Rachel, aged nine, or even Jerry aged ten, had. She had been a wedding present to Mama, and she was known in the neighborhood as "the New York Cat." Jerry was trying to imagine what Gracie's feelings would be if the Pyes did get another pet—a dog.

The one thing that Jerry Pye wanted more than anything else in the world right now was a dog. Ever since he had seen the new puppies over in Speedy's barn, he was not only more anxious than ever to have a dog, he was most anxious to have one of these Speedy puppies. He had the particular one picked out that he would most like to have as his own. This was not easy to do for they were all wonderful. (p. 3)

Economic institutions are featured in one-third of the books of the period.

The workplace is usually nearby, and family members are very cognizant of where the father labors. Particularly in books for boys, role models in different work situations are provided, and the Protestant ethic remains strong.

Political institutions are discussed in 17 percent of the books, usually in historical accounts of this country's founding. Historical descriptions of more recent events, such as the Civil War, World War I, and World War II, are also present in the collection. Religion is discussed in far fewer books (8 percent) than in previous times. Some of the concerns of a religious institution, care of those less fortunate, obedience to authority, are still very much in evidence in books, but in a family rather than a church context. The home has become the major place for moral development. The educational institution is evident in only 4 percent of the books.

In the books of the period satisfaction of needs is placed in the context of the welfare of the group rather than that of the individual. In particular, it is the family group that is of concern. There is little concern with the hereafter and the necessity for temperate behavior to attain eternal salvation.

Human relationships are largely rational and intimate. Rarely do they rely now on a religious belief system. Social consciousness is important, and human relationships tend to be primarily group ones in which people know each other and know what is expected in their respective roles. Goal orientations primarily relate to the group, although much more frequently than before (in 16 percent of the books) individual orientations are found, and individual values are considered legitimate and worthwhile.

In about one-third of the books social stratification among actors is described, about one-half of such books showing an open class structure. When the class structure is presented as closed, an admonition is usually given to the rich to look after the poor.

Needs are still met primarily by conformity to adult norms in 64 percent of the books. Conformity to supernatural norms is found in 12 percent of the books. Needs are also met, now more than in previous periods, by self-direction (in 23 percent of the books). In almost one-fourth of the books there is a focus on social change, change being discussed in the presentation of historical events designed to better the conditions of man, as well as in the presentation of a continuing search for quality of life for all persons.

Satisfaction of needs is obtained in nearly all the books. In this period it is obtained more than ever before, in 40 percent of the books, through the individual's own efforts. In half of the books the family and others close to the individual are instrumental in helping the individual to obtain satisfactions. And in 10 percent of the books God is the source of satisfaction in life.

The main character's view of himself in this period is a positive one. His view of other people is also positive, and the world in general is viewed as a friendly place. Death occurs in far fewer books now and infrequently involves young children.

Four books from this period have been singled out for detailed analysis: Wanda Gàg's *Millions of Cats* (1928) is considered one of the first great American picture books; it is still a favorite of children today. Laura Ingalls Wilder's *Little House in the Big Woods* (1932) marked the beginning of a classic series of books about the nineteenth-century Midwest, which provided a sense of the growth of the country and of the growth of the individual from childhood into adulthood. Lois Lenski's *Strawberry Girl* (1945), about the Crackers in Florida, is one of a group of books on regional values and attitudes in the United States which demonstrate the cultural diversity of the country. E. B. White's *Charlotte's Web* (1952), a superb fantasy, focuses on rural America and on the need for love among all beings. This need is shown on several levels; love and respect between animals in the barnyard are echoed in love and respect between humans—adults and children—around the barnyard.

Millions of Cats

Wanda Gàg grew up in America but with the folk traditions of the Old World. She was born in New Ulm, Minnesota, in 1893. Her father, Anton Gàg, came to the United States with his parents from Bohemia when he was a young boy, and her mother was of Czechoslovakian heritage. Both her parents were artistic, and Gàg, along with her younger sisters and brother, grew up taking drawing as a matter of course. She practiced commercial art as well as fine art and became a regenerative force in the field of children's books beginning with the publication in 1928 of *Millions of Cats*. Included among her books are the retelling of her favorite folk tales, *Tales from Grimm* (1936) and *More Tales from Grimm* (1947). (Further information on Wanda Gàg may be found in Gàg [3], *Horn Book Magazine* [4], and Scott [8]).

Like most of Gàg's books, *Millions of Cats* is of a European peasant tradition, a tradition still to be found in American children's books—with rural scenes, homespun humor, and a clear moral message. The book tells the story of a lonesome old couple, isolated in the hill country, and their quest for a cat. When the wife expresses her desire for a cat, her husband immediately offers to find her one. He goes over the hills to look for a cat and finally finds a hill covered with them. The old man is overjoyed and tries to pick out the prettiest cat. But they are all pretty, and the old man acquires more and more and more cats, many more than he can handle. The story ends well because the man in his innocence asks the cats who is the prettiest cat of all, and the cats in their pride fight to the point of annihilating one another over the issue of beauty. All cats but one are destroyed in this manner. The one remaining cat, then, provides the couple with what they wanted in the first place and also provides the reader with a moral.

The purpose of the book was to entertain. In rural scenes of lyric beauty, both fantasy and humor are found—all those cats! The woodcuts have movement and a joyous rhythm. The locale is, of course, close to home, where life is lived.

The characters are older people. Older people, the lame, the halt, the blind, have always figured in folk tales. They are strong characters because they are distinctive, because they are bolder, often wiser than the ordinary. The animals involved are people in fur—they not only can talk, they can act, vainly, competitively, humbly, just like people.

The most important need of characters was for love, love for people and love for animals, love for old and love for young. Interestingly enough, the needs of the older people did not revolve about medical care or social services, but about loving. There were threats to satisfying needs, psychological and physical. But in the end the needs are satisfied—the lonely old people and the homely little cat comfort and enjoy one another.

The family is the only institution shown, with a husband and a wife and a cat who substitutes for a child. Responsibilities are to one another. Needs are met by self-direction—the old man goes out over the hills and through the valleys to find a cat for his wife. Social change is advocated, a simple change resulting from a simple need.

Needs are satisfied, partly by design (the man goes out to fetch a cat) and partly by chance (all the available cats save one annihilate one another). Characters view themselves and their lives well. They view the world with some uncertainty; present is the sun and rolling hills and fertile valleys and also present is death and distruction.

The Little House in the Big Woods

Laura Ingalls Wilder was born in 1867 in a log cabin on the edge of the big woods of Wisconsin. The place was Lake Pepin. As a child she traveled with her family by covered wagon through Kansas, Minnesota, and Dakota Territory. In her late teens she became an elementary school teacher and later married Almanzo Wilder. In 1894 Mr. and Mrs. Wilder with their child journeyed from South Dakota to a farm in Mansfield, Missouri. There Mrs. Wilder lived until her death at age ninety. (More biographical information is to be found in Colwell [2], *Horn Book Magazine* [5], Smith [9], Wilder [11], and *Top of the News* [13].)

Wilder's first book was published when she was sixty-five. Entitled *The Little House in the Big Woods* (1932), it began the story of five-year-old Laura and her family in the Wisconsin woods. *Farmer Boy* (1933) is the story of Almanzo Wilder's childhood on a New York State farm. *Little House on the Prairie* (1935) tells of the journey westward by covered wagon of Laura and her family. In *On the Banks of Plum Creek* (1937) the family settles in Minnesota, and in *By the Shores of Silver Lake* (1939) it is now in Dakota Territory. *Little Town on the Prairie* (1941) and *These Happy Golden Years* (1945) tell of Laura's teaching career and her marriage to Wilder.

These books move at a slow, deliberate pace, the pace necessary for carving out a new life in a new country. Important in this life is the change of seasons, for the seasons direct to an important degree what one is able to do in a life without central heat and air, without automobile and tractor, and without the countless other indoor and outdoor machines that have made us only talk about the weather. Winter and the sights and sounds and smells of nineteenth-century Christmas in the West are precisely conveyed in this passage from *The Little House in the Big Woods* (New York: Harper and Brothers, 1932):

Christmas was coming.

The little log house was almost buried in snow. Great drifts were banked against the walls and windows, and in the morning when Pa opened the door, there was a wall of snow as high as Laura's head. Pa took the shovel and shoveled it away, and then he shoveled a path to the barn, where the horses and the cows were snug and warm in their stalls.

The days were clear and bright. Laura and Mary stood on chairs by the window and looked out across the glittering snow at the glittering trees. Snow was piled all along their bare, dark branches, and it sparkled in the sunshine. Icicles hung from the eaves of the house to the snowbanks, great icicles as large at the top as Laura's arm. They were like glass and full of sharp lights.

Pa's breath hung in the air like smoke, when he came along the path from the barn. He breathed it out in clouds and it froze in white frost on his mustache and beard.

When he came in, stamping the snow from his boots, and caught Laura up in a bear's hug against his cold, big coat, his mustache was beaded with little drops of melting frost.

Every night he was busy, working on a large piece of board and two small pieces. He whittled them with his knife, he rubbed them with sandpaper and with the palm of his hand, until when Laura touched them they felt soft and smooth as silk.

Then with his sharp jack-knife he worked at them, cutting the edges of the large one into little peaks and towers, with a large star carved on the very tallest point. He cut little holes through the wood. He cut the holes in shapes of windows, and little stars, and crescent moons, and circles. All around them he carved tiny leaves, and flowers, and birds.

One of the boards he shaped in a lovely curve, and around its edges he carved leaves and flowers and stars, and through it he cut crescent moons and curlicues.

Around the edges of the smallest board he carved a tiny flowering vine.

He made the tiniest shavings, cutting very slowly and carefully, making whatever he thought would be pretty.

At last he had the pieces finished and one night he fitted them together. When this was done, the large piece was beautifully carved back for a smooth little shelf across its middle. The large star was at the very top of it. The curved piece supported the shelf underneath, and it was carved beautifully, too. And the little vine ran around the edge of the shelf.

Pa had made this bracket for a Christmas present for Ma. He hung it carefully against the log wall between the windows, and Ma stood her little china woman on the shelf. (pp. 59-61)

Summer was different in the big woods. One had more personal space in the form of the out-of-doors. One had more opportunity to explore the world and to enjoy friends and neighbors. After summer came fall and the season of the harvest. The beautiful harvest has been depicted frequently in nineteenth-century American folklore and art. The harvest of Wilder's books is a good one, but it requires a lot of hard work.

Laura Ingalls Wilder wrote primarily to entertain. The author was also interested in providing her young readers with information on how life was lived by their ancestors. She wanted them to know how their grandparents lived and worked and planned for the future, their own future and the future of their children and their children's children. Wilder's books were not about the country's leaders; they were about the country's people.

These books are reality-oriented; they focus on the home and the family, a family which is white Protestant, of northern European extraction. Relationships between family members—old and young, male and female—are positive and involve strong sets of reciprocal obligations. Because in a life lived in a harsh environment all hands are needed.

A range of needs is discussed in the books, but that particular need which stands out is the need for love—love for the family, but also love and concern for neighbors and friends. There are physical threats to achievement of needs in the woods, but there are no psychological threats. Group life is presented in an almost ideal form.

The family is the most important institution mentioned. It involves not only intimate social relationships and child care but also economic and leisure time activities. Satisfactions are accrued through group effort. If the picture seems a little too perfect, it is still vibrant and plausible. Views of self and people and the world are positive and hopeful. As the seasons change, life continues to grow and develop. There are hostile forces, and the spectre of death is always there; but life itself is celebrated.

Ill. 28: Laura Ingalls Wilder. *The Little House in the Big Woods*. Illustrated by Garth Williams. New York, Harper and Brothers, 1953. [6¼'' x 8¼'']

Strawberry Girl

Lois Lenski was born in Springfield, Ohio, in 1893. She received a bachelor's degree in education from Ohio State University and also studied at the Art Student League. In addition to her children's books, she composed poetry and painted. She was a prolific writer and her autobiography, *Journey Into Childhood,* was published in her seventy-sixth year. Lenski's later years were spent in Tarpon Springs, Florida, where she died in 1974. (See Bird [1] for more details on her life and work.)

Lenski's avowed purpose was to help children see beyond their own world. This she accomplished first with picture books for young children and then with novels for preadolescents. Beginning in 1934 with *Little Auto,* she produced a series of picture books for children, with bold black-and-white illustrations, which described simply but accurately the workings of transportation machines. The author's intense interest in people led her then to a series of books for older children concerned with ways of life in different regions of the country. Before writing each book she lived closely with people of a region. The first of the books, *Bayou Suzette* (1943), presented life in a Louisiana bayou country. *Strawberry Girl* (1945) was concerned with Florida Crackers, *Judy's Journey* (1947) with migrant workers from Alabama who follow the harvest from Florida to New Jersey, *Boom Town Boy* (1948) with persons working in the Oklahoma oil fields, and *My Sack* (1949) with Arkansas cotton pickers.

Strawberry Girl is set in Florida in the early 1900's, when it is still frontier country with vast stretches of unexplored wilderness, woodland, and swamp. There the Crackers live a relatively simple life, fighting an endless battle with nature and wild life. The story centers around the animosity between two Cracker families: the Slaters, old timers in the region, and the Boyers, recent arrivals from Northern Florida, formerly from the Carolina mountains. The Boyers are called "Yankees" by the Slaters, and the Boyer attitudes toward property and progress are ridiculed by the old timers, as in the following passage on fence building (Lois Lenski, *Strawberry Girl,* Philadelphia, J. B. Lippincott Company, 1945):

> "We belong to build us a fence," said Birdie. "We belong to fence in the grove and all the fields, Pa."
> "You mighty right, gal," said Pa.
> It was after the first rails had been split and laid along the outside edge of the strawberry field that Shoestring came along.
> "How you like our new fence?" asked Birdie.
> "Fence? What fence?"
> Birdie pointed to the rails.
> "What you fencin' for?" growled Shoestring.

"What we fencin' for? To keep the Slater hosses and cows out, that's what for!" Birdie's voice rose in shrill anger. "See what that mean little ole cowhorse o' yours done done? See whar he laid down in the middle of our strawberry field and wallered?"

Shoestring began to grin.

"What's funny?" demanded the girl.

"Wal—the bed was so sorry-lookin'," explained Shoestring, "nothin' wouldn't make there, the stawberry plants was all dried up to nothin'—even my ole cowhorse knowed it, so he jest thought it was a good place to waller in!"

Birdie glared

"Think you're funny, don't you?"

"No," said Shoestring. His voice was serious. "I mean it. Strawberries won't never make there."

"Not less'n the neighbors keep their critters out," answered Birdie. "That's why we're fixin' to put up a fence. We're fencin' every acre of ground we own, every inch of field and woods and pasture. See them rails? They're gonna be a fence. Soon as Pa and Buzz get more split, there's gonna be more fence. Hear?"

"Yes," said the boy. When he spoke again, it was in a low, quiet voice. "I wisht you wouldn't fence. If there's ary thing my Pa hates, hit's a fence." He shook his head, frowning, "Ain't nothin' riles Pa more'n a fence."

Birdie stared at him. "Your Pa's got nary thing to do with it."

"Ain't he?" Shoestring looked at her earnestly. "I want to tell you somethin'. Do your Pa fence his fields in, my Pa will make trouble for him. I jest want you to know, that's all."

"What kind o' trouble?" asked Birdie in a scared voice.

"Can't never tell when it's Pa," Shoestring said slowly. "Pa's mean, and when he's drunk, you can't never tell what he'll do."

"He gits . . . drunk?" asked Birdie.

"Yes."

The boy turned and walked away. Birdie stared after him. (pp. 25-27)

As the story progresses, relationships between the Slaters and the Boyers go from bad to worse. The Slaters continue to ridicule Boyer values of planning and hard work. And the Boyers in turn find the Slaters irresponsible and unseemly. Meanwhile Mr. Slater's drinking problem grows, and it is over this crisis that the two families finally come together as neighbors, with understanding and compassion:

The women sat on buckskin rockers on the front porch, Mrs.

[193]

Ill. 29: Lois Lenski. *Strawberry Girl*. Philadelphia: J. B. Lippincott Company, 1945. [5⅞'' x 8⅛'']

Slater with her baby on her lap and Birdie leaned against her
mother's knee. The whippoorwills were calling and the moon shone
with a clear brilliance.

"Things is goin' from bad to worse," sighed Mrs. Slater. "Iffen
hit ain't one thing, hit's two—he's drinkin' so much."

"He won't stop?" asked Mrs. Boyer.

"Nothin' can't stop ary habit like that . . . ."

"Exceptin' to take the liquor away. Where do he get it?"

"The Lord only knows," said Mrs. Slater. "Spends all his
money for it. Never gives none to his family. Do our clothes get
wore out more, they'll fall off us in rags. I been usin' my egg money
for calico for my dresses and overalls for the boys, and now hit's
gone."

"This can't go on," said Mrs. Boyer. "Him drinkin' all the time,
and our men quarrelin' over hogs and cows. We're neighbors and we
belong to live peaceable."

"You mighty right," sighed Mrs. Slater.

"Did the young uns tell you how we saved 'em from the grass
fire, ma'am?" asked Birdie.

Mrs. Slater had heard nothing about it, so Mrs. Boyer told her the
story. She rocked back and forth in her chair. "I'm shore obliged,"
she said. Then she began to cry. "He done set that fire to burn you
folkses out and send you back to Caroliny where you come from."

"I mean!" said Mrs. Boyer. "We like to burnt up, but we ain't
goin' back."

They rocked awhile in silence.

"I hear they're fixin' to hold Camp Meetin' down to Ellis's
Picnic Grounds," said Mrs. Slater. "I'd admire to hear some of the
preachin'. There's nothin' I relish more'n a good noisy sermon. You
reckon we might could go?"

"Why yes," said Mrs. Boyer. "It would pleasure us, too. Do you
have no other way to go, we'll take you-all with us."

"Iffen Sam would only go too . . . " began Mrs. Slater.

"Hit would do him a heap of good," added Mrs. Boyer.

"Ever since I bought me that Bible from the Bible-sellin' feller,"
said Mrs. Slater, "I been thinkin' we belong to get more religion."

"We all belong to git more," said Mrs. Boyer, "to learn how to
love our neighbor."

"Sam, he sometimes goes to the church doin's," said Mrs. Slater,
"but he don't pay no mind to the preacher."

"What he needs is . . . " began Mrs. Boyer.

"A change of heart," added Mrs. Slater. She paused, then she began to sing an old Florida lullaby to her baby. Her soft thin voice melted into the stillness of the night:

" 'Hush, little baby, don't say a word;
Papa's gonna buy you a mockin' bird;
If that mockin' bird don't sing,
Papa's gonna buy you a diamond ring;
If that diamond ring turns to brass,
Papa's gonna buy you a lookin' glass'
If that lookin' glass get broke,
Papa's gonna buy you a billygoat;
If that billygoat runs away,
Papa's gonna buy you a horse and dray.' " (pp. 166-168)

The purpose of *Strawberry Girl* was to promote understanding—understanding of human feelings and human concerns. The setting was the rural South, amidst poverty and a meager environment. Human relationships in the story are primarily between family members and neighbors. Primary group involvement is also found with shopkeepers who, in addition to selling goods, lend money and help their customers in other ways. Major characters are white and poor.

All the basic human needs are of concern to these characters. The need for eternal salvation, and with it the importance of temperance, is discussed. Also focused upon is the need for survival in this life. Love and tenderness, play and curosity are brought out. Achievement needs, in school and in planting, are shown, as is the need for self-actualization in the pursuit of artistic interests. There are real threats to solving needs, deriving from austere physical conditions as well as from human mistrust and fear.

Solutions for obtaining needs are usually found in the family setting, the school and church actively supporting family endeavors. Needs are met by self-direction; in order to survive in that parched land selective crops and innovative planting methods are required. There is, then, an orientation to change—not large-scale change, but small, significant change in everyday patterns of life.

Satisfactions are obtained through the cooperative efforts of family members and ultimately of neighbors. Characters at the end of the book do view themselves and others more positively, and the world has become for them a more hospitable place.

Charlotte's Web

E. B. White was born in Mount Vernon, New York, in 1899 and was educated at Cornell. After service in the First World War he became a reporter for the *Seattle Times,* worked his way to Alaska as a ship's messboy, later took a job in a New York City advertising agency, and finally joined the staff of the humorous literary magazine, *The New Yorker,* for which he has written the "Talk of the Town" column and has set impeccable standards of style. White wrote several books of humor and literary criticism early in his career. His children's books came considerably later: *Stuart Little* (1945), *Charlotte's Web* (1952), and *Trumpet of the Swan* (1970). White is not the only *New Yorker* writer to turn to literature for children; his friend and fellow author James Thurber did so, as did some years later the author/artist William Steig. (See White's *Letters* [10] for comments and concerns over his work.)

Charlotte's Web contains a mixture of reality and fantasy. It tells two stories: One is the story of a child, Fern, of her growing up, and of her changing relationship with family and friends as she grows up. The other story is of a spider, Charlotte, whose love of a fellow creature in the barn, a pig named Wilbur, motivates her to save his life in a wise and witty manner. In the book a range of human emotions are present—joy, sorrow, anger, concern—with love coming through as a unifying force in the actions of all living creatures.

In the beginning of the book the relationship between eight-year-old Fern, her family, and her baby pig, Wilbur, is described with considerable detail. Wilbur is a reluctant gift of Fern's father, and with her mother and father's help, Fern learns to care for and to appreciate her new charge. Fern has quite a bit to learn about the stages in a pig's development.

Concern for other beings in the home is reflected in concern for other beings in the barn. Wilbur learns from a friendly sheep that when he is fat enough, around Christmas time, he will be slaughtered. But he does not wish to die so young! His friend Charlotte understands and responds as follows (E.B. White, *Charlotte's Web,* New York, Harper and Row, 1952):

> Twilight settled over Zuckerman's barn, and a feeling of peace. Fern knew it was almost suppertime but she couldn't bear to leave. Swallows passed on silent wings, in and out of the doorways, bringing food to their young ones. From across the road a bird sang "Whippoorwill, whippoorwill!" Lurvy sat down under an apple tree and lit his pipe; the animals sniffed the familiar smell of strong tobacco. Wilbur heard the trill of the tree toad and the occasional slamming of the kitchen door. All these sounds made him feel comfortable and happy, for he loved life and loved to be a part of the world on a summer evening. But as he lay there he remembered what the old sheep had told him. The thought of death came to him and he began to tremble with fear.
>
> "Charlotte?" he said, softly.
>
> "Yes, Wilbur?"
>
> "I don't want to die."

"Of course you don't,"said Charlotte in a comforting voice.

"I just love it here in the barn," said Wilbur. "I love everything about this place."

"Of course you do," said Charlotte. "We all do."

The goose appeared, followed by her seven goslings. They thrust their little necks out and kept up a musical whistling, like a tiny troupe of pipers. Wilbur listened to the sound with love in his heart.

"Charlotte?" he said.

"Yes?" said the spider.

"Were you serious when you promised you would keep them from killing me?"

"I was never more serious in my life. I am not going to let you die, Wilbur." (pp.52-53)

Charlotte has a plan for saving Wilbur, and the plan works. The plan involves spinning messages about Wilbur on her web. She spins wise and witty signs such as "SOME PIG," "TERRIFIC," and "RADIANT," which all the humans begin to believe about Wilbur. When they believe, they allow him to live out his natural life in dignity and honor.

White's book is now considered a literary materpiece, though it wasn't hailed as such at the time it was first published. Prominent librarians were disturbed by the characters of girl, spider, and pig, but children have always loved them. The book has now been made into a movie.

The purpose of the work is amusement. White's humor and fancy as well as his feeling for all beings make it a very appealing story. The rural setting, talking animals, and a wonderful joke on adults add to the enjoyment.

Characters in the book are both human and animal, and they interact a great deal with each other. The animals are people in fur who show considerable compassion for and understanding of one another, more so than most animal characters. Race and ethnicity are never mentioned in the book; illustrations suggest a world populated with white Anglo-Saxons. There is no sex discrimination among characters; the real star of the book is a *she,* Charlotte A. Cavatica, a beautiful and intelligent gray spider. Affect shown is largely positive, although some negative individuals are present.

The characters are concerned with all human needs, love being focused upon more strongly than others. The major social institution looked to for the solving of needs is the family. Economic and leisure-time activities are seen as part of the family's function. The family includes, as often in rural communities, hired hands and animals as well as parents and children. Relationships between these individuals are rational, intimate, and group oriented.

In this book humans satisfy needs in the performance of ordinary day-to-day tasks in ordinary ways. Animals, though, must perform tasks in more ingenious and self-directed ways in order to survive. Needs are satisfied with the love and help of others. The world is seen as a workable place of friendly beings, in spite

Ill. 30: E. B. White, *Charlotte's Web*. Illustrated by Garth Williams. New York: Harper and Row, 1952. [5⅛″ x 8″]

of uncertainties and change. In the beginning of the book Wilbur is born, and at the end Charlotte dies—the life cycle is shown all of a piece, in a sharp and rich panorama.

The four books just discussed, *Millions of Cats*, *The Little House in the Big Woods*, *Strawberry Girl*, and *Charlotte's Web*, are concerned with understanding and amusement rather than with instruction of one sort or another. They are not focused on the Puritan New England, upper-middle-class tradition, as many books of previous times were. Instead, they point to cultural variation in this vast land. The characters in these books are primarily white Anglo-Saxon, but they exhibit important regional differences that include differences not only in dialect and dress and household furnishings, but, more importantly, differences in attitudes and values. The major focus is not on the individual character, it is on the family unit.

The principal need expressed is for love—of cats, pigs, spiders, but mostly of humans for one another in the family. Love encompasses not only tender feelings and joy but also social responsibility towards others. Needs are satisfied usually through the family, with the benefit of other support systems such as church and school and neighborhood. These support systems vary in organization and function by region. But satisfactions accrue, and America is visualized as a good place for its many peoples.

References

1. Bird, Nancy, compiler. *The Lois Lenski Collection in the Florida State University Library*. Tallahassee: Friends of the Florida State University Library, 1966.
2. Colwell, Eileen. "Laura Ingalls Wilder," *Junior Bookshelf* 26(1962): 237–243.
3. Gàg, Wanda. *Growing Pains: Diaries and Drawings for the Years 1908–1917*. New York: Coward-McCann, c. 1940.
4. Horn Book Magazine, *Wanda Gàg Issue*. Boston: Horn Book, 1947, pp. 157–205.
5. Horn Book Magazine, *Laura Ingalls Wilder Issue*. Boston: Horn Book, 1953. pp. 411–439.
6. Meigs, Cornelia, ed. *A Critical History of Children's Literature*. New York: Macmillan Company, 1953.
7. Praeger, Arthur. "The Secret of Nancy Drew—Pushing Forty and Going Strong," *Saturday Review* 52 (1969): 18–19, 34–35.
8. Scott, Alma. *Wanda Gàg, The Story of an Artist*. Minneapolis: University of Minnesota Press, 1949.
9. Smith, Irene. "Laura Ingalls Wilder and The Little House Books," *Horn Book Magazine* 19 (1943): 293–306.
10. White, E. B. *Letters of E. B. White*, edited by Dorothy Lobrano Guth. New York: Harper and Row, 1976.
11. Wilder, Laura Ingals. *On the Way Home: The Diary of a Trip From South Dakota to Mansfield, Missouri in 1899*. New York: Harper and Row, 1962.
12. "For It was Indeed He." *Fortune* 9 (1939): 86–89, 193–194, 204, 206, 208–209.
13. "Laura Ingalls Wilder, 1867–1967," *Top of the News*, 23 (1967): 264–282.

Chapter 7

1956-1975: "But we can have/ Lots of good fun that is funny!"

During the last twenty years of this time span, while adult caretakers were wringing their hands over the amount of time children sat before the TV tube, publishers were printing more and more books for children. Librarians, with good government subsidies, and parents, with good faith, bought the books in great number. One must assume many were read by children, at least during the TV commercial.

In this period there occurred a change in the purpose for which books were written, and the social background of authors also changed to some extent. Only one of the books in the sample relates to instruction in moral behavior and only three to instruction in social behavior; these latter showing amusing rather than heavily didactic styles.*

Primers, Spellers, and ABC books account for 3 percent of the Library of Congress sample of this time, although they accounted for far more of general publishing output of the period. The ABC's are imaginative and funny and appeal to interests of a child. Katherina Barry's *A is for Anything; an ABC Book of Pictures and Rhymes* (1961) focuses on *A* for anything, *F* for frankfurters, and *H* for Halloween.

A significant development of this time is the introduction of "beginner readers," books for very young children with 200- to 300- word vocabularies. Unlike the sober primers of former times, which were designed for recitation in the classroom, these books, filled with fun and games, are designed for children to read alone at home or in school. Random House published its first beginner book, Dr. Seuss's *The Cat in the Hat,* in 1957. Harper and Row began its *I Can Read* series during the 1950's as well.

Books that instruct in scientific matters account for 9 percent of this sample. In addition to books for the high school student, there are now beginner reader science books in the biological as well as in the behavioral science fields.

Books which focus on understanding, of human beings and the human condition, account for 27 percent of the books of the sample. Earlier in the twentieth century such books (for example, the books of Lois Lenski) highligh-

---

*For changes in book content over time, see Bland [1] and Lystad [6, 7].

ted regional differences. Now, however, the concern is with understanding of differences among racial and ethnic groups and of understanding of social problems—not only problems of racial discrimination but also problems of old age, physical and mental handicaps, and delinquent behavior. Leo Lionni's *Little Blue and Little Yellow* (1959), a picture book for the very young, advocates acceptance of all colors and close human interaction through the simple alliance of forms which happen to be different in hue.

For older children, William Armstrong's *Sounder* (New York: Harper and Row, 1969) focuses on racial discrimination in the South, with the story of a black boy growing up. After his father's death, the boy-child assumes larger responsibilities in the family while still attending to youthful needs for learning and for making sense of his universe:

> "There's plenty of wood, and I must go back to school," the boy told his mother several days after they had buried his father. "Sounder ain't got no spirit left for living. He hasn't gone with me to the woods to chop since Pa died. He doesn't even whine anymore. He just lies on his coffee sacks under the cabin steps. I've dug a grave for him under the big jack oak tree in the stalk land by the fencerow. It'll be ready if the ground freezes. You can carry him on his coffee sacks and bury him. He'll be gone before I come home again."
> And the boy was right. Two weeks before he came home for Christmas, Sounder crawled under the cabin and died. The boy's mother told him all there was to tell.
> "He just crawled up under the house and died," she said.
> The boy was glad. He had learned to read his book with the torn cover better now. He had read in it: "Only the unwise think that what has changed is dead." He had asked the teacher what it meant, and the teacher had said that if a flower blooms once, it goes on blooming somewhere forever. It blooms on for whoever has seen it blooming. It was not quite clear to the boy then, but it was now.
> Years later, walking the earth as a man, it would all sweep back over him, again and again, like an echo on the wind. (pp. 113-114)

Sharon Mathis, in *The Hundred Penny Box* (1975), discusses both blackness and old age in one of the most moving portraits in modern literature.

By far the majority of books of the period (57 percent) are written solely for the purpose of amusement. And there was great, rollicking fun to be had! There was Disney, and there was Seuss. There was also Mother Goose, Cock Robin, and many collections of fairy tales. Amusement was provided in books for all sizes of children. There were picture books, such as Janet Udry's *A Tree is Nice* (New York: Harper and Row, 1956):

> A tree is nice because it has leaves. The leaves whisper in the breeze all summer long.

In the fall, the leaves come down and we play in them. We walk in
the leaves and roll in the leaves. We build playhouses out of the
leaves. Then we pile them up with our rakes and have a bonfire.

There were stories for older children, such as William Steig's *Sylvester and the
Magic Pebble* (1969), which talked of wishes that do come true.

For the teenager there were adventure stories of running away, solving
mysteries, and finding treasures. In E. L. Konigsburg's *From the Mixed-Up
Files of Mrs. Basil E. Frankweiler* (New York: Atheneum, 1967) two children
run away from home to the Metropolitan Museum of Art, where they intend to
live in the English Renaissance section until their parents are truly sorry for
their poor parenting job:

At last they came to the hall of the English Renaissance. Jamie
quickly threw himself upon the bed forgetting that it was only about
six o'clock and thinking that he would be so exhausted that he would
immediately fall asleep. He didn't. He was hungry. That was one
reason he didn't fall asleep immediately. He was uncomfortable,
too. So he got up from bed, changed into his pajamas and got back
into bed. He felt a little better. Claudia had already changed into her
pajamas. She, too, was hungry, and she, too was uncomfortable.
How could so elegant and romantic a bed smell so musty? She would
have liked to wash everything in a good, strong, sweet-smelling
detergent.

As Jamie got into bed, he still felt uneasy, and it wasn't because
he was worried about being caught. Claudia had planned everything
so well that he didn't concern himself about that. The strange way he
felt had little to do with the strange place in which they were sleeping. Claudia felt it, too. Jamie lay there thinking. Finally, realization
came.

"You know, Claude," he whispered, "I didn't brush my teeth."

Claudia answered, "Well, Jamie, you can't always brush after
every meal." They both laughed very quietly. "Tomorrow,"
Claudia reassured him, "we'll be even better organized."

It was much earlier than her bedtime at home, but still Claudia felt
tired. She thought she might have an iron deficiency anemia: tired
blood. Perhaps, the pressures of everyday stress and strain had got-
ten her down. Maybe she was light-headed from hunger; her brain
cells were being robbed of vitally needed oxygen for good growth
and, and . . . yawn.

She shouldn't have worried. It had been an unusually busy day. A
busy and unusual day. So she lay there in the great quiet of the
museum next to the warm quiet of her brother and allowed the soft
stillness to settle around them: a comforter of quiet. The silence

Ill. 31: Janet Udry. *A Tree is Nice*. Pictures by Marc Simont. New York: Harper and Row, 1956. [5⅞'' x 9⅞'']

seeped from their heads to their soles and into their souls. They
stretched out and relaxed. Instead of oxygen and stress, Claudia
thought now of hushed and quiet words: glide, fur, banana, peace.
Even the footsteps of the night watchman added only an accented
quarter-note to the silence that had become a hum, a lullaby.

They lay perfectly still even long after he passed. Then they
whispered good night to each other and fell asleep. They were quiet
sleepers and hidden by the heaviness of the dark, they were easily
not discovered. (pp. 40-42)

In this period authors of books are as likely to be male as female. They are no
longer clergymen but talented writers from a variety of professional backgrounds. Most of their publishing houses are located in New York. All of them
are using commercial presses.

Prose fiction is the predominant form of writing of the period. With the
incredible growth of technology in this century, it is not surprising that science
fiction becomes a popular genre. One of the more talented science-fiction
writers is Madeleine L'Engle, whose *A Wrinkle in Time* (1962) describes with
considerable interplanetary suspense and drama the search of three children
beyond earth for their missing father.

Sixty-four percent of the books of the period are reality-oriented, 24 percent
fantasy-oriented, 12 percent contained both reality and fantasy. Humor is
displayed in 18 percent of the books and is particularly evident in books for
young children. Else Minarik's *Little Bear* series provided humor and gentle
fantasy for the young, with animal characters.

In spite of the fact that by 1950 the country was over 60 percent urbanized,
over 51 percent of the books of the period focus on rural scenes. Another 14
percent of the books describe a combination of urban/rural scenes. The location
is, by and large, the home or other primary group settings (school, workplace,
church, neighborhood) of the characters. Now the environments of poor blacks
and whites as well as those of the middle classes are shown, as in Rebecca
Caudill's stories of Appalachia *Did You Carry the Flag Today, Charley?*
(1966).

The characters in the books of this period are primarily human beings or
humans and animals. There are few books just about animals and few that
include supernatural beings. The social involvement of human characters is, in
about one-third of the cases, with family members alone. The focus, though, is
no longer on smooth positive relationships between parent and child; on the
contrary, negative emotion comes often to the fore, as in the following two
examples.

Joseph Krumgold's *Onion John* (New York: Thomas Y. Crowell Company,
1959) discusses the age-old conflict between father and son. The father wants
his son to prepare for a career in science—first at the Massachusetts Institute of

Technology, then on the moon—a desire prompted by his own youthful dreams of becoming an engineer. The son sees nothing wrong with the small town of Serenity and with working in his father's hardware store. The father finally realizes that his son is growing up and must be allowed to make his own career decisions. Here is the first response of the almost 13-year-old to such liberties:

> My father found the snow shovel and he handed it to me. . . .
> I always get the coal shovel when we dig out after a storm. It's
> smaller. When he gave me the big one, it meant there wasn't any
> doubt that I was grown up.
> "And I'm the one to decide about myself?" I was halfway down
> the driveway, right behind him, cutting a narrow path alongside the
> house.
> He said, "Yes," same as the night before.
> "Well, I've decided," I told him when we reached the sidewalk
> out front.
> "No, you haven't." He heaved the shovelful he had and turned
> around. "You haven't had time to think about it."
> "All the way out here," I told him, "I've had the last ten, twelve
> minutes to think about it."
> "It's the rest of your life you're deciding on. Don't you figure you
> ought to give it a little more time?"
> "That's so!" I leaned on my shovel. "I suppose I ought."
> I gave it until afternoon, when I could get down to the hardware
> store. (p. 223)

Mary Rodger's *Freaky Friday* (New York: Harper and Row, 1972) describes a 13-year-old girl's feeling about her mother's proscriptions:

> I can't stand how strict she is. Take food for instance. Do you
> know what she makes me eat for breakfast? Cereal, orange juice,
> toast, an egg, milk, and two Vitamin C's. She's going to turn me
> into a blimp. . . . She's also very fussy about the way I keep my
> room. . . . A few other things we fight about are my hair . . . and
> my nails which I bite.
> But the biggest thing we fight about is freedom, because I'm old
> enough to be given more than I'm getting. . . . (pp. 4-5)

In another third of the books social involvement of human characters is with both family and other primary groups. Peer group activities are particularly important, and books such as E. L. Konigsburg's *About the B'nai Bagels* (1969) address the American boy's love of organized sports.

Finally, in a third of the books the family becomes involved with secondary institutions such as the courts and welfare offices. In Armstrong's *Sounder* a young boy meets the criminal justice system head on:

A large red-faced man opened the door and said, "You'll have to wait. It ain't visitin' hours yet. Who do you want to see? You'll have to wait." And he slammed the door before the boy could speak.

It was cold on the gray side of the building, so the boy went to the corner near the wall where the people and visitors stood or sat. The sun was shining there. The boy had forgotten it was still Christmas, the waiting seemed so long. A drunk man staggered along the street in front of the courthouse wall, saying "Merry Christmas" to everyone. He said "Merry Christmas" to the boy, and he smiled at the boy too.

Finally the great clock on the roof of the courthouse struck twelve. It frightened the boy because it seemed to shake the town. Now the red-faced man opened the door and let several people in. Inside, the man lined everybody up and felt their clothes and pockets. He jerked the cardboard box from the boy and tore off the top. The boy could hear iron doors opening and closing. Long hallways, with iron bars from floor to ceiling, ran from the door into the dim center of the building. The man with the red face squeezed the cake in his hands and broke it into four pieces. "This could have a steel file or hack-saw blade in it," he said. The he swore and threw the pieces back in the box. The boy had been very hungry. Now he was not hungry. He was afraid. The man shoved the box into the boy's hands and swore again. Part of the cake fell to the floor; it was only a box of crumbs now. The man swore again and made the boy pick up the crumbs from the floor.

The boy hated the man with the red face with the same total but helpless hatred he had felt when he saw his father chained, when he saw Sounder shot. He had thought how he would like to chain the deputy sheriff behind his own wagon and then scare the horse so that it would run faster than the cruel man could. The deputy would fall and bounce and drag on the frozen road. His fine leather jacket would be torn more than he had torn his father's overalls. He would yell and curse, and that would make the horse go faster. And the boy would just watch, not trying to stop the wagon. . . . (pp. 58-60)

Minority characters appear in 23 percent of the books of this sample. Significantly at this time there are a number of books with only black or primarily black characters (8 percent) and a number with only American Indian or primarily American Indian characters (4 percent). Furthermore, when minorities appear together with whites now they are three times as likely to be afforded the same social status; in previous periods they were more often afforded lower status.

Books about minorities won a number of the national literary awards of the time. In the last ten years of the period, three picture books on minority heritages received the Caldecott Medal (awarded annually to the artist of the most distinguished American picture book for children first published in the United States during the previous year) and four novels about minorities received the Newbery Medal (awarded annually to the author of the most distinguished contribution to American literature for children published during the previous year). The Caldecott Medal books are Gail Haley's *A Story A Story* (1970), a West African Anansi tale, Gerald McDermott's *Arrow in the Sun* (1974), a Pueblo Indian tale, and Verna Aardema's *When Mosquitoes Buzz in People's Ears,* pictures by Leo and Diane Dillon, another African animal story (1975). The Newbery Medal books are William Armstrong's *Sounder* (1969), about a black boy growing up in the South, Jean Craighead George's *Julie of the Wolves* (1972), about native Eskimos, Paula Fox's *Slave Dancer* (1973), about slaves in the South, and Virginia Hamilton's *M. C. Higgins, the Great* (1974), about a black boy growing up in the North.

In addition to the increased attention paid to the cultures of racial minority groups, there is increased attention paid to white ethnic customs during this period. A number of Jewish writers have written of their traditions: Isaac Bashevis Singer in *Mazel and Schlimazel; or, The Milk of a Lioness* (1967) and *A Day of Pleasure: Stories of a Boy Growing up in Warsaw* (1969) and Uri Shulevitz in *The Magician: An Adaptation from the Yiddish of I. L. Peretz* (1973). Also during this period a wide range of European traditions was presented by Virginia Haviland in her series of folk tales: *Favorite Fairy Tales Told in Scotland* (1963), *Favorite Fairy Tales Told in Spain* (1963), *Favorite Fairy Tales Told in Poland* (1963), *Favorite Fairy Tales Told in Italy* (1965), *Favorite Fairy Tales Told in Czechoslovakia* (1966).

Male and female characters appear together in most books of the period, males engaging in more exciting and active pursuits than females. Adult and child characters appear together in the majority of books, with the child more prominent than before. Distinctly upper- and lower-class characters appear infrequently, the majority of books containing no class stereotyping.

Animal characters in the books for the most part act as animals, although in one-fourth of the cases they appear as people in fur and in a smaller number of cases they appear as talking animals. The talking animals of Dr. Seuss could be as entertaining as those of Lofting's Dr. Doolittle during an earlier period.

Supernatural beings included God (in 18 percent of the books) and other good and bad spirits (in 7 percent of the books). In this period, unlike others, bad spirits (demons, witches) were as prevalent as good ones (Santa Claus, elves). Just as negative feelings of human characters were discussed more openly now so negative supernatural characters were more often allowed.

The main characters in books of this period more than in any previous period were children (in 46 percent of the sample). The child as a child was focused upon; he or she was no longer treated as a small adult or as a potential angel in heaven. Instead the child was treated as an individual in his or her own right, with needs for love, for adventure, and for self-discovery. Adolescents were main characters in 9 percent of the sample, adults in 21 percent, and animals in 19 percent. Supernatural beings comprised main characters in 4 percent of the books and inanimate objects in 1 percent.

Affect shown by characters was both positive and negative. In this period negative affect was allowed around certain topics which were rarely described previously: hostile child-parent relationships and hostile black-white relationships. Along with the increased openness regarding feelings was increased open discussion around social problems. Problems realted to drug abuse and alcoholism, to mental retardation and old age, were discussed with insight and concern.

The characters in these books focused on expressive needs for love, play, and self-esteem. In few books of the period did characters occupy themselves with the need for eternal salvation (5 percent) or physiological needs (2 percent) or safety needs (13 percent). Love was an important need of characters in 76 percent of the sample, This need included romantic love, familial love, and love for those less fortunate. In Mary Hays Weik's *The Jazz Man*, love of a mother for her deformed son is quietly expressed (New York: Atheneum, 1966):

> One of Zeke's legs was a mite shorter than the other, which gave
> him what his Mama called a ''cute little hop step'' when he
> walked—like a rabbit, she said smiling, making him almost proud of
> it. But other folks, like the kids downstairs, stared at his lame foot
> and made him feel hot and different. One of them even asked why he
> wasn't in school: how old was he? Nine, said Zeke, his heart thump-
> ing. (Why should he tell them he hid in the closet when the school
> man came, looking for children?) After that, he stayed upstairs in his
> room most of the time, and got his fun looking out of the windows.
> (p. 6)

Play, found in 48 percent of the books, was also an important need of characters. Maurice Sendak's *Where the Wild Things Are* (1963) is both witty and wise as it deals in games of imagination, with wild things and magic kingdoms (For a perspective on Sendak's significant contribution to books for children, the reader is directed to Martin [8] and Sendak [9, 10].)

The need for self-esteem is focused upon in a number of books of the sample (58 percent). It provides an underlying theme for characterizations in books on black and American Indian folklore. Gail Haley's *A Story, A Story* (New York: Atheneum, 1970) dramatically presents a West African spider story concerned with small defenseless creatures who outwit others more powerful and succeed against great odds:

> Once, oh small children round my knee, there were not stories on

Ill. 32: Maurice Sendak. *Where the Wild Things Are*. New York: Harper and Row, 1963. [10¼'' x 9¼'']

earth to hear. All the stories belonged to Nyame, the Sky God. He kept them in a golden box next to his royal stool.

Anansi, the Spider man, wanted to buy the Sky God's stories. So he spun a web up to the sky. . . .

So Anansi took the golden box of stories back to earth, to the people of his village. And when he opened the box all the stories scattered to the corners of the world, including this one.

This is my story which I have related. If it be sweet, or if it be not sweet, take some elsewhere, and let some come back to me.

The need to establish reputation and prestige was evident in characters of only 1 percent of the books. Self-fulfillment, expressed in unique ways, was important, however, in 12 percent of the books. Scott O'Dell's *Island of Blue Dolphins* (1960), for example, concerns the Indians of Ghalas who populated an island off the California coast in the early 1900's. The protagonist in the book is caught between pride in her Indian culture and pressure from a Western culture which wants to "civilize" her. Throughout the struggle she maintains her dignity and her sense of purpose.

Characters are not always able to satisfy their needs easily. In 16 percent of the books there are physical threats to satisfaction of needs: threats from war and natural disasters and from handicaps such as mental retardation and senility. Needs still relate primarily to the welfare of the group rather than to the welfare of the individual. In almost all cases they relate to the present rather than to the past or future; the present is seen as the legitimate focus of one's energies and one's concerns.

The family is that social institution to which the characters most often turn for satisfaction of needs. The family is focused upon in 76 percent of the books, and the focus now is less on ideal family structure than on real family situations. In Paula Fox's *Blowfish Live in the Sea* (Englewood Cliffs, New Jersey: Bradbury Press, 1970), adolescent alienation is discussed with clarity and concern, as a young girl describes the effect of her older brother's withdrawal into a world of drugs:

> There were days when I thought Ben looked older than any of us, older even than my father. He looked so tired most of the time. But there were other times when he seemed my own age, times when he was eating something he liked or listening to music he loved. His face could change so quickly. As soon as anyone mentioned college, he'd look away from the person who had asked him—he'd look tired. He'd make up his mind soon, he'd say.
>
> "Don't press him," my mother told my father.
>
> "How can you press air?" my father said once. "When you ask Ben a question, he disappears." My mother said it was a blessing, at least, that the army wouldn't take him. He had something wrong with his right kneecap. He had had a bad accident when he was playing soccer.
>
> Ben must have played soccer years ago when I was still a baby. I watched soccer games in the park. I couldn't imagine Ben ever looking like those boys, running so strongly, hitting the soccer ball with their knees and heads.
>
> When I think of Ben, even when I'm looking straight at him across the supper table, I see a tall thin person in a droopy coat with the collar up. The person's hands are shoved into the coat pockets; the threads that stick out from the places where buttons used to be are a different color from the cloth of the coat. When he walks, the person looks down at his feet as they move forward in cracked muddy boots. (pp.10-11)

The family as depicted in books of the period consists primarily of father and mother and children, although in 7 percent of the cases other relatives are also in the home, and in 10 percent of the cases children are in foster care or in institutions. Interpersonal difficulties among adult relations as well as among parents and children are brought up; Sharon Mathis' *The Hundred Penny Box* (New York: The Viking Press, 1975) tells the story of a family's accommodations to an elderly relative:

> Michael had heard his father and mother talking in bed late one night. It was soon after they had come from going to Atlanta to bring back Aunt Dew. "She won't even look at me—won't call my name, nothing," his mother had said, and Michael could tell she had been crying. "She doesn't like me. I know it. I can tell. I do everything I can to make her comfortable—" His mother was crying hard. "I rode half the way across this city—all the way to Mama Dee's—to get some homemade ice cream, some decent ice cream. Mama Dee said, 'The ice cream be melted fore you get home.' So I took a cab back and made her lunch and gave her the ice cream. I sat down at the table and tried to drink my coffee—I mean, I wanted to talk to her, say something. But she sat there and ate the ice cream and looked straight ahead at the wall and never said nothing to me. She talks to Mike and if I come around she even stops talking sometime." His mother didn't say anything for a while and then he heard her say, "I care about her. But she's making me miserable in my own house."
>
> Michael heard his father say the same things he always said about Aunt Dew. "She's a one-hundred-year-old lady, baby." Sometimes his father would add, "And when I didn't have anybody, she was there. Look here—after Big John and Junie drowned, she gave me a home. I didn't have one. I didn't have nothing. No mother, no father, no nobody. Nobody but her. I've loved her all my life. Like I love you. And that tough beautiful boy we made—standing right outside the door and listening for all he's worth—and he's supposed to be in his room asleep."
>
> Michael remembered he had run back to his room and gotten back into bed and gotten up again and tiptoed over to the bedroom door to close it a little and shut off some of the light shining from the bathroom onto Aunt Dew's face. Then he looked at Aunt Dew and wished she'd wake up and talk to him like she did when she felt like talking and telling him all kinds of stories about people.
>
> "Hold tight, Ruth," he had heard his father say that night. "She knows we want her. She knows it. And baby, baby—sweet woman, you doing fine. Everything you doing is right." Then Michael could hear the covers moving where his mother and father were and he knew his father was putting his arms around his mother because sometimes he saw them still asleep in the morning and that's the way they looked. (pp. 10-11)

In the majority of books mother and father jointly make decisions about the child. When one parent makes decisions alone, it is just as often the mother as the father. Parents take care of and discipline the child together, and they spend considerable time with him. In this sample of books, not only are the attitudes and feelings of parent to child expressed, also expressed, sometimes with great humor, are the attitudes and feelings of child to parent.

Important during this period was the institution of leisure, described in 46 percent of the books. Birthdays and dress-up and make-believe were given proper attention, as in Else Minarek's *Little Bear* and Dr. Seuss' *Happy Birthday to You*.

Another institution of significance was the economic one, discussed in 34 percent of the books. Occupations of fathers were often investigated, particularly in stories with adolescent male characters. In Emily Neville's *It's Like this, Cat* (New York: Harper and Row, 1963) an adolescent boy acquires respect for his lawyer-father when he finds him genuinely interested in helping people:

> "Pop," I say, "there's this guy I met at the beach. Well, really I mean I met him this spring when I was hunting for Cat, and this guy was in the cellar at Forty-six Gramercy, and he got caught and. . . ."
>
> "Wha-a-a-t?" Pop puts down his paper and takes off his glasses. "Begin again."
>
> So I give it to him again, slow, and with explanations. I go through the whole business about the filling station and Hilda and NYU, and I'll say one thing for Pop, when he finally settles down to listen, he listens. I get through, and he puts on his reading glasses and goes to look out the window.
>
> "Do you have this young man's name and address, or is he just Tom from The Cellar?"
>
> I'd just got it from Tom when we were at the beach. He's at a Y in Brooklyn, so I tell Pop this.
>
> Pop says, "Tell him to call my office and come in to see me on his next day off. Meanwhile, I'll bone up on City educational policies in regard to juvenile delinquents."
>
> He says this perfectly straight, as if there'd be a book on the subject. Then he goes back to his newspaper, so I guess that closes the subject for now.
>
> "Thanks, Pop." I say and start to go out.
>
> "Entirely welcome," says Pop. As I get to the door, he adds, "If that cat of yours makes a practice of introducing you to the underworld in other people's cellars, we can do without him. We probably can anyway." (pp. 64-65)

Ill. 33: Sharon Mathis. *The Hundred Penny Box*. Illustrated by Leo and Diane Dillon. New York: Viking Press, 1975. [7⅞″ x 9⅞″]

Political institutions are prominent in 21 percent of the books. They tend to be institutions of the past, dealing with the American Revolution or the Civil War. F. N. Monjo has written several stories of our country's founding; his *Poor Richard in France* (1973) gives a grandson's eye view of Benjamin Franklin's substance and style.

Religious institutions are described in 11 percent of the books. They are not always in the Judeo-Christian tradition; in Jean Craighead George's *Julie of the Wolves* (1972), a book about culture in transition, Eskimo gods are invoked.

Eleven percent of the books of this period deal with the educational establishment, often through a child's eye. In Mary Rodgers', *Freaky Friday* (New York: Harper and Row, 1972) the adolescent heroine fancies herself as her Mother, attending a school conference with the principal, the school psychologist, and her homeroom teacher. The conference goes like this:

> "Yes. Let's see now. Winter report. Math, 72. 'Annabel has been having trouble mastering the techniques of long division. With more diligent application and attention to detail, however, we shall hope for a higher degree of accuracy in the future. Talks in class. H.M.' That's Harvey Mills.". . .
>
> "French, 68. 'Although Annabel is developing a charming French accent, we would wish for more clarity in the written assignments. Her Petit Cahier is in deplorable condition and she cannot, or will not, comprehend the plus-que-parfait. Madame Murphy.' You know Madame Murphy, don't you, Mrs. Andrews?". . .
>
> "American History and Current Events, 65.". . ."' 'Annabel can always be counted upon to make a lively and enthusiastic contribution to class discussion. Outspoken (sometimes to the point of belligerence) on such topics as our environment and the Women's Liberation Movement. She is occasionally inclined to be a touch intolerant of the other fellow's viewpoint. Nevertheless, she is to be commended for her passion!
>
> " 'Unfortunately, Annabel's interest in our country's past is not commensurate with her concern for its future . . . ' " Mr. Dilk looked up. "I do enjoy Sophie Benson's reports. She puts things so nicely, don't you think?" (pp. 77-78)

The majority of characters in this period show a strong sense of responsibility to others, particularly to others in their family. In 21 percent of the books, however, characters focus on responsibility to themselves alone. More now than at any other time the self is looked upon as an entity with legitimate demands and adequate competencies to meet these demands. For young children play is seen as an important demand, and there are all sorts of creative ideas offered to meet the need for play. For adolescents the questioning of old truths and experimenting with new ideas are seen as important demands, and adolescent development and social problems are addressed sensitively and cogently.

Use of stimulants—drugs and alcohol—is mentioned in only 5 percent of the books of the period. When mentioned at all it is placed not in the context of decrying an evil practice but is put in the context of understanding individual problems which led to escape behavior. Drug abuse was a major problem among American youths of this time period; in one book, Paula Fox's *Blowfish Live in the Sea* (1970), the drug use of son is linked to the alcohol use of the father in a moving picture of family dissolution.

Social relationships of characters in books of the time are largely rational and intimate, oriented to the group. In Eveline Ness's *Sam, Bangs, and Moonshine* (1966), a father helps his young daughter, Sam, differentiate between dreams and reality, so as to relate meaningfully to her best friend. Sam has sent her friend out in a storm in search of a nonexistent baby kangaroo. When the friend returns safely, after near disaster in the storm, Sam resolves to accept the difference between "moonshine," or fantasy, and the commonplace world she lives in.

In this period one-fourth of the books show social stratification among characters. Half of these books depict social mobility between classes, with the traditional American dream of rags to riches; the other half deal with the inequities of life for the poor, who are often part of a minority.

More than in any other previous time, needs of characters are met by self-direction—in 33 percent of the books. In 50 percent of the books they are met by conformity to adult norms, in 10 percent by conformity to supernatural norms; the remaining books show combinations of such solutions. Self-direction is encouraged in books for young children, as in William Steig's *Dominic* (1972), the story of an indomitable dog who faces great danger in his altercations with the Doomsday Gang. But does Dominic mind? No. And does he overcome all obstacles? Yes. And self-direction is encouraged in books for adolescents—when the youth struggles, really struggles, to find his or her place in the world. In Jean Craighead George's *Julie of the Wolves* (1972), the struggle is made even more difficult when Julie and her father, Kapugen, meet after a long absence. Julie has remained an Eskimo, her father has become an American. It would seem that they can no longer live in harmony, and Julie must reject him absolutely. But she does not.

In this period, more often than in previous ones, characters seek to satisfy their needs through social change. A change orientation is seen in books about minorities who fight hard for justice and equity. It is seen in books about adolescents who have values about the world different from their parents and who strive to uphold them. Change is focused upon in one-third of the books.

Satisfaction of needs does occur through the individual's own efforts and through those of his family. Even when large problems are brought up, they are not left unresolved. In Paula Fox's *The Slave Dancer* (New York: Bradbury,

1973) a young Southern boy is captured by slave traders and forced to sail to Africa and return on the filthy, overcrowded, prison ship. The boy is treated miserably, and he sees only abject misery for four months. But in the end he escapes from the ship, and he survives. The reader is left with the notion that it is possible to survive, to change his circumstances so that his existence not only becomes more tolerable but indeed more meaningful. This passage on the boy's homecoming expresses both determination and hope:

> By late afternoon, I was walking down Chartres Street toward Jackson Square. I looked like a muddy scarecrow but I didn't attract much attention, only a warning look from a lady sliding along beneath her parasol, and a vague smile from a riverboat captain who, having long since begun his day's drinking, allowed everything strange to amuse him.
>
> I opened the door to our room as I had done in my imagination a hundred times. I took my first step inside. I heard a shriek, a cry. Betty and my mother and I stood silently for a moment, then we ran toward each other with such force I felt the little house shake in all its boards and bricks.
>
> We talked through half the night. I learned of their frantic search which had followed my disappearance, how even that very day my mother had questioned venders in the market as she had done every day since I'd been gone. My mother often wept, not only because I, whom she'd thought dead, had been returned to her, but at the story of *The Moonlight*. When I described how the slaves had been tossed into the shark-filled waters of Cuba, she covered her face with her hands and cried, "I can't hear it! I can't bear it!"
>
> It did not take long, to my surprise, for me to slip back into my life as though I'd never left it. There were signs—brooding looks from my mother, Betty's way of speaking softly to me as though I was an invalid, and, most startling, the change in Aunt Agatha who treated me now with affection and never called me a bayou lout. My mother guessed that the shock of my disappearance had changed her into what she had once been, a slightly soured but not bad-hearted woman. I was back in my life, but I was not the same. When I passed a black man, I often turned to look at him, trying to see in his walk the man he had once been before he'd been driven through the dangerous heaving surf to a long boat, toppled into it, chained, brought to a waiting ship all narrowed and stripped for speed, carried through storms, and the bitter brightness of sun-filled days to a place, where if he had survived, he would be sold like cloth.
>
> I found work on the Orleans Bank Canal which was to eventually connect New Orleans to Lake Pontchartrain. That might have kept

me occupied and earning my keep for some time, but I grew restless
and began to think about what profession would suit me, and what
would be available to one who could not afford much schooling.

At first, I made a promise to myself: I would do nothing that was
connected ever so faintly with the importing and sale and use of
slaves. But I soon discovered that everything I considered bore,
somewhere along the way, the imprint of black hands. (pp. 173-174)

The main characters of the books of the period view themselves positively;
they view other people positively as well. In general people are seen as
controlling their own lives, and the world is seen essentially as a good and
supportive place, but one in which individuals have to work together for the
good of all. In 27 percent of the books death is present, but it does not destroy
the hope and the joy in life.

As was done earlier, two books from the period have been singled out for
detailed analysis: *The Cat in the Hat*, by Dr. Seuss (Theodor Seuss Geisel) and
M. C. Higgins, the Great, by Virginia Hamilton. The books are markedly
different in content and style, and yet both are important landmarks of their
time.

Dr. Seuss' *The Cat in the Hat* was one of the most widely read books for
children of this era. It was a favorite among beginner readers, available not only
in the library and the book store but in countless drug and grocery store stands
throughout the country. It pointed the way to a different kind of reader—a book
of only 223 words, attuned to the interest of the child, calculated to entertain
him royally. The child was lured into reading, into becoming an active participant in the learning process, by an incredible cat with a tall hat and two incredible
things (named appropriately, "Thing 1" and "Thing 2"). Seuss' lively imagination has helped countless children, including slow readers, to learn to read far
sooner than they might have otherwise on sober and didactic fare.

Wirginia Hamilton's *M. C. Higgins, the Great* is one of a growing number
of books about the black experience. A brilliant novel, it won both the Newbery
Medal and the National Book Award for children's books in its year of
publication. Increasingly, writers of minority backgrounds are turning to their
cultures to focus on the social values and life styles they hold important. Blacks
have been most prolific in this regard; many of their books are written of the
past and speak of social injustices in the South. Hamilton's books, however,
are about the present and discuss the lives of blacks in the North. Her characters
have strength and dignity and survival power.

The Cat in the Hat

Theodor Seuss Geisel was born in 1904, in Springfield, Massachusetts, and
was educated at Dartmouth College and Oxford University. After a year

traveling in Europe, he returned to the United States and worked as a magazine cartoonist and satirist. Later he spent four years in Hollywood as a screen artist and followed this with a highly successful advertising career. He was the creator of a memorable series of advertisements for "Flit" mosquito repellant ("Quick, Henry, the Flit!").

Restless with the advertising world, Geisel tried his hand at picture books for children. *And To Think I Saw It on Mulberry Street,* published in 1937, was his first major children's book. Forty years and forty odd books later, they are still coming and still being read voraciously. Geisel's distaste for the commonplace and preference for a touch of anarchy, as well as his predictable style, has brought criticism from teachers and librarians, but children enjoy both his predilections and his sense of humor.

The Cat in the Hat (New York: Random House, 1957) was the first of Random House's Beginner Book Series. Some books of the series were written by Geisel and some by other authors; together they have sold approximately fifty million copies in the United States and several million in Britain as well. Geisel writes under the pseudonym of "Theo Le Sieg" as well as of "Dr. Seuss;" the latter name he gave to himself during his journalistic period when he wanted a name to append to a series of articles supposedly written by a wise old man.

In addition to writing books for children, Geisel has written several screen plays, including that for the animated color cartoon *Gerald Mc Boing-Boing,* which won an Academy Award in 1951. Today he lives in a converted windmill in La Jolla, California. (For discussion of Seuss, see Davis [2] and Lingeman [5].)

The Cat in the Hat begins on a gloomy note: two young children are left alone at home for a whole day. Their mother is out; no adult supervision or stimulation is offered. Furthermore it is a cold and wet day, so there is no chance for playing outdoors. The older child speaks:

> So all we could do was to
> Sit!
>   Sit!
>   Sit!
> And we did not like it.
> Not one little bit.
> And then
> Something went BUMP!
> How that Bump made us jump!
> We looked!
> Then we saw him step in on the mat!
> We looked!

And we saw him!
The Cat in the Hat!
And he said to us,
"Why do you sit there like that?
I know it is wet
And the sun is not sunny.
But we can have
Lots of good fun that is funny! (pp. 3-7)

The children's fish warns them against this unusual intrusion, especially while their Mother is out. But then the Cat shows the children all manner of amazing tricks, which result in complete uproar everywhere. The fish tries to take over and commands the Cat to leave the house. The Cat does not wish to leave:

"But I like to be here,
Oh, I like it a lot!"
Said the Cat in the Hat
To the fish in the pot.
"I will NOT go away. I do not wish to go!
And so,"said the Cat in the Hat.
"so
    so
        so . . .
I will show you
Another good game that I know!"
And then he ran out.
And, then, fast as a fox,
The Cat in the Hat
Came back in with a box.
A big red wood box.
It was shut with a hook
"Now look at this trick,"
Said the cat.
"Take a look!"
Then he got up on top
With a tip of his hat.
"I call this game FUN-IN-A-BOX,"
Said the cat.
"In this box are two things
I will show to you now.
You will like these two things,"

Ill. 34: Theodor Seuss Geisel. *The Cat in the Hat,* By Dr. Seuss (pseud.).
New York: Random House, 1957. [6½'' x 9'']

Ill. 35: Theodor Seuss Geisel. *The Cat in the Hat*, by Dr. Seuss (pseud.). New York: Random House, 1957. [6½'' x 9'']

Said the cat with a bow.
"I will pick up the hook.
You will see something new.
Two things. And I call them
Thing One and Thing Two. (pp. 27-33)

Thing 1 and Thing 2, predictably, only increase the pandemonium by flying kites in the house and knocking down just about everything.

Then the mother approaches, her foot can be seen out the window. The Cat in the Hat, though, is not irresponsible; he immediately takes away Thing 1 and Thing 2. With the help of an extraordinary four-armed cleaning machine, he tidies up the house quickly, picking up from the floor in no time a cake, a rake, mother's new gown, milk, strings, books, dish, fan, cup, ship, and the fallen fish. Following this, he disappears. Mother comes in the door (you only see a foot and a leg) and says to her children:

"Did you have any fun?
Tell me, what did you do?" (p. 60)

The book ends before the children decide whether or not to tell all.

The purpose of *The Cat in the Hat* is to engage the reader, to entertain him so that indeed he will want to read on, to develop reading skills. Repetition and rhyme are used to facilitate word usage, and the familiar surroundings of home enable the reader, despite all the fantasy and fanfare, to remain secure.

Human and animal characters are involved in diverse ways. A boy and a girl make up the human component, and a variety of animals are also shown. Mother's voice is heard on the second to last page, but her face is never seen. The main character is the cat himself, a cat with the imagination and wit and impulsiveness of a lively child.

The basic need, exhibited by human and animal characters, is for play and adventure. There are no problems in solving such needs as long as creative ability lasts. Needs are satisfied through leisure in a family setting. Only the children, though, are in the home. The mother, we are told, is our for the day, and the father is not in evidence either, leaving the children to care for themselves. Needs are met by the surprising entrance of a cat with a zest for life and innovative ways of living; the children are innocent bystanders, which allows them to enjoy the mad and wonderful scene with hardly any feelings of guilt. And the message is clear—if the world is bleak, change it, create a new world! Everyone can have fun that is funny, even on lonesome, cold, wet days.

M. C. Higgins, the Great

Her maternal grandfather was born a slave, in the Kentucky-Tennessee area, and ran away with his mother, her great grandmother, to settle in Jamestown,

Ohio; Virginia Hamilton grew up in that area. She attended Antioch College and left for New York for a period of fifteen years during which she sang in obscure nightclubs, studied at the New School, wrote, and made friends with musicians, artists, and other writers. In New York she met and married the poet and anthologist Arnold Adoff. Now they live with their two children in Yellow Springs, Ohio, back in the area of her ancestors, near family and friends.

Hamilton's intimacy with generations of black families and her interest in black history are evidenced in all her novels—*Zeely* (1967), *The House of Dies Drear* (1968), *The Planet of Junior Brown* (1971), and *M. C. Higgins, the Great* (1974). *M. C. Higgins, the Great* is a story of persons who are black and poor and who live in the Appalachian hill country of Ohio, where coal companies have for too many years stripped the land of its beauty and its usefulness. But it is more than the story of the black and the poor; it is the story of all who survive painful obstacles to growth and self-actualization. (For insights into Hamilton's work, see Hamilton [3] and Heins [4].)

"M. C. Higgins, the Great," is the name given to a thirteen-year-old boy by his father, in partial jest, when the boy meets his father's challenge to swim the Ohio River. M. C. has a lot of challenges to meet, living as he does at the edge of a strip-mine area. He understands this, and he worries about himself and his family. Early in the book he is shown in his favorite place, on top of his gleaming, forty-foot pole. He sits there and watches over his younger sister and two younger brothers *(M. C. Higgins, the Great,* New York: Macmillan, 1974):

> The kids, Lennie Pool, Harper and Macie Pearl, always swam in the lake on a hot morning. The lake water could be cold as ice; it had blue holes and grottoes emerging into pools a short distance from it.
>
> Squinting, M. C. saw the children wade gingerly in the water and then swim out. They were like fish, gliding and diving. After a while a few town kids drifted over the hills and down to the lake. Half afraid of water, they splashed in the shallows along the shore.
>
> M. C. let his pole sway gently. He caught a sudden guest of breeze. He continued to sit more comfortably now, for he did have to watch out for the kids over in the lake. He had to wait for the dude. And he let the thought of a lone stranger, a girl in the woods, slip out of his mind again.
>
> Macie Pearl and M. C.'s brothers could swim well enough to care for themselves in the water. But if one of them did commence to drown. . . .
>
> Don't think about it.
>
> M. C. frowned.
>
> They don't know how lucky they are. Swimming. Playing. Without a worry for food or nothing.

His mother, Banina, was off cleaning houses. Jones, his father, worked as a laborer in the steelyard at Harenton when somebody was sick, like today. A whole month could go by and often did before someone became ill. Whenever work was scarce and food was low, M. C. didn't count on his rabbit traps.

Depend on them, we'd starve.

He hunted with a burlap sack, a rock or two and a paring knife. He had no dog, and so he had taught himself how to be the hunter. He would read animal signs around trees or in wetlands and along streams where they came to drink. Hunting was hours and hours of stalking, of blind trails, of studying the ground and listening. It could be bloody, too. But he could hunt well when he had to, using the paring knife to skin and gut the animal.

When M. C. couldn't be around sitting on his pole to watch the kids, he made them stay inside the house, sometimes for hours. He had taught Macie Pearl to sit in the parlor for as long as it took him. She wouldn't even move her hands.

"I can't hunt so good," he told her, "if I'm not positive you are safe here. I can't catch me a shameful thing if you be running the hills or swimming the lake without me to watch."

Whatever Macie Pearl thought about during the long, half-hungry hours when she had to sit, she could do it because M. C. had told her to.

They stay safe. They listen to me.

Now M. C. kept watch over the lake, straining his eyes so, that they began to ache. He shifted his gaze back to the hill range. Hills rolled eastward and became faded with haze. (pp. 29-30)

Even in the midst of pleasant activities, such as sitting on top of his pole and swimming in the lake and hunting rabbits, M. C. is never able to rid himself of the nagging fear of the spoil heap on Sarah's Mountain. His home is at the foot of the mountain, and the spoil is oozing down slowly to destroy it. M. C.'s fear is heightened when a storm comes; he fears for himself and for his family. But he carries on.

Hamilton's purpose in *M. C. Higgins, the Great* is to provide the reader with understanding of the human condition and of human competence to meet this condition. On the one hand, she mourns the situation of the poor and the powerless; on the other hand, she extols the human being himself. No one dies in the book. But M. C.'s efforts to stay alive, to preserve respect and meaning in life are central to the narrative.

The characters in the story are free and live in the North, but their roots are in slavery in the South. The main character, Mayo Cornelius Higgins, is a teenager of uncommon curiosity and strength. He has concern with the need to survive on a physical level, with the need to love and be loved, to play, to master complex skills. That's a lot for a young man to worry about, but he is "M. C. Higgins, the Great."

The family is the principal institution through which needs are approached; family members work together for economic survival, they play together, and they love and care for each other. The mother holds the steady job; the father works only intermittently when he can find work, staying home the rest of the time to cook and care for his children. There is no ill feeling between spouses; there is on the contrary, expression of romantic love. When the two parents are home together, they care for the children together.

Satisfactions occur in the books through individual and family efforts. The main characters view themselves well, and they view people, their people, well. They are in control of their own lives even though they need to consider family, past and present, to plan for the future—for it is within the family that they find courage and determination to go on.

Hamilton's *M. C. Higgins, the Great* and Geisel's *The Cat in the Hat*, though they differ in many ways, are alike in breaking new ground in this period. Hamilton introduces in children's literature a strong new character, like herself, black and resolute in a white world. Geisel introduces a new form of reading, simple and appealing to children. The books are alike, too, in that both authors pay tribute to the child—one by portraying a child of considerable complexity and ability and the other by challenging the child/reader so that he or she will grow in competence and confidence. In books of the period the child is taken into the society as a person. The child is encouraged to become involved to the degree to which he or she is able and is afforded dignity and purpose, whether he or she is black or white, rich or poor, northerner or southerner. The child is important as himself or herself.

References

1. Bland, David. *A History of Book Illustration: The Illuminated Manuscript and The Printed Book.* Berkeley: University of California Press, 1969.
2. Davis, David C. "What the Cat in the Hat Begat," *Elementary English* 48 (1957): 677–679, 746.
3. Hamilton, Virginia. "Newbery Award Acceptance," *The Horn Book Magazine* 151 (1975): 4:337–343.
4. Heins, Paul. "Virginia Hamilton," *The Horn Book Magazine* 41 (1975): 4:344–348.
5. Lingeman, Richard. "Dr. Seuss, Theo Le Sieg," *The New York Times Book Review,* November 14, 1976, pp. 23, 48.
6. Lystad, Mary. "From Dr. Mather to Dr. Seuss: Over 200 Years of American Children's Books," *Children Today* 5 (1976): 3:10–15.

7. Lystad, Mary. "The Adolescent Image in American Books for Children: Then and Now," *Children Today* 6 (1977): 4:16–19, 35.

8. Martin, C. M. "Wild Things," *Junior Bookshelf* 31 (1967): 359–363.

9. Sendak, Maurice. "The Qualities that Make for Excellence in Children's Literature," *Hofstra University Reading Conference* (1967), p. 7–10.

10. Sendak, Maurice. *Questions to an Artist Who is Also an Author: A Conversation between Maurice Sendak and Virginia Haviland.* Washington, D.C.: Library of Congress, 1972.

Chapter 8

Changing Social Values

In the first chapter several questions were posed about the presentation, in American books for children, of social values and their change over time. The first question, concerning the value of egalitarianism, was: have the social backgrounds of characters in books become more culturally diverse and their social conditions more equal in accordance with the spirit of the new country over the years? The second question concerned the value of self-expression. The question was: have the needs of characters changed over the years, did they become less concerned with survival and more with self-fulfillment as the country grew and prospered? The third question concerned the value of freedom of choice around the way needs were satisfied, specifically, the question was: are there more social institutions available to individuals through which to satisfy needs, and are these social institutions viewed as more adaptable over time? A final question, concerned with satisfaction of needs, was also addressed: are needs met more often by characters in books in later years, accompanied by greater feelings of self-worth and control over the environment?

Each of these questions was looked at from an historical perspective. Did such values, important as *reasons* for declaring a revolution and for forming a new country, become expressed more clearly and more strongly in books for children as the country grew and developed? As the country progressed, did it hold up to its children other ideas and hopes for the future?

The Value of Egalitarianism

First examined was whether characters were presented as of equal or unequal status in books. All persons were supposed to be born equal in the new land; but were some more equal than others by virtue of their racial, age, sex, and social-class statuses? Were some afforded more opportunities and more knowledge because of such statuses? In particular the investigation focused upon the handling of minority, child, female, and economically disadvantaged characters in books.

In terms of racial minorities, inequalities are immediately evidenced in books by virture of the absence of clearly identifiable minorities in most works in early years. Table 8-1 gives a breakdown by time period of those books which had no identifiable minority characters, those which had principally minority characters, those which had minority characters appearing with white characters but in lower statuses, and those which had minority characters along with whites with no status differentials. Until the 1950's, few books featured minority characters, except during one period after the American Civil War (1876–1895) when minority characters appeared in numbers and were shown with lower statuses. The ravages of war and a country divided left the society unable to provide the child with anything but the old stereotypes of minorities as lazy and stupid. It took another sixty years to reverse the trend.

By the 1950's a substantial number of books included minority characters. In the thirteen books of the 1956–1975 sample which focused upon them, nine were about blacks and four about American Indians. Most of these books are novels, set within an historical context.

Racial stereotypes were strong at the turn of the eighteenth century and continued strong even after the Civil War. Books were aimed at the white Protestant; when the black slave or the American Indian was spoken about or to, such heathens generally appeared as candidates for conversion. Converting the Indians was of sufficient concern that *The Triumphant Deaths of Pious Children* was published in 1835 in the Choctaw language by missionaries of the American Board of Commissioners for Foreign Missions.

Even in the latter part of the nineteenth century, stereotyped pictures of

Table 8.1. Presentation of Minority Characters in Books by Publication Date (percent)*

Publication Date	No Identifiable Minority Characters	Minority Characters Appearing Substantially Alone	Minority Characters With Lower Status than Whites	Minority Characters With Same Status as Whites	N
1721–1795	100	0	0	0	100
1796–1815	95	0	4	1	100
1816–1835	92	0	4	4	100
1836–1855	85	0	14	1	100
1856–1875	81	0	16	3	100
1876–1895	67	0	30	3	100
1896–1915	80	1	17	2	100
1916–1935	88	3	5	4	100
1936–1955	88	3	6	3	100
1956–1975	76	13	3	8	100

*p<.001

blacks and other minorities show them to be lazy and incompetent persons. An example is the counting book, *Simple Addition by a Little Nigger* (published by McLoughlin Brothers, c.1860), which starts Out:

> One little nigger feeling rather blue,
> Whistled out another nig, and that made 2.

Another well-known example of racial stereotyping is Annie Fellows-Johnston's *The Little Colonel* (1896), set in the Old South after the Civil War and characterizing the Negro as a childlike human being.

By the mid 1900's the primary focus of books was still on white actors. The here-and-now of racial interaction, of racial conflict and cooperation, was only beginning to be addressed; but the number of talented writers of minority-group backgrounds entering the children's book field was growing. Writers such as Lucille Clifton, Nikki Giovanni, Eloise Greenfield, Virginia Hamilton, and John Steptoe added the insight and vitality needed in this area. These authors were at home in poetry and prose, and their writing showed a keen understanding of human nature as well as of cultural differences.

Equality among characters was also looked at in terms of sex differences. Table 8.2 gives the presentation of characters by sex in books. Most books throughout the years dealt with both male and female characters; only in the early years of the country did a substantial number of books focus solely on boys, and that at a time when only boys usually attended school.

However, the books differed in their presentation of what boys and girls do.

Table 8.2. Presentation of Characters by Sex in Books by Publication Date (percent)*

Publication Date	Male Characters Appearing Substantially Alone	Female Characters Appearing Substantially Alone	Both Sexes, With Lower Status for Female	Both Sexes, With Same Status for Female	N
1721–1795	11	0	29	60	100
1796–1815	4	1	13	82	100
1816–1835	3	2	5	90	100
1836–1855	1	0	6	93	100
1856–1875	0	0	2	98	100
1876–1895	1	0	1	98	100
1896–1915	0	0	2	98	100
1916–1935	2	4	2	92	100
1936–1955	2	1	1	96	100
1956–1975	1	0	1	98	100

*$p < .001$

In early years books for boys contained friendly advice on how to succeed at work; books for girls concentrated on how to be pleasant and kind and gentle at home. The table of contents of *Useful Lads: or, Friendly Advice to Boys in Business*, published by the American Sunday School Union in Philadelphia in 1847, for instance, gives such chapter headings as Personal Habits and Appearance, Punctuality and Exactness, Obedience, Honesty, Truthfulness, Industry, Temper and Behavior, and Sundry Cautions. The advice offered young girls, on the other hand, is represented by the author's admonition in *Little Lucy: or the Pleasant Day, An Example for Little Girls*, published by S. B. Babcock in New Haven in 1840:

> Let all my little readers strive, like Lucy, to be kind, gentle and
> affectionate, and to do all that is in their power to make their friends
> happy; they will then find that doing their duty has increased their
> own happiness, and every day will be to them A Pleasant Day.

Later, in the nineteenth century, books continued in their stereotyping of boys and girls, with boys appearing more active and adventuresome. Male characters such as those of Horatio Alger worked hard and achieved admirably in worldly pursuits, while female characters were submissive and proficient with the needle.

Into the twentieth century boy and girl characters still emerge differently in books for children. Boys, especially white boys, are more involved in achievement roles. The black boy achieves in one particular area: professional sports. There are scores of sports series published on the lives of male football, baseball, basketball, and hockey stars, and books on black stars do discuss the problems of poverty and race which the black athlete has to overcome in order to succeed. The girl of any color is, by and large, denied success in professional work, although she can achieve in interpersonal relationships and in family situations. In the more recent past strong female characters appear more frequently. Jean Craighead George's *Julie of the Wolves* (1972) is a book about a remarkably resourceful girl who manages to survive parental abandonment, attempted rape, and life on the tundra lost amidst the wolves. Mary Rodgers' *Freaky Friday* (1972) is about a spunky young female who takes on the role of her mother only to realize that being a responsible adult is not always easy or always fun.

Equal handling of age differences among characters was also examined. Except for the eighteenth century, when adults appeared alone in half of the books, both children and adults usually appeared together. In terms of character focus, adults were twice as often focused upon as main characters as were children in the 1700's. Adults continued to be main characters more often than did children until the latter half of the nineteenth century, when children began to receive more attention. By the 1950's children were seen twice as often as main characters as were adults. Adolescents were never as frequently main

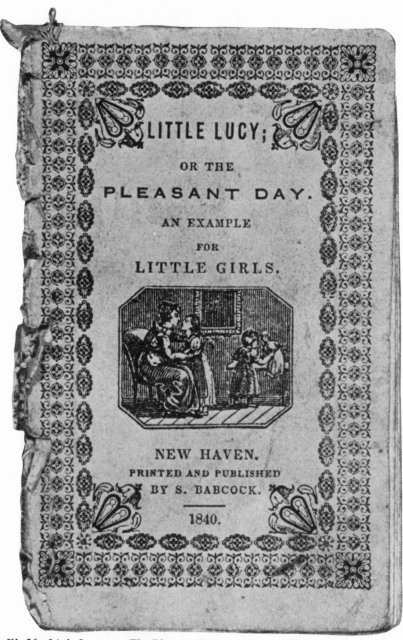

Ill. 36: *Little Lucy; or, The Pleasant Day, an Example for Little Girls.* New Haven, S. B. Babcock, 1840. [2⅞″ x 4⅜″]

Ill. 37: Mary Rodgers. *Freaky Friday*, cover by Edward Gorey. New York: Harper and Row, 1972. [6½'' x 9½'']

characters as adults or children—it was as if this developmental period was unimportant or didn't exist, except in the latter part of the nineteenth century and early part of the twentieth when there were family novels for girls and work novels for boys and a number of series books on adolescent characters that carried the same actors through many different adventures.

There was, then, a real shift from the early years in which children were perceived only in adult terms to the twentieth century where they were given center stage in books written about them. Concomitant with the shift in number of books which focused on children was the shift in the way children were presented. They were, in early years, presented as miniature adults to be socialized into adult roles; even the clothes they wore were copies of adult attire, unsuited to play or to just wriggling about. Adult attitudes towards children were expressed often and openly, but children's attitudes towards adults were expressed infrequently and only in positive terms. It was much later that children's natural feelings and wants were admitted, that they were allowed to be themselves, disheveled appearance and all. It took the 1960's and 1970's to permit presentation of a significant proportion of child characters with negative feelings and with revolutionary ideas.

Examined too were inequalities as expressed in the descriptions of characters from upper, middle, and lower social classes. All classes were shown in books for children throughout our country's history; every period and community had its rich and its poor. In early years status differentials were addressed in one-third of the books, where the rich were admonished to attend the poor, as in an early *New England Primer* (New Haven: S. Babcock, c.1830):

Be never proud by any means,
  Build not your house too high,
But always have before your eyes,
  That you were born to die.

Defraud not him that hired is
  Your labor to sustain;
But pay him still without delay,
  His wages for his pain.

And as you would that other men
  Against you should proceed,
Do you the same to them again,
  When they do stand in need.

Impart your portion to the poor,
  In money and in meat,
And send the feeble fainting soul,
  Of that which you do eat.

Ask counsel always of the wise,
  Give ear unto the end,
And ne'er refuse the sweet rebuke
  Of him that is your friend.

Be always thankful to the Lord,
  With prayers and with praise,
Begging of him to bless your work,
  And to direct your ways. (pp. 22-23)

By the mid-nineteenth century approximately half of the books discussed status differentials between rich and poor, and the discussion had changed character somewhat. While the rich were still advised to help those less fortunate, the poor were advised to improve themselves, as in Horatio Alger's *The Young Salesman* (Philadelphia: John C. Winston, 1896):

Loammi Little, for this was the name of the red-haired boy, regarded Scott with curiosity mingled with surprise.

"What is your name?" he asked, abruptly.

"Scott Walton."

"I have never heard of you, though I have heard pa say that a cousin of his married a man named Walton. Where is your father?"

"He is dead," answered Scott, sadly. "He died on the voyage over."

"Humph!" said Loammi, in a tone far from sympathetic. "I suppose you are poor."

"I am not rich," replied Scott, coldly.

He began to resent the unfeeling questions with which his cousin was plying him.

"If you have come over here to live on pa, I don't think he will like it."

"I don't want to live on any one," said Scott, his cheek flushing with anger. "I am ready to earn my own living."

"That's the way pa did. He came over here a poor boy, or rather a poor young man."

"I respect him the more for it."

Status differentials were considered less frequently by the mid-twentieth century, in one-fourth of the books. The focus was primarily on the lower classes, poor and often minority persons, and the inequities they faced in terms of economic opportunity. Hamilton's *M. C. Higgins, the Great* (New York: Harper and Row, 1974) describes the situation of a black day laborer in a distressed coal mining area. Here attention is not directed at the individual poor person, to encourage him to better his lot, or the individual rich person, to encourage him to help the less fortunate, but at a social system which is seen as unjust and demeaning.

The Value of Self-Expression

The second area focused upon is the presence of expressive materials among characters in the books. In the new land persons were supposed to have new opportunity to develop as people, to follow the beat of their own drummer. Did characters then focus on expressive needs (love, play, self-actualization) or on traditional achievement needs (eternal salvation in the next world, strength and achievement, reputation and prestige in this world)? The handling of human needs—which ones were emphasized, problems presented in solving needs, relationships of individual to group needs—were explored in the books over the two-hundred-year period.

Table 8.3 shows the basic human needs expressed in these books for children by time periods. For the first hundred years the need for eternal salvation in the next life was strong; also strong was the need for strength and achievement in this life. The two needs were, of course, related—for the individual was to pray and to work hard for the Lord. Economic success in this life showed the Lord's pleasure in one's efforts and boded well for eternal salvation in the next. Worldly goods thus became a sign that salvation was at hand. The following quotation from an early *New England Primer* (New Haven: S. Babcock, c.1830) says it clearly:

> See first, I say, the living God,
>   And always him adore,
> And then be sure that he will bless
>   Your basket and your store.
>
> And I beseech Almighty God
>   To replenish you with grace,
> That I may meet you in the heavens,
>   And see you face to face. (p. 23)

This logic was found not only in the *New England Primer* but also in numerous catechisms and bibles of early America.

The need for eternal salvation and strength and achievement lessened as the years went on. On the other hand, expressive needs—need for love, play and adventure, self-actualization—increased over the years. Love of parent for child, romantic love, and love for neighbor were all found in these volumes. Books concerned with imaginative play, games, and adventure and intrigue appeared more and more frequently as time went on. And the need for self-actualization, very infrequently found until the 1900's, increased thereafter, especially in books for adolescents where teen-aged characters talked openly about their feelings for their parents and their goals for the future. Two recent examples are Paula Fox's *Blowfish Live in the Sea* (1970) which focuses on a young white girl, and Virginia Hamilton's *M. C. Higgins, The Great* (1974), which shows a young black boy.

Table 8.3. Basic Human Needs Expressed in Books by Publication Date
         (percent)*

Publication Date	Eternal Salvation	Physiological and Safety Needs	Love	Play and Adventure	Strength and Achievement	Reputation and Prestige	Self-Actualization	N
1721–1795	56	9	15	4	69	14	5	100
1796–1815	51	15	35	5	64	7	3	100
1816–1835	64	13	40	2	46	3	4	100
1836–1855	73	3	61	4	59	2	3	100
1856–1875	72	2	78	17	72	1	4	100
1876–1895	42	15	81	31	78	1	1	
1896–1915	24	14	68	33	71	10	6	100
1916–1935	6	22	65	43	57	8	9	100
1936–1955	7	29	75	46	58	2	14	100
1956–1975	6	16	77	49	59	2	13	100

N.B. The percentages per time period add up to more than 100% because most books focused on more than one discernible need.

*p<.001

The presentation of needs of characters in books over the years was examined not only in terms of which needs were more frequently expressed but also in terms of problems overcome in solving needs. For if the character faces considerable obstacles to achieving his goals, and if indeed he is shown as incompetent to achieve on his own, the message given is one of self-doubt. If one has self-doubts, one is less likely to experiment with self-expression.

Table 8.4 shows problems described in solving needs in books, by publication date. The table indicates that the number of books throughout the years which mention concrete threats from the outside stayed relatively constant. However, a dramatic shift took place over the years in the proportion of books which showed threats to obtaining goals derived from the character's basic inability to achieve on his own. Books of the eighteenth and the nineteenth centuries, especially publications from the Sunday School presses, stressed the character's dependence on others, principally on God and the family. By the twentieth century, the individual's own ability to solve his problems is emphasized. The individual is shown as competent and in control, able to set forth and explore and enjoy.

The presentation of needs in books was, finally, examined in terms of the relationship of individual to group needs. Table 8.5 shows the relationship of needs of individual characters to those of other characters over time. The table shows, in general, an increase in number of books which relate individual to group needs for the 200-year period. There is a decline in this relationship during sixty years of the nineteenth century (1816–1875), a period when Sunday School presses flourished and when the need to do God's will was

Table 8.4. Identification of Problems in Solving Needs in Books by Publication Date (percent)*

Publication Date	Physical or Psychological Threats from Outside	Inability of Character to Achieve Needs on His Own	No Problem if Character Works at it	N
1721–1795	14	50	36	86
1796–1815	14	35	51	78
1816–1835	12	65	23	83
1836–1855	15	78	7	86
1856–1875	12	65	23	96
1876–1895	9	48	43	93
1896–1915	27	23	50	87
1916–1935	24	7	69	85
1936–1955	19	6	75	87
1956–1975	20	9	71	83

*$p < .001$

paramount. By the twentieth century, however, a solid majority of the books focused on the individual and on the significant others around him, principally members of his nuclear family. Love and play, of course, are needs which involve others intimately. But strength and achievement needs also involve others if the individual shares his resources as a matter of principle.

The Value of Freedom of Choice

The third value area to be examined concerns freedom of choice for characters as expressed in the books. Freedom was an important concept at the time of the Revolution and remained an important ideal in the years to come. These books for children were looked at, then, in terms of whether or not they offered freedom to pursue goals through a variety of social institutions, whether or not the institution closest to the child, his family, was ordered democratically, and whether or not institutions were shown as rigid or as adaptable to the needs of people.

With regard to the first focus on the variety of social institutions, Table 8.6 shows that there was indeed a mix of institutions shown in the books from the eighteenth century on to the present. In early years the religious institution was paramount. Bibles and religious tomes were numerous, and the child was reminded sternly and often of his debt to God, as in *A New Hieroglypyic Bible* (printed and published by the Booksellers, 1796):

NURSERY FINGER PLAYS

XVII. — MAKING BUTTER.

Skim, skim, skim,
  With the skimmer bright;
Take the rich and yellow cream,
  Leave the milk so white.

Churn, churn, churn,
  Now 'tis churning day;
Till the cream to butter turn
  Dasher must not stay.

Ill. 38: Emilie Poulsson. *Finger Plays for Nursery and Kindergarten.*
Boston: D. Lothrop Company, 1893. [6¼″ x 9¼″]

Table 8.5. *Needs of Individual Characters as Related to Those of Other Characters in Books by Publication Date (percent)**

Publication Date	To Self Alone	To Self and Others	To Self, Others, and God	To God Alone	N
1721–1795	1	39	48	12	89
1796–1815	2	35	50	13	78
1816–1835	3	20	38	39	82
1836–1855	1	15	54	30	86
1856–1875	0	29	55	16	96
1876–1895	14	56	28	2	93
1896–1915	4	67	28	1	87
1916–1935	11	86	3	0	85
1936–1955	13	83	4	0	86
1956–1975	7	88	3	2	83

$*p<.001$

1 Peter ii.25

For ye were as Sheep going astray; but are now returned unto the Shepherd and Bishop of your souls. (p. 111)

2 John ver. 3

Grace be with you, mercy, and Peace from God the Father, and from the Lord Jesus Christ the son of the Father, in truth and love. (p. 114)

Romans XV.13

Now the God of Hope fills you with all joy and Peace in believing, that ye may abound in hope through the power of the Holy Ghost. (p. 95)

Education was also important in early years. It was seen as another social system for civilizing the child: as shown in the following excerpt concerning the advantages of education, from John Kingston's *The Reader's Cabinet* (Baltimore: John Kingston, book-seller, Samuel Magill, printer, 1809):

It brings children into order. Such is the state of human nature, that we plainly see that those who are not educated are wild and rude, and although some, after receiving a good education, are very disorderly, yet the regular discipline and instruction of schools have brought multitudes to be prudent and orderly all their lives. (pp. 1-2)

As the nineteenth century wore on the institution of the family became more and more important, and it remained important in the twentieth century. In

*Table 8.6. Social Institutions Focused upon in Books by Publication Date (percent)**

Publication Date	Political	Economic	Leisure	Family	Religious	Educational	N
1721–1795	26	29	23	32	57	43	100
1796–1815	17	22	17	42	52	24	100
1816–1835	20	16	9	52	72	19	100
1836–1855	18	24	12	65	79	15	100
1856–1875	14	31	28	82	70	18	100
1876–1895	8	24	48	88	46	7	100
1896–1915	22	30	53	74	26	9	100
1916–1935	17	36	64	59	7	3	100
1936–1955	17	34	65	74	8	4	100
1956–1975	21	34	46	76	11	11	100

N.B. The percentages per time period add up to more than 100% because most books focused on more than one social institution.

*$p < .001$

early years the emphasis was on the white, middle-class family; discussed was the need for duty and decorum, as in George Alfred's *The American Universal Spelling Book* (Staunton, Virginia: printed by Isaac Collett, 1811):

Rule 2 of behaviour to the family

2. If you have sisters or brothers, it is your duty to love them; they will love you for it, and it will be pleasing to your parents and pleasure to yourselves. (p. 157)

Sometimes duty to God came before duty to family, as in this classic scene from Martha Finley's *Elsie Dinsmore* (New York: M. W. Dodd, c.1867) in which Elsie's father asks her to play the piano and sing on Sunday; Elsie refuses to do so:

"Stay, Horace," she said, "you had better not send for her."

"May I be permitted to ask *why*, madam?" he inquired in a tone of mingled surprise and annoyance.

"Because she will not sing," answered the lady, coolly.

"Pardon me, madam, but I think she will, if I *bid* her do it," he said with flashing eyes.

"No, she will not," persisted Mrs. Dinsmore, in the same cold, quiet tone, "she will tell you she is wiser than her father, and that it would be a sin to obey him in this. Believe me, she will most assuredly defy your authority, so you had better take my advice and let her alone—thus sparing yourself the mortification of exhibiting before your guests your inability to govern your child."

Mr. Dinsmore bit his lip with vexation. (p. 237)

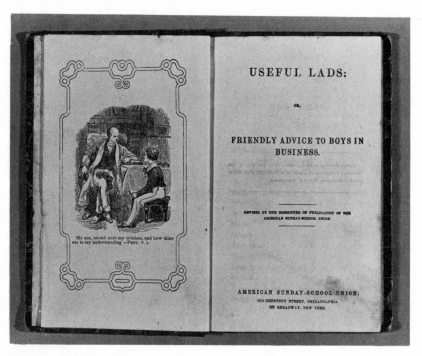

Ill. 39: *Useful Lads; or, Friendly Advice for Boys in Business.* Philadelphia: American Sunday School Union, 1847. [6¾″ x 5½″]

In the twentieth century, family life was shown with fewer restrictions and with more understanding of family dynamics. The family constellation was often described from a child's point of view, as in Paula Fox's *Blowfish Live in the Sea* (New Englewood Cliffs, New Jersey: Bradbury Press, 1970), where a young girl talks about her feelings and concerns about an older brother:

> I didn't want him to get angry at me. Sometimes I felt like one of the pillows on the living room sofa, a pillow which each member of the family punched a little as he passed by. (p. 10)

> He never took the elevator—he said it was too crowded in the morning, full of zombies going to work, and he made up a story about someone he called Gluemaster who glued people together so they could go to jobs they hated. He said the glue began to melt in the afternoon and by evening when all the people came home, they were real again, with human faces. . . . (pp. 17–18)

Not only were activities around the family more important over time, activities around leisure were also more important over time. From the middle of the nineteenth century leisure activities and peer-group relationships acquired a real legitimacy in books for children. Such books allowed child characters great freedom to explore and to be themselves; Beatrice Schenk De Regniers in *A Little House of Your Own* (New York: Harcourt, Brace, 1954) provides a good example of such liberties, in relation to secret hideaways to be by one's self, to play, to dream. Such hideaways may be under the dining room table, way up in a tree, or in a big box.

Political and economic institutions are not focused upon to a great extent over the years. When political institutions are shown, they are usually shown in the context of considerable social change—the American Revolution, the Civil War. Slower and quieter times go relatively unnoticed. Economic institutions gain in importance around 1850, when Horatio Alger and the creators of other male heroes show the male reader how to succeed in the free enterprise system. The free enterprise system remains important in about a third of the books through the twentieth century; about the middle of the twentieth century, though, it is looked upon more critically, in terms of inequities and injustices to the poor, especially the poor who are members of minority groups.

Indeed, then, there were a variety of social institutions presented to the child, those allowing the most freedom of expression (the family/leisure) becoming the most frequently mentioned in books over time. Also looked at was how the institution with which the child was primarily involved, the family, was organized. Table 8.7 shows how it was organized in terms of child care; it was organized similarly in terms of family decision-making and discipline. From the table it is evident that parents have usually shared responsibility for child care. The father has infrequently been the principal caretaker. The mother took major responsibility in a substantial number of cases in the nineteenth and early twentieth century—before, during, and after the Victorian era, the female was glorified and at the same time confined to the home to carry out her child-care role. The care of the child by others was infrequent in any period.

Finally, institutions were examined in terms of their adaptability to change, of whether or not they permitted innovation in structure and function to serve the needs of characters more effectively. Table 8-8 shows institutional orientation towards the status quo or towards change in books over time. There is a significant shift in emphasis in books over the years from an almost total focus on maintenance of the status quo, to some focus on social change. Social change was advocated for all types of institutions, but particularly for political and economic ones. In early years, such change dealt primarily with the American Revolution. Later, in the nineteenth century, it included the Civil War. In the twentieth century social change in regard to the handling of

Table 8.7. *Individual who Cares for the Child in the Institution of the Family in Books by Publication Date (percent)**

Publication Date	Principally Father	Principally Mother	Father and Mother Together	Other Relative	N
1721–1795	10	7	80	3	31
1796–1815	11	15	72	2	34
1816–1835	12	36	50	2	42
1836–1855	15	23	57	5	62
1856–1875	9	9	77	5	76
1876–1895	2	20	68	10	50
1896–1915	2	38	54	6	40
1916–1935	10	29	49	12	31
1936–1955	5	8	85	2	35
1956–1975	11	17	63	9	43

*$p < .001$

Table 8.8. *Institutional Orientation to Status Quo or to Social Change in Books by Publication Date (percent)**

Publication Date	Status Quo	Institutional Change	N
1721–1795	95	5	91
1796–1815	93	7	80
1816–1835	93	7	83
1836–1855	95	5	86
1856–1875	88	12	94
1876–1895	83	17	94
1896–1915	79	21	85
1916–1935	80	20	83
1936–1955	76	24	85
1956–1975	66	34	82

*$p. < .001$

minority-group relationships, but not in warlike terms, is addressed in superb novels about blacks, Mexican-Americans, and American Indians.

There are books, particularly of the twentieth century, concerned with social change in the institution of the family, where the need for more flexible relationships and greater understanding between family members is discussed openly. And there are also books in this century about change in patterns of leisure; Dr. Seuss provides good examples of this change as he transforms zoos and circuses and birthdays into nontraditional modes. Few changes are allowed in the structure of religious or educational institutions in books for children; in the early books such institutions were rigidly defined in terms of structure and function, in later books they are infrequently focused upon.

Satisfactions in Life

It has been demonstrated that books for children stressed to a greater degree egalitarianism, expressivity, and freedom of choice over the years. Did these books also, then, show more satisfactory outcomes over time? The answer is *no*, for even in the earliest times satisfactions were obtained in most books. Directed to children, the stories almost always ended happily ever after; even when a character died, he usually went straight to heaven and eternal bliss.

Table 8.9 shows how satisfaction of needs was obtained—through the efforts of the individual character alone, through the help of his family, other persons, and God, through God's goodness and mercy alone. The table shows a change over the years as the importance of God's help decreased and the importance of human help, including the individual's own resources, increased. In early years the child was to look for help to his elders—family members, other persons, God. Especially were they to look to God as indicated, for example, in *The Boy's own Book of Amusement and Instruction* (Providence: Cory and Daniels, 1835):

> Oh, who is that laughing, and singing, and skipping about so
> merrily? It is little Flora; the happiest child almost in all the city.
> Flora always looks good humored; and that is the reason we all love
> her. She looks very pretty; and that is because she is good.
>   "God, our Heavenly Father, gave Flora this improvable mind,
> and gave her too all else that makes her happy. This good God will
> love my child if she tries to do well; and He will give her more and
> more knowledge."

Table 8.9. Satisfaction of Needs, by the Individual Help Involved, in Books by Publication Date (percent)*

Publication Date	Only the Character in question	Combination of Family and Others	Combination of Family, Others, God	Only God	N
1721–1795	12	11	43	34	83
1796–1815	4	25	43	28	75
1816–1835	5	18	29	48	80
1836–1855	1	11	54	34	85
1856–1875	7	20	52	21	94
1876–1895	12	49	34	5	82
1896–1915	26	35	31	8	86
1916–1935	35	41	15	9	83
1936–1955	26	48	16	9	83
1956–1975	28	46	13	13	79

*p. < .001

Ill. 40: William Steig. *Farmer Palmer's Ride*. New York: Farrar, Straus and Giroux, 1974. [8¾'' x 10½'']

Later, children were to look to the family for support and satisfaction. William Steig's *Farmer P.almer's Ride* (1974) concerns Farmer Palmer's strenuous ride to market and back in his wagon pulled by his ass, Ebenezer. Though the ride to market is uneventful, the ride home involves many mishaps. Despite thunder and rain, a broken wagon, and Ebenezer's sprained hock, Farmer Palmer does manage to arrive back home, exhausted. His family is out to greet him with hugs and kisses, laughter and joy, for they have worried about him and are grateful for his safe return.

Also examined in terms of satisfaction in life was the threat of death in books. The spectre of death was indeed frequently found in books of the eighteenth and nineteenth century. (See Table 8.10.) The lengthy discussions early on of the deaths of pious children served two purposes: to impress upon the child the possibility, yea the probability, of early death and to encourage him to perform acts defined as pleasing to God, since he was likely to meet God in person soon. In the twentieth century death is found less often in books and is brought up for other reasons: to describe the social isolation of the old, particularly the disabled old nearing death, and to describe the life cycle, with death as much a part of the continuum as birth.

Through the years, then, books have changed in content, but similarities are apparent as well. In terms of egalitarianism, minority characters appear more often in the twentieth century as central figures and with status equal to whites. Very obvious sex stereotyping diminishes substantially over the years; women continue, nevertheless, to do less exciting and demanding tasks up to the present. Young children are focused upon more often in books over time, especially after the beginning of the nineteenth century. And, finally, differentiation of characters by social status becomes less prominent in the twentieth century; poverty is no longer looked upon as the fault of the individual but as the fault of the social system and its opportunity structure.

Table 8.10. The Presence of Death in Books by Publication Date (percent) *

Publication Date	Present	Absent		N
1721–1795	76	24	،	100
1796–1815	74	26		100
1816–1835	69	31		100
1836–1855	73	27		100
1856–1875	66	34		100
1876–1895	49	51		100
1896–1915	62	38		100
1916–1935	26	74		100
1936–1955	18	82		100
1956–1975	27	73		100

*p. < .001

The value of self-expression increased as nineteenth- and particularly twentieth-century books focused on human needs for love and play and self-actualization. More and more satisfactions of needs were obtained through the character's own resources; the character was seen as capable and willing. Finally, such needs related more and more to the character himself and his relationships to significant others rather than to an unknown God and his restrictive proscriptions.

Characters in books always had freedom to explore goals through a variety of social institutions. In early years religious and educational institutions were most important, and they were narrowly structured. Later, leisure and family institutions were stressed,and they became less and less structured. Within the institution closest to the child, his family, mother and father tended to participate together in child care from earliest times. In the twentieth century social institutions were presented as less rigid, closed structures than they were formerly, and social change was advocated to a significant degree.

There are, then, real shifts in books for children to more humanitarian values. All peoples, not just white Protestants, are much more in evidence now. Individual economic success is considered less important, and self-expression is considered more important. The present-day individual is often encouraged to change institutions to fit his need rather than just to accept them.

These findings from books for children parallel recent studies of attitudes and values of young people in our society. Lystad [7], in a study of young adults in the early 1970's, found them very concerned with equality, especially as regards equality of opportunity for the poor and for minorities. These individuals were not overly worried about achievement, about choosing traditional occupations of high incomes and prestige; they were, instead, interested in occupations which allowed creative expression and free time to do their own thing. They were involved with all social institutions, but particularly those of leisure and the family. And they were involved with such institutions critically—expecting to change them as they needed changing.

Other researchers provide similar findings on attitudes and values of adolescents and young adults of the 1960's and 1970's (these individuals were reading the children's books of the 1940's and 1950's). With regard to the value of equality, Keniston [5] found among youth of socially fortunate upbringings an unusual capacity for nurturent identification, for empathy and sympathy with the underdog. Flacks [2] also found among advantaged youth focus on such themes as egalitarianism and populism.

In terms of the value of self-expression, Winthrop [9] reported among youth less concern with competition, success, and power, and more with the establishing of personal identity and authentic relationships with other persons. Whittaker [8] found an emphasis on self-expression, doing one's own thing as a legitimate and important activity in its own right.

Freedom of choice is extolled, as Carey [1] points out, in the words of the popular songs of the young. Keniston [4, 5] and Lipset [6] have documented their alienation from traditional institutions and their commitment to political and economic change. Greeley [3] has shown their revitalized interest in religion, with an emphasis on individual rather than on institutional behaviors.

Along with these changing social values there is changing public concern now with the child and his family. Major child and family advocacy groups have addressed needs for public support for the poorest families, social services for all families, programs for child health and safety, and opportunities for parents to combine jobs and parenthood. The next chapter will discuss changing views of the child and of how the child should be cared for, as indicated by books for children and also, briefly, as indicated in social programs for children that are presently being developed and debated.

References

1. Carey, James. "The Ideology of Autonomy in Popular Lyrics: A Content Analysis." *Psychiatry* 32 (1969): 150–164.
2. Flacks, Richard. "The Liberated Generation: An Exploration of the Roots of Student Protest." *Journal of Social Issues* 23 (1967): 52–75.
3. Greeley, Andrew. "There's a New-time Religion on Campus." *New York Times Magazine,* June 1, 1969.
4. Keniston, Kenneth. *The Uncommitted: Alienated Youth in American Society.* New York: Harcourt, Brace and World, 1965.
5. Keniston, Kenneth. "The Sources of Student Dissent." *Journal of Social Issues* 23 (1967): 180–137.
6. Lipset, Seymour, and Altbach, Philip. "United States Campus Alienation." *New Society* 8(206) (1966): 361–463.
7. Lystad, Mary. *As They See It: Changing Values of College Youth.* Cambridge, Massachusetts: Schenkman Publishing Company, 1973.
8. Whittaker, David, and Watts, William. "Personality Characteristics of a Nonconformist Youth Subculture." *Journal of Social Issues* 25 (1969): 65–89.
9. Winthrop, Henry. "The Alienation of Post-industrial Man." *Midwest Quarterly,* 9 (1968): 121–138.

Chapter 9

Changing Views of Children and of Socialization

Just as there were, in books over the years, changes in social values, there were changes in views of children and of the ways in which they should be socialized. The topics focused upon in this chapter are changes in the importance given to the child as a child, the time orientation provided the child, the social responsibility placed upon the child, the ways in which he or she was urged to carry out such responsibility, and, finally, the self-esteem afforded the child.

The importance given to the child increased over the centuries. In the eighteenth century adults made up the majority of main characters in books for children. They were the role models, the examples of excellence. Later the child achieved center stage—primarily the young child, with adolescents only occasionally starred. Table 9.1 shows the shift in emphasis on main characters over time. Until the late 1700's the child was usually described in texts as an imperfect adult, one who had not yet learned to be quiet and neat and clean and prompt and task oriented. Illustrations furthermore showed the child in adult clothing—a kind of uncomfortable looking midget. Books of politeness and virtue were plentiful, and the same amount of politeness and virtue were required of the child as of the adult.

The 1800's showed a growing interest in adolescent characters. Adolescents during this time period were indeed entering adult roles—boys went to work on the farm or in town as factory workers, apprentices, or clerks. In addition to Horatio Alger, several other authors wrote how-to-succeed series for boys. Girls in adolescence performed household chores with skill and with diligence.

By the 1900's the child as a dirty, fun-loving, noisy creature came to the fore. Children and their dogs, their friends and neighbors, were shown frequently in books on small-town life. Later in the century ethnic differences in how children experienced life were brought out, and values and attitudes of black children, Mexican-American children, and American Indian children were shown.

As the child's importance grew, and as the child gained acceptance as a child rather than as a prospective adult, the time orientation provided him changed

Table 9.1. Main Characters in Books by Publication Date (percent)*

Publication Date	Child	Adolescent	Adult	N
1721–1795	28	0	72	53
1796–1815	46	0	54	56
1816–1835	49	2	49	66
1836–1855	47	1	52	69
1856–1875	34	27	39	91
1876–1895	46	18	36	83
1896–1915	33	35	32	79
1916–1935	55	15	30	66
1936–1955	61	5	34	66
1956–1975	59	13	28	71

*p<.001

from an emphasis on the future, on adult achievement roles in this life and the next, to an emphasis on the present, on love and on play, as well as achievement, now. Nowhere is this difference clearer than in the works of Dr. Mather and Dr. Seuss. Dr. Mather looked at children not as children, not even as adults, but as servants of the Lord. They were, thus, passing through this world on their journey to the next, as shown in Mather's "A Token for the Children of New-England," an addition to James Janeway's *A Token for Children* (Boston: Printed and Sold by Z. Fowle, 1771):

> If the Children of New-England should not with an Early Piety, set themselves to Know and Serve the Lord Jesus Christ, the God of their Fathers, they will be condemned, not only by the Examples of pious Children in other Parts of the World, the publish'd and printed Accounts whereof have been brought over hither; but there have been Exemplary Children in the Midst of New-England itself, that will rise up against them for their Condemnation. It would be a very profitable Thing to our Children, and highly acceptable to all the godly Parents of the Children, if, in Imitation of the excellent Janeway's Token for Children, there were made a true Collection of notable Things, exemplified in the Lives and Deaths of many among us, whose Childhood hath been signalized for what is virtuous and laudable. (pp. 107-108)

At the other end of the two-hundred-year time spectrum, the child is seen as a child. He is urged, not to be mindful of life after death, but to be mindful of life right now. He is urged to do his own thing, to enjoy, as in Dr. Seuss's *Happy Birthday to You* (New York: Random House, 1959):

> I wish we could do what they do in Katroo.
> They sure know how to say "Happy Birthday to You!"

In Katroo, every year, on the day you were born
They start the day right in the bright early morn
When the Birthday Honk-Honker hikes high up Mt. Zorn
And lets loose a big blast on the big Birthday Horn . . .

The Great Birthday Bird!
And, so far as I know,
Katroo is the only place Birthday Birds grow . . .
And whether your name is Pete, Polly or Paul,
When your birthday comes round, he's in charge of it all . . .

"Today," laughs the Bird, "eat whatever you want.
Today no one tells you you cawnt or you shawnt.
And, today, you don't have to be tidy or neat.
If you wish, you may eat with both hands and both feet.
So get in there and munch. Have a big munch-er-oo!
Today is your birthday! *Today you are you!* . . .

Come on! Open your mouth and sound off at the sky!
Shout loud at the top of your voice, "I AM I!
ME
I AM I!
And I may not know why
But I know that I like it.
Three cheers! I AM I!"

Table 9-2 shows the time orientation provided characters in books over the years. There is a significant shift in focus, from an early emphasis on delayed gratification and the future, particularly during the era of the Sunday school presses, to a later emphasis, from 1875 on, toward immediate gratification and the present. By the beginning of the twentieth century persons were no longer born to die, but to live—with spirit and with imagination. As the twentieth century continued, book characters were provided more and more opportunities to pay attention to themselves, to their day-to-day activities and needs. Instead of didactic catechisms describing the lives of saints and martyrs, there were simple stories of ordinary people doing ordinary things—learning how to whistle, jumping rope, climbing trees, discovering their world.

Not only were later books for children focused to a greater extent on activities of the present, they were also focused to a greater extent on responsibility to oneself and to significant others. Table 9.3 gives the direction of social responsibility placed on characters over the years.

More and more characters in books for children were allowed to look inward to their own needs and desires as well as to pay attention to the social needs of others, particularly others within the family group. God, once the major focus of social responsibility, became far less important. God was not forgotten, to be

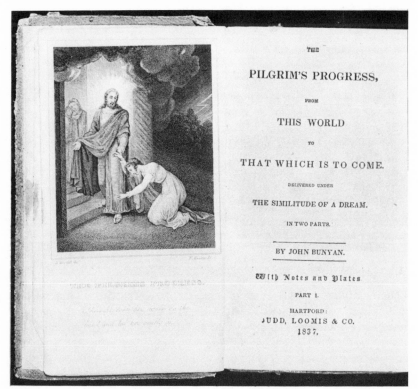

Ill. 41: John Bunyan. *The Pilgrim's Progress.* Hartford: Judd, Loomis and Company, 1837. [5½'' x 5'']

Table 9.2. Time Orientation of Characters in Books by Publication Date (percent) *

Publication Date	Past	Present	Future	N
1721–1795	1	43	56	88
1796–1815	2	53	45	79
1816–1835	1	21	78	83
1836–1855	0	30	70	77
1856–1875	0	47	53	92
1876–1895	0	63	37	93
1896–1915	0	81	19	80
1916–1935	0	95	5	84
1936–1955	0	99	1	87
1956–1975	1	96	3	78

*$p < .001$

Table 9.3. Social Responsibilities of Characters in Books by Publication Date (percent)*

Publication Date	Oneself	Others	Combination of Others and God	God	N
1721–1795	3	6	62	29	78
1796–1815	9	20	40	31	54
1816–1835	11	11	24	54	65
1836–1855	6	8	30	56	53
1856–1875	14	11	47	28	80
1876–1895	14	23	59	4	70
1896–1915	17	17	62	4	86
1916–1935	16	52	31	1	83
1936–1955	18	52	30	0	83
1956–1975	23	52	23	2	73

*$p < .001$

sure, but when He appeared in later books, He reinforced responsibility to His children, that is, to other humans.

The family group changed over the years. In earliest years large nuclear families were often depicted—with a distinguished father, serene mother, sometimes a grandparent or grandaunt, and many offspring interacting in the parlor. The roles of parents and children were formal and inflexible, as shown in this description of proper child behavior in the home (*The Child's Spelling Book* [Hartford: printed by John Babcock, 1800]):

1. Make a bow always when you come home, and be instantly uncovered.

2. Be never covered at home, especially before thy parents or strangers.

3. If thou art going to speak to thy parents, and see them engaged in discourse with company, draw back and leave thy business until afterwards; but if thou must speak, be sure to whisper.

4. Never speak to thy parents without some mark of respect, viz. sir, madam, &c, according to their quality.

5. Dispute not, nor delay to obey thy parents' command.

6. Come not into the room where thy parents are with strangers, unless thou art called.

7. Quarrel not nor contend with thy brethren or sisters, but live in love, peace and unity.

8. Insult not, but be courteous towards the servants.

9. Grumble not, nor be discontented at any thing thy parents appoint, speak or do.

10. Bear with meekness and patience, and without murmuring or sullenness, thy parents' reproofs or corrections; nay, though it should happen that they be causeless and undeserved. (pp. 103-104).

The consequences of *not* doing such are seen in works such as Lucy Watkins' *Sophy, or, The Punishment of Idleness and Disobedience* (1819) which concerns a child who ignores the advice of her mother, runs away from home, is taken advantage of by others and finally dies of hunger. In the Victorian era the scene was more of the same white, middle-class tradition, with considerable interaction between family members, and considerable restrictions on children. Rebecca Clark's *Little Prudy* is a sterling example (*Little Prudy*, by Sophie May, pseud. [Boston: Lee and Shepard, 1864]):

"No, my dears," said grandma, "I couldn't consent to let you go strawberrying 'up by the Pines' as you call it. It is Mr. Judkin's mowing-field."

"But, grandma," said Grace, "Johnny Gordon went there yesterday; and there wan't any fuss about it."

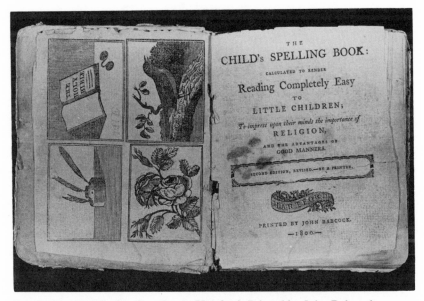

Ill. 42: *The Child's Spelling Book*. Hartford: Printed by John Babcock, 1800. [7¼'' x 4¾'']

"Then you may be sure Mr. Judkins did not know it," said grandma. "If he should catch any children in his field, he would be sure to given them a severe scolding."

"Besides," chimed in Aunt Madge, "Prudy isn't fit to walk so far—she isn't very well."

"No, she is quite out of sorts," said grandma. "So if you must go somewhere, you may take your little baskets and go out in the meadow on the other side of the cornfield. Only take good care of Prudy; now remember."

"Grandma always says that over," said Susy, as the three children were on their way to the meadow; "and Aunt Madge always says it too—'take care of Prudy!' As if she were a little baby."

"That is all because she cries so much, I presume," said Grace, looking at poor Prudy rather sternly. "I did hope, Susy, that when Horace went down to the 'crick' fishing, you and I might go off by ourselves, and have a nice time for once. But here is 'ittle Pitcher' right at our heels. We never can have any peace. Little Miss Somebody thinks she must follow, of course."

"Yes, that's the way it is," said Susy. "Some folks are always round, you know."

"Now, Susy," said Prudy, forcing back her tears as well as she could, "I guess you don't love your little sister, or you wouldn't talk that way to me."

They gathered strawberries for a while in silence, Prudy picking more leaves than berries, and sometimes, in her haste to keep up with the others, pulling up grass by the roots. (pp. 44-47)

Only in recent years have the black family and the single-parent family been described with any frequency. When they are described, they are described with honesty and compassion and joy, as in Lucille Clifton's *Some of the Days of Everett Anderson* (1970) and its sequels. Everett Anderson is black and he lives with his working mother in a tall apartment building. He sometimes wishes his father were there too. But he is a boy full of joy and of tricks and he has a mother who loves and cares—and that is enough for comfort and laughter.

In carrying out family and other primary group roles, characters in books for children throughout the years generally conformed to well-established, traditional norms. As Table 9.4 shows, until the end of the nineteenth century over half of the books stressed conformity to rules and regulations set forward by God and by adults. Conformity to adult norms alone become very important only at the beginning of the twentieth century. In the twentieth century, also, more characters showed self-direction and innovation in carrying out their roles.

Conformity to supernatural norms was expressed most clearly in early-

*Table 9.4. Manner in which Needs are Met in Books by Publication Date (percent)**

Publication Date	Self-Direction	Conformity to Adult Norms	Conformity to Adult and Supernatural Norms	Conformity to Supernatural Norms	N
1721–1795	3	41	34	22	91
1796–1815	10	21	46	23	79
1816–1835	10	17	31	42	83
1836–1855	3	12	44	41	83
1856–1875	11	25	41	23	95
1876–1895	17	39	41	3	94
1896–1915	22	53	21	4	85
1916–1935	19	61	3	17	83
1936–1955	24	63	1	12	85
1956–1975	32	54	3	11	82

*p<.001

nineteenth-century books of the American Sunday School Union. Rules for both religious and social behavior, particularly temperance behavior, were presented, and God's will was cited as the sole reason for attending to them. A typical example is found in *The Still and the Spring* (Philadelphia: American Sunday School Union, c.1825):

> "What is that running out of the hill? It does not look like rum."—"No, my child, it is pure, sweet water. It flows out of the side of the rock. That is a spring or fountain. See how it sparkles in the sun as it dashes into the stone basin."—"May I drink some of it?"—"Yes, it will do you good this warm day. That is the best liquor in the world. You need not be afraid to drink it. Taste how cool it is. It is as clear as crystal. The sheep, and cows, and birds, and insects, all come here to drink. This never makes any one drunk. The blessed Creator gives it to us in abundance. . . .
>
> "Remember this, that you must never drink any thing which will make you drunk. Drunkards are great sinners, and, if they do not repent and let their liquor alone, they must perish forever. If you never taste these bad drinks, you will never be a drunkard."—"Father, I am determined that I will never drink a drop of them. I will love the clear, pure spring, and keep away from the poisonous still." (pp. 6-8)

The need to conform to adult norms around social relationships was shown in the many nineteenth-century discourses on politeness and model behavior, a direct holdover from class-oriented societies in Britain and Europe. An illustration is taken from *The Daisy; or, Cautionary Stories in Verse, Adapted to the Ideas of Children from Four-to-eight Years Old* (Philadelphia: Henry F. Anners, 1839) which cautions:

> Good little boys should never say,
> "I will," and "Give me these;"
> O, no! that never is the way,
> But, "Mother, if you please."
>
> And "If you please," to sister Ann
> Good boys to say are ready;
> And "Yes, Sir," to a gentlemen,
> And "Yes, Ma'am to a lady.

In the latter half of the nineteenth century and certainly in the twentieth, a greater number of books for children allowed characters self-direction and creativity in meeting their own needs; this was expecially true of books focusing on male characters. In the nineteenth century, William T. Adams wrote many books about boys who had high adventures here and abroad. Rebecca Clark's works about girls, on the other hand, allowed them to go out West but were still quite circumspect in approach.

In the twentieth century Eleanor Estes' series of stories on the Pye family, who explored their own neighborhood with energy and ingenuity, were instantly popular. More recently, innovative modes of survival are frequent in books focusing on minority characters struggling to overcome discrimination and deprivation. Virginia Hamilton's books all focus on black survival in a white world. Hamilton's *The Planet of Junior Brown* tells the story of Junior Brown, a 300-pound musical prodigy with a neurotic, overprotective mother, and Buddy Clark, a loner who lives by his wits because he has no family. The two have been truant from their eighth grade classroom all semester; most of the time they have hidden in the school building in a secret cellar room, behind a false wall, where Mr. Pool, the janitor, has made a model of the solar system. Their self-direction, involving intelligence and wit, helps to overcome a barren, punitive environment.

As time progressed, more books for children depicted main characters with strong feelings of self-esteem and of competence to perform on their own. Table 9.5 shows how characters viewed themselves in books over two hundred years. Early books of the eighteenth and most of the nineteenth century emphasized God as the main provider of strength and competence. *The New England Primer* (New Haven, Published by S. Babcock, c.1830) was one of a plethora of books which took the view that man was very much in need of God's help:

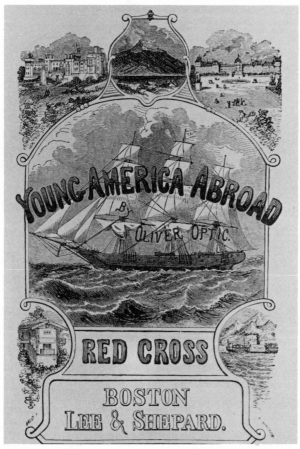

Ill. 43: William T. Adams. *Young America Abroad.* Boston: Lee and Shepard, 1867. [4¼″ x 6¾″]

Q. What doth God require of us that we may escape His wrath and curse due us for sin?

A. To escape the wrath and curse of God due to us for sin, God requireth of us faith in Jesus Christ, repentance unto life, with the diligent use of all the outward means whereby Christ communicateth to us the benefits of redemption.

Q. What is faith in Jesus Christ?

A. Faith in Jesus Christ is a saving grace whereby we receive and rest upon Him alone for salvation, as he is offered to us in the gospel. (pp. 52-93)

THE PIGEON PIE.

Page 60.

Ill. 44: Rebecca Clark. *Dotty Dimple out West*. Boston: Lothrop, Lee and Shepard Company, 1868. [4½'' x 6½'']

Books of the later part of the nineteenth century emphasized human social groups, particularly the family group, as the source of support and nurture. The family provided emotional support, physical sustenance, and guidance in work and play. Child characters in books looked homeward. Even at the beginning of the twentieth century Frank Baum's Dorothy, in between fabulous adventures down the yellow brick road, kept saying she wanted to go home again.

Ill. 45: Eleanor Estes. *Ginger Pye*. New York: Harcourt, Brace, 1951. [5″ x 4¾″]

In the late nineteenth and in the twentieth century a significant number of books featured characters with high self-esteem and with high competency to go off on their own. An example in nineteenth-century books is Mark Twain's Tom Sawyer, a young adolescent who was indeed assured and creative, in spite of occasional setbacks. This passage, concerning Tom's amorous adventures, serves to illustrate (*The Adventures of Tom Sawyer*, 1876):

> About half past nine or ten o'clock he came along the deserted
> street to where the Adored Unknown lived; he paused a moment; no
> sound fell upon his listening ear; a candle was casting a dull glow
> upon the curtain of a second-story window. Was the sacred presence
> there? He climbed the fence, threaded his stealthy way through the
> plants, till he stood under that window; he looked up at it long, and

Table 9.5. *Main Characters View of Self in Books by Publication Date (percent)* *

Publication Date	Competent on his own	Competent but needs help of Other Persons	Competent but needs help of Other Persons and God	Competent but needs help of God	N
1721–1795	6	28	19	47	68
1796–1815	2	33	33	32	72
1816–1835	4	19	28	49	79
1836–1855	1	12	54	33	84
1856–1875	7	19	52	22	94
1876–1895	12	48	35	5	82
1896–1915	26	35	31	8	86
1916–1935	35	41	14	10	83
1936–1955	25	48	16	11	82
1956–1975	28	47	12	13	79

*p<.001

with emotion; then he laid him down on the ground under it, disposing himself upon his back, with his hands clasped upon his breast and holding his poor wilted flower. And thus he would die—out in the cold world, with no shelter over his homeless head, no friendly hand to wipe the death damps from his brow, no loving face to bend pityingly over him when the great agony came. And thus she would see him when she looked out upon the glad morning, and oh! would she drop one little tear upon his poor, lifeless form, would she heave one little sigh to see a bright young life so rudely blighted, so untimely cut down?

The window went up, a maidservant's discordant voice profaned the holy calm, and a deluge of water drenched the prone martyr's remains!

The strangling hero sprang up with a relieving snort. There was a whiz as of a missile in the air, mingled with the murmur of a curse, a sound as of shivering glass followed, and a small, vague form went over the fence and shot away in the gloom. (pp. 40-41)

An example of a twentieth-century child character with aspirations and ability appears in Maurice Sendak's *The Sign on Rosie's Door* (1960). Rosie, the heroine, stages and directs spellbinding variety shows for the neighbor children. Included in her productions are Arabian dancing girls, lovely lady singers and other performers of great talent. The neighbor children both participate and enjoy.

These changing views towards children in books for the young—allowing them more importance, more self-determination, and more self-esteem—have their parallels in changing public attitude and debate around children. There are today numerous advocacy groups on national, state, and local levels which stress the fundamental worth of the child and his family, and which argue for their needs as well as their autonomy. On the national level, a National Academy of Sciences Report, *Toward a National Policy for Children and Families* [6], and the first report of the Carnegie Council on Children, *All our Children: The American Family under Pressure* [5], resulted in a public-policy document, *The Children's Political Checklist* [2]. This document focuses on the child and his primary support groups, and it puts forth specific goals for a new child-and-family policy for the nation (Education Commission of the States, et al., *The Children's Political Checklist* [Denver: Education Commission of the States, 1977]):

We believe the goals of a new child and family policy should be:

1. to provide maximum choice for parents about the ways they can bring up their children;

2. to provide maximum information to all parents so that these choices will be informed ones;

3. to keep families together and interdependent in times of crisis;

4. to provide a range of family support services which are accessible to all families equitably;

5. to assure maximum parent participation and authority in planning and implementing family services;

6. to provide for responsible community-based evaluation of public and private programs;

7. to recognize and reinforce diversity and pluralism in family life and values, responding to economic and social changes that affect family life;

8. to be sure that all policies have been considered in the light of the cost of doing nothing, the cost of alternatives, and long-term consequences.

Most of all, we believe that the needs of young children should always be considered in the context of the needs of their families—and, in particular, their parents. There is a place for the traditional belief that parents can, should and will sacrifice their own needs in order to meet the present and future needs of their children. At the same time, we recognize that it is the physical and mental well-being of parents that creates the family climate which, in turn,

nurtures the development of young children. It cannot be too carefully guarded.

As a nation, we are currently undergoing a re-examination of our
social policies for families and children. We have a heritage of
previous efforts, some of which have worked, some of which have
not, all of which, in some way, have shaped our current attitude. We
do not have a consensus but we do have an exciting moment in our
social history where there is support for a new surge of creativity in
social policy development. A new national debate begins. The most
important thing we can do for our children is to get involved in that
debate—in essence, to get involved in the political process, the
politics of children. We can, through joint discussion and action,
provide a clearer demand for public policies for children and their
families, and state what those policies should be. We hope that this
book provides a basis for accelerating that demand and enhancing
your informed participation. (p. 36)

In addition to changes in public attitudes on the importance of children there
are changes in public attitudes on how to socialize children. With regard to a
time orientation for the child, current child-care literature focuses on present
needs, particularly for love and affection, rather than on future needs, for
achievement in later life or in another life. Fraiberg [3] and others emphasize
the importance of the mother-child bond for developing healthy, secure human
beings. Educational opportunities for the young child, especially the poor, the
minority, the handicapped child, are of major concern now (see Bell [1] for an
overview of changes in American education). Child labor, on the other hand, is
obsolete, and the child is not encouraged to work at all, as Goldstein [4]
indicates, until late teenage or sometimes late twenties.

The social responsibility placed upon the child in the twentieth century is far
less directed towards God and far more towards others, particularly others in
the family. Solnit [9] points out that, with improved nutrition and medical care,
children's survival and development to adulthood within the family became
more common. Now parents can invest more in each child as a carrier of their
hopes for the future, and consequently they could ask for more in return from
the child. Norton and Glick [7] show the long-term trend towards the small
family, both in terms of fewer families with large numbers of children in the
home and in terms of the recent rise of single-parent families. The geographic
isolation of these nuclear families from relatives makes family members more
interdependent.

The ways in which a child is urged to carry out family and other responsibilities have also changed over time. Conformity to adult norms, particularly
family norms, is still encouraged. With the different family migrations of this
country over the years, many different family norms have been and continue to

be observed (see Sudia [10] for trend data). Self-determination in carrying out responsibility has gained in importance in the last several decades, partly because children are left alone more as mothers enter the work place. Self-determination is particularly encouraged in the area of play and recreation, which is viewed now as critical to the mental and physical health needs of the child. Recreation is looked upon more and more, Reynolds [8] points out, as an integral part of child and youth development.

Finally, the desire of the public to provide the child with self-esteem is found in increased public pressure for Federal programs related to child health and child development. Of particular concern are programs for the poor child, who is often a member of a minority, and the physically handicapped child, to afford him adequate skills and opportunities so that he will feel good about himself. The Federal government's participation in the field of child health care stems only from the early twentieth century, but interests and activities in this area have increased over the years (see Waserman [11]). In 1909 the first White House Conference on Children was called by President Theodore Roosevelt. As a result of the recommendations of this conference, the Children's Bureau was established in 1912 for the purpose of investigating and reporting upon matters relative to the welfare of children among all social classes. The Children's Bureau, by publicizing needs of children related to health care, helped to make possible the passage in 1921 of the Sheppard-Towner Act for the Promotion of the Welfare and Hygiene of Maternity and Infancy; this act, in effect until 1929, established a precedent for Federal grants-in-aid to states for child and adult health programs. The Social Security Act of 1935 directly affected child health through its Title V provision for extensive programs for maternity care and care of infants and children, as well as for a full range of medical services for handicapped children. The Social Security Act continues to be an active force in the area of children's health. In 1962 the National Institute of Child Health and Human Development was established as a part of the National Institutes of Health to conduct and support research and training relative to maternal health and human development. And still another major Federal thrust is Head Start, the program for economically disadvantaged preschool children, launched in 1965 by the Office of Economic Opportunity. Head Start's comprehensive health care program provides medical, dental, mental health, and nutritional services for hundreds of thousands of children a year.

This country's bicentennial saw further public attention devoted to the child and his needs. In 1976 several reviews of the changes that have occurred in family life, child care, and child welfare services in this country over two hundred years were published; these documents, a number of which have been cited in this brief overview, evoked more public discussion and debate. But focus on the child did not end at the end of that year. Soon afterwards preparations began for a White House Conference on Families and another

White House Conference on Children and Youth, and public concern about children's needs and social policies to affect these needs continues. The commitment remains.

References

1. Bell, T. H., compiler. *A Nation of Learners*. Washington, D.C.: U.S. Government Printing Office, 1976.
2. Education Commission of the States, et al. *The Children's Political Checklist*. Denver: Education Commission of the States, 1977.
3. Fraiberg, Selma. *Every Child's Birthright: In Defense of Mothering*. New York: Basic Books, 1977.
4. Goldstein, Harold. "Child Labor in America's History." *Children Today* 5(3) (1976): 30-35.
5. Keniston, Kenneth, et al. *All Our Children: The American Family Under Pressure*. New York: Harcourt, Brace and Janovich, 1977.
6. National Research Council. *Toward a National Policy for Children and Families*. Washington, D.C.: National Academy of Sciences, 1976.
7. Norton, Arthur, and Glick, Paul C. "Changes in American Family Life." *Children Today*, 5(3)(1976):2-4, 44.
8. Reynolds, Jean. "Two Hundred Years of Children's Recreation." In *Two Hundred Years of Children*, edited by Edith H. Grotberg. Washington, D. C.: U. S. Department of Health, Education, and Welfare, DHEW Publication No. (OHD) 77-30103, 285-321, 1977.
9. Solnit, Albert. "Changing Psychological Perspectives About Children and Their Families." *Children Today*, 5(3) (1976):5-9, 43.
10. Sudia, Cecelia. "Historical Trends in American Family Behavior." In *Two Hundred Years of Children*, edited by Edith H. Grotberg. Washington, D.C.: U.S. Department of Health, Education, and Welfare, DHEW Publication No. (OHD) 77-30103, 41-59, 1977.
11. Waserman, Manfred. "An Overview of Child Health Care in America." *Children Today*, 5(3) (1976):24-29, 44.

Chapter 10

Into the Third Century

Predictions are indeed hazardous. It is difficult enough to interpret the important issues of the present, about which something is known, let alone speculate on the important issues of the future, about which nothing is known for sure. But predictions evoke ideas and plans which are necessary in providing groundwork for optimal developments in the future.

A brief review of the history and current trends in books for children in other countries may facilitate the prediction of new directions in this country. Books for children from Great Britain, Western Europe, the Soviet Union, and the People's Republic of China seem useful. The former two areas are very like America's in social values and political structure, the latter two are less so in these matters.

As mentioned earlier, eighteenth-century books in Britain and Europe produced numerous editions of Catechisms and Bibles; many are found in the Library of Congress collections. For example:

> Crouch, Nathaniel, *Youth's Divine Pastime. Part II. Containing Near Forty More Remarkable Scripture Histories, with Spiritual Songs and Hymns of Prayer and Praise. Turn'd into English Verse.* 6th ed., London, C. Hitch, 1749.

> Meilan, Mark Anthony, *Sermons for Children: Being a Course of Fifty-two, on Subjects, Suited to their Tender Age, and in a Style Adapted to an Understanding of the Rising Generation. Being an Attempt to Counsel and Improve the Heart, by Occupying the Imagination, with a Hymn Annexed to each Discourse.* London, Printed for T. Hockham and T. Longham, 1789.

> *History of the Bible. An Abridgment of the History of the Holy Bible.* Glasgow: Printed by J. and W. Roberts, 1795.

Britain also published a goodly number of words of instruction on behavior, spelling, reading, and science which came to America. Among others:

> *Youthful Portraits; or, Sketches of the Passions: Exemplifying the*

Dignity, and Inculcating the Advantages of Virtue. London: Printed for E. Newbery, 1796.

The Royal Primer: Or, An Easy and Pleasant Guide to the Art of Reading. Authoriz'd by His Majesty King George II. To be used throughout His Majesty's dominions. Adorned with cuts. London: Printed for J. Newberry, at the Bible and Sun, in St. Paul's Church-yard, 1760.

Turner, Richard. *A New and Easy Introduction to Universal Geography. In a Series of Letters to a Youth at School.* Illustrated with copper-plates. The 4th ed., considerably enl. Dublin. Printed by P. Byrne, 1787.

So, too, were some books of amusement published in eighteenth-century Britain and Europe and imported to the New World. Thus:

Defoe, Daniel. *The Wonderful Life and most Surprising Adventures of Robinson Crusoe of York, Mariner, Containing a Full and Particular Account.* Faithfully epitomized from the three volumes, and adorned with cuts suited to the most remarkable stories. Glasgow, R. Smith, 1762.

Dodsley, Robert. *Dodsley's Select Fables of Aesop and other Fabulists.* Dublin, Printed for T. and J. Whitehouse, 1763.

Perrault, Charles. *Histories or Tales of Past Time, Told by Mother Goose, with Morals Written in French by M. Perrault and Englished by G. M. Gen.* 8th edition. Salisbury, Printed and sold by Collins and Johnson, 1780.

In the beginning of the nineteenth century in Britain and Europe didacticism declined in strength, and the fairy story gained in respectability. In Germany folk literature took hold with the publication of tales by Christopher von Schmid, Johann Peter Hebel, the Brothers Grimm, and others; in Denmark and Western Europe the works of Hans Christian Anderson reached larger and larger audiences. Poetry for children appeared in England, notably Ann and Jane Taylor's collection, *Original Poems for Infant Minds* (1804), and William Roscoe's *The Butterfly's Ball* (1807). Later in Germany Dr. Henreich Hoffman's comic *Struwwelpeter* (1845) arrived, and frivolity in England became truly acceptable with Edward Lear's *A Book of Nonsense* (1846) and Lewis Carroll's *Alice in Wonderland* (1865). In the late 1800's books from America by James Fenimore Cooper, Harriet Beecher Stowe, Mark Twain, and Joel Chandler Harris became known throughout Europe and were popular for their specifically American characterizations.

By the twentieth century in Britain and Europe there were more and more books whose purpose was either amusement or understanding, and there was increasing exchange of books across the Atlantic. Many translations of foreign-language books now receive simultaneous publication in England and America now, and talented writers and artists from England and Europe have come to America to live and to work, including Roger Duvoisin, Hugh Lofting, Beni Montresor, and Feodor Rojankovsky. Conversely, a number of American writers and artists have been well received abroad—among them Frank Baum, Walt Disney, and Laura Ingalls Wilder. Literary linkages between the countries thus remains strong. For further discussion of books for children published in Britain and in Europe over the years, see Haviland [2,3], Hürlimann, [4,5] and St. John [10]; information on specific authors and artists can be found in Doyle [1], Kingman [6] and Mahoney-Miller [7,8].

Modern British and European books for children show social values similar to those of modern American books for children. Egalitarianism is expressed, not in terms of racial groups—few of these books show variations from traditional European racial types—but in terms of the presentation of sex, age, and social-class differences. The British author P. L. Travers presents in *Mary Poppins* (1934) not only the world's most beguiling nannie, but a woman who is highly competent, self-determined, and spirited. The Swedish author Astrid Lindgren's *Pippi Longstocking* (1945) shows a young girl with amazing strength (she picks up her horse with one arm) and resourcefulness (with no parents to help her, she takes care of herself extremely well). The elderly and the handicapped are prominent in current European books; in their uniqueness they lend strength and drama to the story line. They are often depicted as persons from whom the young might well learn, as in the work of the Swedish author Max Lundgren. Lundgren's *Matt's Grandfather* (1970) concerns an elderly man who maintains youthful dreams in spite of considerable odds. The dignity of all men, regardless of their social class and social role, is seen throughout the work of the British author-artist Charles Keeping, whose books reflect the London street market area of his childhood (*Joseph's Yard*, 1969).

More recent British and European books focus on expressive values of love, play, and self-actualization, as do recent American books for children. Early in the twentieth century Beatrix Potter, a gentle Englishwoman, produced the first of a series of books; it was entitled *The Tale of Peter Rabbit* (1902). The books featured a group of animal characters who, like children, were interested in affection, fun and games, and adventure; they are as popular today as they were when originally published. Another early-twentieth-century picture book still cherished in European households is Swedish author Carl Larsson's *At home* (1904). This book idealizes genteel family life, with parents and children interacting intensely and happily with one another. From France, Antoine de Saint-Exupéry's *The Little Prince* (1945) focuses on a child, a figure of love and imagination, who courageously leaves his asteroid home to fly to earth;

here he makes friends with a stranded airman in the Sahara Desert in a poignant and poetic tale.

Finally, in twentieth-century British and European books, as well as American books, is found a concern for freedom—freedom to pursue goals through a variety of social institutions and freedom to change these institutions. This concern is shown in stories by European authors painfully aware of how many times their countries have almost lost individual freedom. Child labor, war, and other forms of social persecution are addressed with openness and with compassion. In England child labor has been attacked in moving portrayals from the time of Charles Dickens (1812–1870). In Germany Liza Tetzner's series of books, *Die Kinger aus Nr. 67* (nine volumes, 1933–1949) takes up persecution and homelessness in one of the saddest periods of human history. Tetzner's books show war not in its moments of heroism but in its moments of horror and argues strongly through its child characters for cooperation and peace. In France Jean de Brunhoff wrote a series of picture books concerning an ideal welfare state. The first of the series, *The Story of Babar, the Little Elephant*, appeared in 1931. Although de Brunhoff died a few years afterwards, the series was started up again in 1945 by Jean's son, Laurent de Brunhoff, and continued into the 1960's. Popular in Europe and America, it advocates, simply but eloquently, love, kindness, and social justice.

Just as there are similarities in cultural values between current books from Britain and Europe and those from America, there are also similar views of children among these countries. The child as a child is focused upon in modern European books, especially in the more recent ones by picture book author/artists such as Ludwig Bemelmans of France, Bruno Munari of Italy, Jóse Sánchez-Silva of Spain, and Celestino Piatti of Switzerland. The child is not expected to be a miniature adult, and his rights are protected against exploitation in work and against political bondage. He is urged to act responsibly to his neighbor, especially in those books pointing out social injustices, and he is allowed self-direction. As in modern American books for children, self-esteem is freely given.

The Soviet Union was the first modern European country in which the control of book production was taken over by the state; this control occurred after the Revolution of 1920-28. One by one all the countries of the Eastern bloc have followed suit. In Russia the author of children's books is part of the Soviet educational system, and his first aim is to spur the reader on in the service of the fuller development of the community. This aim of the Russian author does not mean that all Russian books for children are ponderously didactic—far from it. The best books are exciting and colorful and show good and bad, industry and foolishness, heroism and cowardice. But even the most adventurous and entertaining contributes to the main stream of Communist thought. In this sense, then, Soviet books, with the exception of the old fairy tales, are all political. These features are also found in books from the People's Republic of China, although the Chinese works are more limited in scope than are the Russian ones. Additional information is available on Russian books from Hürlimann [4] and Morton [9] and on Chinese books from Salisbury [11].

When recent Russian and Chinese books are looked at from the perspective of social values, differences between them and American, British, and European books are apparent. In terms of the value of egalitarianism, no minority groups are shown in Russian and Chinese books. Class differences are also missing. Sex and age variations are present, but little note is taken of these differences; males and females, old and young, work together, to the best of their abilities, for the good of the State. Every one has equal status and equal opportunity to perform services.

An example of such egalitarianism is found in a collection of poems by the Russian poet Samuil Marshak, *The Rainbow Book* (translated and published in English in 1974). Marshak is one of the founders of Soviet literature for children, and this book contains his own favorite poems, written at different periods of his life. One of the poems discusses "Good Manners" and includes admonishments about being quiet when chewing food, remembering to say "hello," and not arguing, squabbling or fighting. It reminds the reader to obey his elders, to be polite and respectful of others. Another poem, "About one Schoolboy and Six Poor Marks," points out the shame and guilt which come from laziness at school. Laziness as a cardinal fault is brought up in other poems as well. A Chinese book by Miao Yin-tang, entitled *Good Children* (translated and published in English in 1977), presents a similar lesson. Good children, according to this book, present flowers to working women on International Working Women's Day, help others, especially the elderly, are thoughtful to their friends, wash their own clothes, play only after doing their homework, repair toys for tiny tots, and are thorough in their job.

The value of self-expression, very prominent in recent American, British, and European books, is not prominent in recent Russian and Chinese books. Instead these latter books focus on traditional achievement goals, and such goals are related firmly to the well-being of the group rather than to the well-being of the individual.

The Russian book, *Merry Rhymes for Little Ones,* compiled by N. V. Agurova (published in English 1961) expresses group concerns clearly. The first group of verses, presented under the general heading of "Labour," concerns the dignity and importance of workers. The last poem in this group, "Good Advice," reminds the child, once he has begun a task, not to leave it until he has completed it. For labor, great or small, should be done well or not at all. A Chinese book, Yang Yi and Liang Ko's *I Am on Duty Today* (published in English 1966) tells the story of a little girl who gets up happily with the sunrise and goes quickly off to school. While there she changes water in the goldfish bowl, arranges chairs, tidies the bookshelf, and puts toys in their places so as to have everything ready for class to begin. Though a child, she assumes responsibility with an adult sense of order and purpose.

The third value to be explored in recent Russian and Chinese books, a value of importance to American, British, and European books in the twentieth century, is freedom—freedom to pursue goals in a variety of social groups, and freedom to change such groups. Russian and Chinese books do not advocate such freedoms. The major social group discussed is the state, and individuals are to subordinate individual needs and goals for the good of the state. Changing the state, its goals and its direction, is never brought up.

A Russian book of poems by the well-known poet Sergei Mikhalkov, *My Friend* (published in English 1960), praises the state and the status quo. An example of such tribute is seen in the poem, "Successors," which links the goals of children to those of adults in a statement of national purpose. It tells of an incident when busy adults from several walks of life—miners, musicians, physicians, generals—are driving their cars to important places. They have to stop to allow a group of children to cross the street, and instead of being annoyed at the delay, they look with pride at these children. These are the future defenders of the Soviet cause, the future workers and makers of laws! "Worthy successors," says the traffic militiaman who crosses them. Among Chinese books, there are a number of biographies of children who have shown selfless devotion to country in small and in large ways. The biography, *Stories from Hu-Lan's Childhood*, by Chun Li (published in English 1966), focuses on a revolutionary heroine during the Chinese People's War of Liberation. It tells of Hu-lan's experiences as a little child in aiding a Chinese soldier during the bitter period of the War of Resistance against Japan. Through Hu-lan's care, along with that of other villagers, the wounded soldier recovered quickly and was able to return to the battlefront.

Just as social values expressed in books from Russia and China differ from those expressed in books from America, Britain, and Europe, so do the views of children and socialization differ. In Russian and Chinese books the child is looked on as a child, but he is supposed to emulate adult behavior to the best of his ability. His responsibility is to the group, and it is the group, or state, that is extolled. A Chinese book which portrays this spirit well is Hsieh Chi-Kuei's *Hello! Hello! Are You There?* (published in English 1965). In that book two children, former neighbors who now live in different parts of China, call on the phone and compare experiences. Fang Fang now lives in north China. He describes to Sa Sa the cold, his ice-skating activities after school, his father's work as a woodcutter in the north woods. Sa Sa, now living in south China, explains that it is quite warm there. She and her friends play in water to cool off; her father is a tapper on a rubber plantation. The two agree that though north and south China are different in many ways, they are similar in purpose and in commitment as they work for socialist goals. Both Russian and Chinese books carry a message of pride in the nation, of confidence and hope for the nation's future, which their people are to share at all ages.

This brief perspective of developments in other cultures shows once again the close relationship between a country's political and social ideology and its books for children. It is likely that American society in the future will continue to idealize values of egalitarianism, self-expression, and freedom of choice. It is also likely that it will concern itself even more with the gaps between ideal and reality—with racism, sexism, poverty, with the absence of warm supportive environments as well as opportunities for growth and development, with social choice and social change. American books for children then can be expected to continue to express these values, but to define them differently over time and to explore different ways to express them over time.

With regard to egalitarianism, of particular concern at present in America is the presentation of minority group members in books. Focus on the dignity and worth of minority peoples is only two decades old in America. There is much catching up to be done, and minority authors/artists are doing the catching up. The black experience in this country and the black heritage in Africa are boldly and respectfully described to even young audiences. The collaborations of Verna Aardema and Leo and Diane Dillon (*Why Mosquitoes Buzz in People's Ears*, 1975, and *Who's in Rabbit's House*, 1977), as well as works of Virginia Hamilton, are particularly noteworthy. In Margaret Musgrove's *Ashanti to Zulu*, with pictures by Leo and Diane Dillon (1976), the diversity and strength of black cultures is glowingly portrayed. The letter *A* focuses on the Ashanti people, in particular Ashanti weavers and their bright kente cloth; the intricacy and symbolism attached to their designs are described. The letter *B* focuses on the Baule people, their history and their legends. *C* is for the Chagga and the way Chagga children are socialized; their coming-of-age rites are explained clearly and simply.

Also of concern in American books for children now is the equality of the sexes. Women are increasingly shown as more competent in more fields. In fiction, female characters are often feisty and imaginative and are active outside of the home. In nonfiction, women and even young girls with exacting careers are characterized. Author-photographer Jill Krementz in *A Very Young Dancer* (1976) and *A Very Young Rider* (1977) focuses upon the rigors of professional life and the exhilaration of competition for adolescent girls. Krementz's message of encouragement to females is not unlike the messages of encouragement to males in the many books on how-to-succeed in business and how-to-succeed in athletics, from the works of Horatio Alger on. In *A Very Young Rider* Krementz writes from the point of view of a ten-year-old (New York, Alfred A. Knopf, 1977):

> I don't know if I'll ever make the United States Equestrian Team when I grow up, but I really want to. I started riding when I was

Ill. 46: Margaret Musgrove. *Ashanti to Zulu: African Traditions*. Pictures by Leo and Diane Dillon. New York: The Dial Press, 1976. [10¼″ x 12¾″]

three. I'm ten now. My name is Vivi Malloy. My pony's name is
Ready Penny. She's a chestnut and I've had her for two years. I ride
her in horse shows in the medium pony hunter division. She's 13.1
hands high. A hand is four inches, and you measure a horse from the
ground to its withers. That's the place at the base of the neck where
the mane starts. A large pony can be as tall as 14.2 hands. After that
it's a horse and you can't show it in pony classes. . . .

What I love the most is competing in horse shows around the
country. I compete in about fifteen major shows a year—in spring,
summer, and fall. I don't show in the winter because most of the
good showing is in Florida and I have to be in school.

Showing takes a lot of time, especially getting ready. Before each
show I have to clean my tack . . . clean it really well. First, I clean
the leather of my saddle and bridle with saddle soap—this keeps the
leather moist so it doesn't crack and break. Then I polish the metal
parts of my bridle: the bit, the rings, and all the buckles. Mom says
I'm good at that.

Interest in self-expression continues to be evidenced in American books for
children. Love as well as play and self-actualization are recurrent themes
throughout this century. In recent books the interaction of love, of caring for
others, and play, of development of self, is more in evidence than ever before.
An example of this interrelationship is found in William Steig's novel for
children, *Abel's Island.* The story concerns a mouse, Abel, who, at the outset,
leads a secure life, with a comfortable allowance from his generous mother and
with a lovely, attentive wife, Amanda. One stormy day flash flood waters carry
him away and dump him on an uninhabited island, from which he is unable to
escape. Faced with the daily challenges of subsistence in a hostile environment,
he reexamines the easy way of life he has always accepted and discovers
survival and artistic talents that hold promise of a more meaningful life when he
does return to his dear Amanda. He does return, a wiser and more responsible
person (New York: Farrar, Straus, and Giroux, 1976):

When at last he came out of the water and touched the shore he
had been yearning toward for the whole round of a passing year, he
experienced a burst of astounding joy. He lay on the longed-for
ground, flooded with ecstatic feelings of triumph and well-being.
Then he broke into uncontrollable laughter. He was a free mouse!

In a while he started upstream, walking along the bank, where no
tall grass obstructed the way. His thoughts were full of the future,
but they were also full of the past. He was imagining ahead to
Amanda, and beyond her to his family, his friends, and a renewed
life in society that would include productive work, his art; but he was
also remembering his year on the island, a unique and separate

segment of his life that he was now glad he had gone through, though he was also glad it was over. (pp. 106-107)

He reached the edge of town at night. He was in Grover Park. The soft gas lamps were lighted. It was a hot night, and the park was full of townsfolk, outdoors after dinner to keep cool, strolling on the graveled walks, chatting on the benches, laughing, watching the children romp and frisk about. How wonderful, after the year alone in the woods, to see this model of civilized society, the town where he was born. He recognized many faces; he was back where he belonged. But he stayed in the shadows to avoid being seen.

Then, suddenly, whom should he see! She, herself, Amanda! Sitting on a stone bench in a perfectly everyday way.

How could he keep from rushing out and holding her dearness in his arms? He managed to restrain himself. There were others on the bench and on the walk. He had waited a year; he could wait a bit longer. Their reunion should be theirs alone. He hurried quietly home, avoiding any encounter.

Home! He grasped the graceful railing and bounded up the steps. He still had the keys in his ragged pants. He opened the door. (pp. 114–116)

For younger children, Dr. Seuss/Theo Le Sieg and other humorists continue to relate caring for others to having fun. Le Sieg's *Hooper Humperdink . . .? Not Him!* (1976) features a young man in the process of planning a party. He decides early on not to ask Hooper Humperdink to the party, for he had so many more exciting friends in the world. The host plans all sorts of entertainment for his guests, and the event becomes more and more extravagant. But in the end, of course, he does invite Hooper; he does not leave him out. Although Dr. Seuss/Theo Le Sieg could hardly be considered didactic, his message of concern for others is clear.

A concern with freedom—freedom to pursue goals through a variety of social institutions and freedom to change these institutions—also continues to be expressed in books for children. Freedom to be a child, to hope and dream, is clearly evidenced in Eloise Greenfield's book of poems, *Honey, I Love* (1978). Freedom to question traditional social institutions, particularly family and economic ones, and to develop new institutional forms is increasingly expressed. Katherine Paterson's *Bridge to Terabithia*, for example, concerns a family of professionals who leave Washington, D.C., for a rural area of West Virginia in order to live a new kind of life. The parents openly question consumer values and ask their child to do the same. In the following passage the child explains to a West Virginia schoolmate about their decision to move (New York: Thomas Y. Crowell Company, 19??):

She talked about Arlington, about the huge suburban school she

Ill. 47: William Steig. *Abel's Island*. New York: Farrar, Straus and Giroux, 1976. [4¾'' x 7¾'']

I'll ask Charlie, Clara, Cora.
Danny, Davey, Daisy, Dora.

Ill. 48: Theodor Seuss Geisel, *Hooper Humperdink . . .? Not Him!*
Illustrated by Charles E. Martin. New York: Random House, 1976. [6⅜″ x
8⅞″]

used to go to with its gorgeous music room but not a single teacher in
it as beautiful or as nice as Miss Edmunds.

"You had a gym?"

"Yeah, I think all the schools did. Or most of them anyway." She
sighed. "I really miss it. I'm pretty good at gymnastics."

"I guess you hate it here."

"Yeah."

She was quiet for a moment, thinking, Jess decided, about her
former school, which he saw as bright and new with a gleaming
gymnasium larger than the one at the consolidated high school.

"I guess you had a lot of friends there, too."

"Yeah."

"Why'd you come here?"

"My parents are reassessing their value structure."

"Huh?"

"They decided they were too hooked on money and success, so
they bought that old farm and they're going to farm it and think about
what's important."

Jess was staring at her with his mouth open. He knew it, and he
couldn't help himself. It was the most ridiculous thing he had ever
heard.

"But you're the one that's gotta pay."

"Yeah."

"Why don't they think about you?"

"We talked it over," she explained patiently. "I wanted to come,
too." She looked past him out the window. "You never know ahead
of time what something's really going to be like."

The bus had stopped. Leslie took May Belle's hand and led her
off. Jess followed, still trying to figure out why two grown people
and a smart girl like Leslie wanted to leave a comfortable life in the
suburbs for a place like this.

They watched the bus roar off.

"You can't make a go of a farm nowadays, you know," he said
finally. "My dad has to go to Washington to work, or we wouldn't
have enough money . . . ."

"Money is not the problem."

"Sure it's the problem."

"I mean," she said stiffly, "not for us."

It took him a minute to catch on. He did not know people for
whom money was not the problem. (pp. 31-33)

Undoubtedly, the future will see, in book content for children, changes in the
social values expressed and also in views of the child expressed. Two directions
are already apparent: (1) increasing concern with the child who needs special

help in order to achieve competence, the child who needs special stimulus to reach his potential; (2) increasing concern that all children become aware of the nature and importance of social relationships. These changes in book content are coming about mainly because of a concern with the heretofore underserved child—principally the child of poverty and the physically or emotionally handicapped child.

The major educational approach to helping this underserved child now is not through books—he needs help before he gets to school, before he learns to read—but through television programming. Television is accessible to large numbers of children, poor and rich, young and not-so-young. Television programs for children, though, do have book products. It is unlikely that any of the volumes emanating from the Sesame Street or the Electric Company or Misterogers Neighborhood or Captain Kangaroo television shows will be placed in the Rare Books Section of the Library of Congress; they are not considered of special literary consequence. But they are placed for sale on countless drug store, grocery store, and bookstore shelves. And they are read by or read to a large number of children, reinforcing information these children have heard and seen on TV.

These books are designed to motivate the child to read and to think; they deal with basic perceptual skills (letters, numbers, shapes, opposites). The TV programs from whence they come, of course, also have these goals and make careful use of motivation and retention research to get their messages across. A popular set of books from the Children's Television Workshop is *The Sesame Street Little Library* (1977); it consists of four volumes by Kay Wood: *The Monsters' Alphabet*, *Ernie and Bert's Counting Book*, *Big Bird's Shape Book*, and *Grover's Favorite Color*. The books use objects that are familiar and interesting to the child in order to engage him or her in the learning experience. *The Monsters' Alphabet*, which features muppets from the Sesame Street program, is an example of the approach: *A* stands for accordian, *B* for bull-dozer, *C* for cookie, and *Z* for zipper.

Other popular books from these TV programs for children discuss human relationships. From the Misterogers' Neighborhood program comes *Mr. Rogers' Neighborhood* (1974), *Mr. Rogers Talks About the New Baby, Fighting, A Trip to the Doctor, Going to School, Haircuts, Moving* (1974). Sesame Street has produced *People in Your Neighborhood* (1971) and *People in My Family* (1971). In *People in Your Neighborhood* attention is given to the kinds of work people do to help one another. The functions of the garbageman, the doctor, the bus driver, the baker are explained in ways that are understandable and that give dignity to all occupations.

To emphasize egalitarianism, this book, it should be noted, contains persons whose skin colors are orange, pink, green, purple, blue, and various shades of yellow to brown. The highly respected profession of dentistry is represented by a female dentist; the highly respected profession of medicine is represented by a

Ill. 49: Jeffrey Moss. *People in Your Neighborhood.* Illustrated by Leon
Jason Studios and featuring Jim Henson's Muppets, A Sesame Street book.
Racine, Wisconsin: Western Publishing Company, Children's Television
Workshop, 1971. [8″ x 8″]

black doctor. And there is a green fireman. The community background shows
both lower- and middle-class housing.

Besides these basic texts Sesame Street has produced books of fairy tales,
Mother Goose rhymes, puzzles, and stories and songs. The Electric Company
offers a book of jokes and a book of riddles, to entice, cajole, push the young
child into basic learning.

While changes can be anticipated in books for children in the future,
continuities can be anticipated as well. Two probable ones are a continued
celebration of life and a continued interest in family life. These interests have
always been present in American books for children, and they remain the

Ill. 50: Margot Zemach. *To Hilda for Helping*. New York: Farrar, Straus and Giroux, 1977. [7¼″ x 8¾″]

energizing spirit for many. The 1977 Caldecott award, for the most distinguished American picture book for children published in the previous year, was presented to Peter Spier for *Noah's Ark* (1976). This book of glorious pictures superbly reproduced is indeed a celebration of living. The story comes from the Bible, Spier's texts from the Dutch poet Jacob Revius, who lived from 1586–1658.

Interest in family life is seen in books of fiction and nonfiction, of prose and poetry, of information and amusement. If present and future books prove to be less didactic than older ones, they will nonetheless be as committed. Margot Zemach, a teller of Yiddish folktales, in her first book of modern fiction for children, deals with kindness and gentleness as well as strong sibling rivalry, all in one family, in *To Hilda for Helping* (New York: Farrar, Straus, Giroux, 1977):

> Every night, when it was dinnertime, Gladys and Rose found lots of things to do. Hilda always set the table and she didn't complain.
>
> One day her father said she should have a medal for helping, so he made one for her out of a tin-can top. On the medal he wrote in red and green letters: TO HILDA FOR HELPING. There was a safety pin attached to the back.
>
> Hilda wore the medal all the time. Rose didn't care about Hilda's medal, but it made Gladys mad. Every time she saw the medal, it made her madder.
>
> Sometimes she hollered at Hilda. Sometimes she pushed her, and she wouldn't let Hilda use any of her things.

Both the continuities and changes in book fare for the young reflect concern for people, for their uniqueness, and for their well-being. Increasing focus in books on cultural diversity, on expressive needs, and on freedom of choice for all people, encourages children to explore and question, to do and be. In such ways can they actively participate in their own society. To be wished for also in books for children is the persistence of love and magic, of goodness and hope, of fun that is funny. For with these offerings literature confirms old truths and carries out a search for new, thereby enriching the lives of all, old and young alike.

References

1. Doyle, Brian, ed. *The Who's Who of Children's Literature*. New York, Schocken Books, 1968.
2. Haviland, Virginia. "The Wide World of Children's Books: A Library of Congress Exhibition for International Book Year." *The Horn Book Magazine* 48(1972):241-248.

3. Haviland, Virginia. *The Wide World of Children's Books: An Exhibition for International Book Year*. Washington, D.C.: Library of Congress, 1972.

4. Hürlimann, Bettina. *Three Centuries of Children's Books in Europe*. Translated and edited by Brian Alderson. New York: The World Publishing Company, 1968.

5. Hürlimann, Bettina. *Picture-Book World*. Translated and edited by Brian Alderson. New York: The World Publishing Company, 1969.

6. Kingman, Lee, Foster, Joanna, and Lontoft, Ruth. *Illustrators of Children's Books, 1957-1966*. Boston: The Horn Book, 1968.

7. Mahony, Bertha, Latimer, Louise, and Folmsbee, Beulah. *Illustrators of Children's Books, 1744-1945*. Boston: The Horn Book, 1947.

8. Miller, Bertha Mahony, Viguers, Ruth, and Dalphin, Marcia. *Illustrators of Children's Books, 1946-1956*. Boston: The Horn Book, 1958.

9. Morton, Miriam. *A Harvest of Russian Children's Literature*. Berkeley: University of California Press, 1967.

10. St. John, Judith. *The Osborne Collection of Early Children's Books. 1566-1910*. Toronto: Toronto Public Library, 1958.

11. Salisbury, Harrison. "Now It's China's Cultural Thaw." *The New York Times Magazine*, December 4, 1977, pp. 49, 106-128.

Permissions/Acknowledgments